Making a Leadership Change

Thomas North Gilmore

Making a Leadership Change

How Organizations and Leaders Can Handle Leadership Transitions Successfully

Jossey-Bass Publishers

San Francisco • Oxford • 1989

MAKING A LEADERSHIP CHANGE
*How Organizations and Leaders Can Handle
Leadership Transitions Successfully*
  by Thomas North Gilmore

Copyright © 1988 by: Jossey-Bass Inc., Publishers
                     350 Sansome Street
                     San Francisco, California 94104
                              &
                     Jossey-Bass Limited
                     Headington Hill Hall
                     Oxford OX3 0BW

Library of Congress Cataloging-in-Publication Data

Gilmore, Thomas N.
  Making a leadership change.

  (Jossey-Bass management series) (Jossey-Bass public
administration series)
  Bibliography: p.
  Includes index.
  1. Organizational change. 2. Leadership. I. Title.
II. Series. III. Series: Jossey-Bass public administra-
tion series.
HD58.8.G55   1988   658.4'063   88-42789
ISBN 1-55542-114-8 (alk. paper)

Manufactured in the United States of America

The paper in this book meets the guidelines for
permanence and durability of the Committee on
Production Guidelines for Book Longevity of the
Council on Library Resources.

JACKET DESIGN BY WILLI BAUM

FIRST EDITION
    First printing: October 1988
    Second printing: November 1989

Code 8836

A joint publication in
The Jossey-Bass Management Series
and
The Jossey-Bass Public Administration Series

For Sally, Walker, and Justin

ᘓ *Contents*

ᴄ·ᴐ Preface

Experts and laypersons alike acknowledge the critical importance of good leadership to the success of any firm, organization, or institution. Yet, paradoxically, as increasing change and complexity make good leadership more important, leaders are also becoming more vulnerable and accountable to stakeholders. The average tenure of leaders in a variety of organizations is decreasing. A new leader will arrive, begin to understand the business—its technology, finances, and people—only to leave shortly thereafter, perhaps attracted by better opportunities elsewhere or perhaps asked to resign owing to a gap between the company's expectations and the leader's performance. Given this increasingly tenuous situation, organizations must learn to strategically manage leadership transitions.

The term *transitions* is used here to mean all the stages from an organization's perception of the need for new leadership through the arrival and successful joining of a new leader. Many books have focused on leadership, but few have addressed in a concrete way how an organization assesses its strategic situation; translates this assessment into a profile of a desired candidate; actively recruits, screens, and hires the candidate; and manages the critical period when the new leader takes charge. Many books separate this process into discussions of strategic planning, executive recruitment, and transformational leadership. However, *Making a Leadership Change* treats leadership transition as an integral process. The approach is organized around the temporal sequence of leadership change, with careful consideration of the perspectives of different stakeholders. This integrated approach enables an organization to capitalize on the opportunity afforded by a leadership change to impart relevant, new values and behavior.

Audience

Changes in leadership fascinate us all, in part because we may identify with those whose lives and careers are fatefully influenced by the change. From the struggle of a middle-aged son with his elderly father for the control of a small family business to the transitions at the White House, each situation holds a certain fascination for us. This book is not only for those who are fascinated by these processes but also for those who see the potential for actively guiding leadership transitions so that they result in the hoped-for improvements and in minimal damage to people's careers, hopes, and lives.

This book is particularly directed at those charged with overseeing leadership changes, either at the organizational or unit level. Practical advice is given that will aid clear thinking during stressful moments in the life cycle of an organization, and suggestions are made about what to be aware of during the uncertainty that surrounds a leadership transition. This book can also assist employees and managers in understanding the overall picture of leadership transition, the role of the new leader, and the dynamics of the interaction between the new leader and the existing staff.

Theoretical background as well as practical advice are included. Conceptual frameworks can help make sense of these difficult periods in organizational life. For each stage of the process, specific advice is offered that will help those in responsible roles manage change effectively. This specific advice may also help those who are simply victims or beneficiaries of a leadership change gain insights about how to have greater influence over the process.

This book is written for practitioners: members of boards, staff members serving on search committees, managers coping with key vacancies in their organizations, talented leaders who are interested in being effective as they take progressively larger, more complicated assignments. In addition, those in both consulting and academic fields will find the book of value. The division of labor among executive search firms, strategy consultants, and organizational development experts is ineffective because a successful leadership transition requires the talents of those in each area. Consultants can benefit from seeing the interrelation of these divisions. Leadership transitions and the accompanying stresses are infrequently researched, perhaps because academics often must depend on the organizational leader, who is in the process of transition, for information and access. Thus academics may find this book helpful in framing research directions about organizational change processes. The aim of this book is to contribute to an understanding of leadership transitions by actively joining in the action research tradition with those who are struggling with these issues in the world of practice.

Examples in the book have been drawn from my practice and from the literature on a wide variety of organizations: profit-making, governmental, academic, health care, and nonprofit. Although the examples and the book's central focus are on leaders at the top of organizations or major divisions, many of these ideas are useful for managers at the work group level.

I have used the term *appointing authority* to indicate the individual or group lawfully authorized to hire the leader. For many organizations this authority would be the board of directors. In other firms the appointing authority will be an executive who may or may not be the direct supervisor of the individual being hired. The leader hired will often be the appointing authority for the next level of executives. Thus the processes described in this book are useful for each successive level of the hierarchy that is actively recruited as part of a new leadership mandate.

I have used the term *leader* to stress the strategic aspects of managing: setting direction, infusing the organization with purpose, choosing priorities, and defending the integrity of the unit. Even for transitions in units of the organization, it is useful to think of these changes as leadership transitions rather than as managerial succession. By so doing the organization can take advantage of the opportunity these changes offer.

Overview of the Contents

Part One examines the increasing importance of leadership and the paradoxical increase in leadership instability. Chapter One reviews why leadership is so necessary and why the very processes that make leadership important also make leaders vulnerable. Chapter Two explains the transition process and explores why organizations fail to use transitions strategically or to search actively, despite the acknowledged importance of good leadership. The central argument of Chapter Two is that far too many organizations are fundamentally unprepared for managing an effective transition, even under the best of circumstances, and that this lack of preparation can often lead to the mishandling of a strategic moment.

Part Two addresses the major stages in an active leadership search. Chapter Three discusses how the appointing authority can think strategically about an organization's direction and the key tasks for a new leader. Chapter Four concerns the translation of strategic considerations into specific qualities desired in a candidate. In organizations, the act of selecting a new leader opens up a wide range of implicit and explicit issues that the organization must face in its future. Given the rate of technological and organizational change, the organization will require someone with significantly different qualities than the prior leader. Appointing authorities often have difficulty concretely envisioning the needed leadership qualities. Chapter Five presents a model of an active search—the process of working through sources to develop a rich list of actual candidates for the position—and addresses the advantages and disadvantages of outside assistance in the recruiting process. Chapter Six focuses on the final stages of screening and selection and argues forcefully for the use of particular methods of background screening and interviewing that focus on historical data. Chapter Seven addresses the important issue of interim, or acting, leaders. Without effective use of interim leadership, appointing authorities often will not be able to use the active methods presented here.

Part Three focuses on the processes of transition after the new leader is designated. Chapter Eight confronts the myth of new beginnings and explores how the new leader's past as well as the past leader's performance affect the early stages of the transition. Chapter Nine explores the psychological process of joining between a new leader and the existing staff. Three typical traps that new leaders and existing staff often find themselves in are explicated. The pace and focus vary according to the type of leader chosen, but in all cases, a leader's initial decisions are intensely scrutinized by those inside and outside the organization. Chapter Ten focuses on the critical task of assembling a team; the new leader now acts as the appointing authority, recycling through the stages of the process that brought him or her to power. Establishing who one can trust and getting the right mix of outsiders and insiders in the newly emerging dominant coalition are major tasks during the early months.

Part Four tackles four major issues confronting a new leader: setting a direction, reorganizing, building working alliances, and managing change. Each is the subject of a chapter. Chapter Eleven looks at the effect of the leader's vision on the staff. What existing activities must be reaffirmed in order to gain support for new initiatives? What are the seemingly easy changes that an outsider may think of as "quick victories" but that insiders realize will consume a disproportionate amount of effort? How does the leader learn what is necessary to make decisions early?

Intertwined with determining the strategy is the rethinking of organizational structures. Chapter Twelve reviews the pros and cons of reorganizing and suggests charting responsibilities as a process for examining organizational structure. Many staff view the first reorganization as motivated by the new leader's desire to put his or her "stamp" on the organization rather than a strategically motivated move that fits with the organization's mission. How can one reorganize in ways others will perceive to be mission linked?

Chapter Thirteen addresses the issue of building and maintaining working alliances, especially with one's boss. Often new leaders are so intent on taking control of the organization that they fail to manage upward and keep a viable working arrangement with their superiors. The structured process of role negotiation is presented as a way of maintaining good working relationships, despite the stress of transition.

As the new team takes shape and an appropriate structure is developed, an inevitable tension arises between the capacity of the new regime and its aspirations. The arrival of a new leader elicits pet ideas and projects from the major camps in an organization. Consequently, leadership transitions are fertile moments with an inevitable excess of good ideas that are presented at a time when the system is not operating at full capacity. Bottlenecks result, and the hope that surrounded the arrival of the new leader begins to fade and turn to cynicism. Chapter Fourteen deals with the critical pacing and timing of the change process.

Chapter Fifteen, the final chapter, concludes by briefly suggesting some consequences of leadership transitions and arguing that we need to stay closer to the deeper issues transitions bring up if we are to use them strategically for organizational and individual development.

Acknowledgments

I am deeply indebted to the many new leaders and subordinates who have shared so freely with me their triumphs and tragedies as they worked through the difficult issues involved in leadership transitions. I have been particularly fortunate over the past few years to have received generous support from the Edna McConnell Clark Foundation to develop the Program on Correctional Leadership and Innovation at the Wharton School, University of Pennsylvania. Through this grant, I have been privileged to work with Kenneth Schoen, the justice program officer, and with many dedicated leaders in the particularly difficult field of corrections. In the context of this project, I have worked closely first with John Isaacson and subsequently with Ted Ford Webb, who have been my tutors in the art and science of executive recruiting. Isaacson, in particular, has been both a practitioner and theoretician of recruiting, and I have benefited immeasurably from long conversations about his beliefs and from discussions about actual cases in his practice, some of which I have used in this book. Peter Bell, president of Edna McConnell Clark Foundation, and John Coleman, former president of the same foundation, have been solid supporters of this project.

During the years of project work that are the basis for this book, I have benefited immeasurably from Larry Hirschhorn's help in conceptualizing and writing about my experiences. As a friend and colleague, he has modeled the ability to link theory and practice in his own writings as well as supported me throughout this project. Thomas Burns, Burton Cohen, James Krantz, and Don Ronchi shaped many of the ideas during projects on which we worked together. Vincent Carroll, president of the Wharton Center for Applied Research, has strongly backed the writing of the book.

Throughout the book's development, many other colleagues have generously given their time to review parts or all of the manuscript. Michael Austin, Gary Carini, Katherine Farquar, Franklin Farrow, Robert Keidel, Steven Kelban, Joseph McCann, Gordon Moyer, Michael Rubin, Linda Carrick Torosian, and John Valentine have all made valuable contributions. Other readers include Peter Bell, John Calhoun, Paul DeMuro, Peter Digre, Robert Doughty, Gordon Kamka, Franklin Lindsay, James Lytle, Larry Meachum, Geno Natalucci-Perschetti, Chase Riveland, Ellen Schall, Robert Schwartz, Richard Seiter, and Ann Sheetz, each of whom has shared insights from the world of practice. Many nursing executives who have participated in the Johnson & Johnson–Wharton Fellows Program in Management for Nurses have shared their insights about taking leadership roles in the quickly changing health care industry. Agnieszka Baumritter has ably served as my research assistant on the project. Catherine Brundage, Michelle Henry, and Marie Paro cheerfully typed, printed out, and proofed seemingly endless drafts during the book's development.

During early drafts, William Moore was an invaluable help in editing chapter by chapter and served as a sounding board for different ideas about the effective presentation of the book's argument. When a first draft was completed, Nina Gunzenhauser skillfully edited and reshaped the entire manuscript, helping me sharpen the argument and link the different sections effectively. Her skill helped me better understand my own ideas.

Moving to the deeper roots of this project, I want to acknowledge Eric Trist, who introduced me to the world of organizations and has continued to guide my practice in the action research tradition.

Finally, I want to honor the sacrifice and support I received from my family—Sally, Walker, and Justin—during the long gestation and realization of this project.

Philadelphia, Pennsylvania   Thomas North Gilmore
August 1988

ᖆ The Author

Thomas North Gilmore is a vice-president of the Wharton Center for Applied Research, a private consulting firm that operates in cooperation with the Wharton School of the University of Pennsylvania. The Center's mission is to help clients identify and resolve strategic issues that are linked to the successful adaption of the organization to its emerging environment. Gilmore has worked for clients ranging from America's largest industrial enterprises to small nonprofit organizations. He has consulted extensively in government, especially in leadership transitions of governors and senior executives.

Gilmore received his B.A. (1966) degree from Harvard College and his Master's of Architecture (1970) from the University of Pennsylvania. He is currently adjunct associate professor of health care systems and a senior fellow of the Leonard Davis Institute of Health Economics, University of Pennsylvania.

Gilmore has written extensively on issues of organizational consultation and strategic planning, including four chapters in *Cutting Back: Retrenchment and Redevelopment in Human and Community Services* (1973). He is particularly interested in the adaptation of organizations to emerging, highly uncertain environments and how leaders learn from their experiences under these conditions. Along with his colleague, Larry Hirschhorn, Gilmore was one of the first to explore the application of family systems theory to organizational issues, and he is a founding member of the International Society for the Psychoanalytical Study of Organizations.

Making a Leadership Change

The New Reality of Leadership Turnover

The rate of leadership turnover is increasing, and the norm of organizational loyalty is weakening. Organizations risk a succession of new leaders, each of whom do not serve long enough to fully implement a new strategy. On the positive side, new leaders offer a powerful way for new values and behaviors to enter an organization, to revitalize working alliances, and to stimulate rethinking of outdated assumptions. In earlier times, the intergenerational process of death and succession was the major mechanism of adaptation and change. Mechanized farming evolved in America not because the father suddenly realized its benefits, but because the son went to agricultural college, returned to struggle with his father, and finally took over the family farm and introduced dramatically different methods.

Such natural succession processes are giving way to a maturing and more rapidly changing executive labor market. Who will take charge of any organization is less and less predictable, as future challenges may require dramatically different skills than the loyal heir apparent has developed. All involved in leadership transitions will need to become more skilled in successfully managing each of the major phases of the process, from the triggering decisions that create the vacancy all the way through the process of the effective joining of a new leader with the existing staff.

How each of the steps is handled will make a significant difference in the steps that follow as well as in the quality of the ultimate outcome—a new leader at the helm. Care and time invested in these critical steps will pay significant dividends to the future health and vitality of the organization.

1

Part One

The New Realities of
Leadership Turnover

Chapter 1

Increased Leadership Turnover: Problem or Opportunity?

Leadership is paradoxical: We need it most when circumstances make its emergence and effective exercise most difficult. The rate of change in the wider society is accelerating. Toffler (1971) refers to its effect on humans as *future shock,* and Schon (1971) asserts that we are in an era in which change is not simply a manifestation of a transition from one period of stability to another but endemic. As our world becomes more complex, pluralistic, and interdependent, and as the pace of change quickens, we become increasingly dependent on authentic leaders who can guide society's organizations through the adaptations that are needed to ensure continued vitality. Yet these very same factors are causing a shrinkage in the tenure of top executives. For any number of reasons, new leaders often move on before they have had time to set a new direction, translate it into the operations of the organization, and work through the conflicts—both inside and outside—that inevitably accompany the changes.

As circumstances shift dramatically within the time span of a leader's tenure, the stakeholders in an organization must judge the leader's fitness to meet the current challenges. Thus the question of tenure can be two-sided: Is he leaving too early? Has she stayed too long?

Few long-term studies of leaders' length of tenure have been made, perhaps because we have paid too little attention to leadership succession issues. In one sample of the top two executives of one hundred very large corporations, however, the number of

resignations for reasons other than retirement was found to have
nearly tripled, from an average of 3.3 per year during the years 1960–
1964 to an average of 9.8 in 1980–1983 (Jennings, cited in "Turnover
at the Top," 1983, p. 104).

Causes of Increased Leadership Turnover

Many of the reasons for the increased turnover in leadership
can be found in external forces. Today, many more stakeholders
believe they have legitimate claims on our organizations (Freeman,
1984). Each group pushes to steer the organization in the directions
it feels are most important. Environmentalists want low levels of
pollution. Consumers want fuel efficiency. Labor unions want job
security and better benefits. Shareholders want earnings. Communities want employment. Minority groups want equal opportunity.
The mission of an organization is not unilaterally decided but
negotiated, both implicitly and explicitly, with outsiders who give
it the necessary resources (sanction, legitimacy, funds, staff, and so
on) and who consume its products and services. Formulating an
organization's mission has become increasingly difficult, but it is
critical. Failure to get the mission right can mean the decline or
even the death of the organization. Short tenure has two consequences on the formulation of mission: First, no single leader has
adequate time to work through the multiple interests. Second, each
shift in leadership destabilizes the alignment of stakeholders.

The identification and protection of an organization's
boundaries are becoming more problematic. Hostile and friendly
takeovers are redrawing the institutional landscape. Outsiders do
not hesitate to use the power of the courts to call into question
internal policies and practices. Bankruptcies, in which outsiders
take over critical internal functions, are more frequent (and
paradoxically are beginning to be used as a final tactic in the battle
to retain control).

Both a result of the acceleration of leadership change and a
factor contributing to it is the rapidly growing executive recruitment industry. As shifts occur, recruiters actively solicit talented
executives for attractive positions in other firms, creating new
vacancies in the process.

These external forces in turn create pressure within the organization. As institutional investors demand short-term performance, directors take greater part in deciding the overall strategy of the firm and in hiring and firing its leaders. In part they are hoping to avoid lawsuits over failure to protect the financial interests of shareholders. Such suits are estimated to have quadrupled in the last decade, and a 1986 survey of *Fortune* 1,000 companies revealed a 506 percent increase in director-liability premiums (Bivens, 1987).

Other sources of instability at the top can be found in rapidly changing technologies, deregulation, or other environmental changes. These may call for new strategies that an executive who formerly functioned well simply cannot cope with.

As organizations become larger and more complex, a critical task of leadership is to manage the internal differences that arise: differences between headquarters and field, among functions, among types of employees, between proponents and opponents of new initiatives. Today there is less trust in leaders to resolve conflicts. Followers question leaders' authority. They use internal grievance processes, external administrative or court actions, or shareholder suits to pursue the issue further. Therefore, conflicts persist and debilitate the organization. Company loyalty is weaker, and people are more likely to resolve conflicts by exiting rather than staying to work through their issues (Hirschman, 1970). The result is fragmentation and splintering. No longer is there an expectation that one's career will be within a single company. A few years ago job-hoppers were looked at askance; today, those who have *not* changed companies are regarded with suspicion: are they aggressive enough for top positions?

Note the self-exciting aspects of these trends. Stockholders pressure a board. The board in turn pushes for short-term performance, which may create the conditions for a future drop in earnings because of failure to invest in necessary research and development. A new leader is brought in. Those who were considered but did not get the job become available for other jobs. The new leader makes substantial changes in the top team, both attracting talent from the outside and exporting executives who do not fit with the new style and strategy. Each of those changes in turn causes more executive-level turnover.

Effects of Increased Leadership Turnover

The effects of leadership changes can be both positive and negative. These transitions are opportunities for organizations to look back and look ahead, to think about their environments and to respond by selecting a leader whose strengths match the new challenges. They are occasions for importing new ideas and values.

On the positive side, the selection of a particular leader makes a telling statement about the issues an organization faces. When John Sculley, a Pepsi-Cola executive with a marketing background, was chosen as chief executive officer (CEO) of Apple Computer, Inc., his choice sent a clear, credible message to all observers about a change in direction at Apple that a simple announcement of a new consumer/marketing orientation could not have conveyed. Hiring Sculley was not merely a way to implement a new policy at Apple, any more than electing Ronald Reagan was the implementation of a conservative shift in this country. In each case, the leadership change embodied and enacted the shift. The new leaders *are* the strategy.

On the negative side, the shorter tenure of leaders creates problems. Top teams and working alliances are often not in place long enough to work through the changes that are introduced. The leader who comes from outside the organization takes longer to get on top of the business. Just when the leader has begun to understand the business deeply and to set a new strategy, events lead to his or her departure, and the entire process starts over again.

In 1979, Thomas Vanderslice was brought into GTE to make the necessary changes in an industry in turmoil because of deregulation. By 1983, two-thirds of the top ninety executives had been moved or newly recruited from outside. A plan was beginning to guide the strategy. Then Vanderslice departed abruptly when the chairman reneged on a promise to step down, and observers wondered if the new directions were sufficiently institutionalized to sustain the changes ("Turnover at the Top," 1983). If four years is too short a time, what is happening at all the companies whose leaders depart, willingly or unwillingly, after only one or two years?

In many of our institutions, leaders have particular difficulty establishing control because of constraints over hiring and firing key people. For example, it takes years for a university president to gain control over appointments because of tenure and the decentralized power of departments. Yet presidents are now serving on average only seven years (Hechinger, 1986). By way of contrast, the transformative presidency of Theodore Hesburgh at Notre Dame was thirty-four years, of Charles Eliot at Harvard forty years, and of Wallace Sterling at Stanford nineteen years. Will anyone survive effectively at the helm of universities for such tenures in the future?

Similarly, in hospitals both CEOs and nursing executives have to cope with autonomous professionals in the form of doctors. Turnaround in this field is not easy. Yet directors of nursing have an average tenure of 3.4 years (Freund, 1985), so a key link among the significant groups in the hospitals is likely to change before a major initiative will be finished. In public-sector settings where political appointees turn over rapidly, the permanent civil service bureaucracy begins to become decoupled from the ever-changing leadership, maintaining its own momentum and blunting the opportunities for new leaders to make an authentic difference by establishing new policies and programs.

In a sense, figures for average tenures understate the instability, because the critical variable is the duration of key relationships among top executives—and they are becoming significantly shorter. For example, it has been calculated that in the federal government 29 percent of cabinet secretary–undersecretary relationships during the 1960s and 1970s lasted less than a year and 39 percent of undersecretary–assistant secretary links did not last a year. In both cases roughly a third of the relationships lasted two years, and only one third more than two years (Heclo, 1977). Recent data suggest these patterns are continuing: the median service of presidential appointments is still around two years, with a third staying for less than eighteen months (National Academy of Public Administration, 1985).

As the tenure gets shorter, the likelihood increases that the leader will depart without completing any changes. Followers also suffer. As people experience a succession of leaders, none of whom serves long enough to see a set of ideas through to realization, they find it difficult to have an intelligent sense of their institutional history. One of the most damaging results is the cynical belief that leaders can no longer make a difference. In a large division of the Department of Health, Education, and Welfare (HEW), a new commissioner had arrived in the final year of the Carter presidency, filled with hopes for the division. The unit had had several leaders in the first three years, and people knew that, because Carter was probably a one-term president, this new leader would also soon depart. Because they had been burned once too often, they disengaged from him—even though they were drawn to his ideas and the changes he proposed.

Paradoxically, by withholding their commitment in such a situation, people create conditions that may make the relationship fail. A "wait and see" stance inadvertently becomes subversive, creating yet another failure to deepen the cynicism.

The Importance of Transitions: Three Premises

Recent interest in leadership, one of the most extensively studied areas of organization and management, has gone beyond academia—witness the large number of books on the bestseller list. Much of the focus of this work has been on how a leader can motivate, inspire, direct, and change an organization (Burns, 1978; Peters and Waterman, 1982; Levinson and Rosenthal, 1984; Peters and Austin, 1985; Bennis and Nanus, 1985). Yet a critical precondition for successful inspiration and change is that the right person be selected as leader.

This book has three premises:

1. Leadership does make a critical difference.
2. Leadership transitions are particularly significant moments in an organization's history.
3. We often dramatically underinvest in these high-leverage opportunities, relying on luck rather than intelligent strategies for success.

Let us examine each of these premises more closely.

Leadership Does Make a Difference. Increasingly, both practitioners and writers in the academic community are drawing a dis-

tinction between leaders and managers. According to Bennis and Nanus (1985, p. 33), "leaders do the right things," while managers "do things right." Zaleznik (1978) richly develops the distinction (see Table 1). He characterizes leaders as "obsessed by their ideas, which appear visionary and consequently excite, stimulate and drive other people to work hard and create reality out of fantasy" (Zaleznik in Wysocki, 1984, p. 1).

Table 1. Differences Between Leaders and Managers.

	Leaders	*Managers*
Necessary characteristics	Imagination; ability to communicate; creativity; readiness to take risks; willingness to use power to influence the thoughts and actions of others.	Persistence; tough mindedness; intelligence; analytical ability; tolerance; good will.
Attitudes toward goals	Have personal, active goals; shape ideas; seek to change the way people think about what is desirable, possible, or necessary.	Have impersonal goals that arise from organizational necessities; respond to ideas.
Conceptions of work	Create excitement; develop fresh approaches to long-standing problems; open up issues; project ideas into images that excite people and only then develop choices that give the projected images substance.	Formulate strategies; make decisions; manage conflict; negotiate, bargain, compromise, balance; limit choices.
Relations with others	Intuitive, empathetic, intense; concerned with what events and decisions mean to people.	Prefer working with others, with a low level of emotional involvement in these relationships; role oriented; concerned with how to get things done.
Sense of self	Feel separate; work in organizations, but never belong; inward.	Joiners, sense of belonging.

Source: Abstracted from Zaleznik, 1978.

One role of the leader is to shield the organization from ambiguity and uncertainty so that people can do their work. Leaders absorb uncertainties and transform them into directions that give meaning to the work of others. This buffering function was addressed in a recent workshop where participants developed analogies to explore the relationship of leaders to followers. They offered the usual metaphors, such as coach to players, along with more unusual ones such as yeast to bread. One comparison suggested a different conceptualization of the leader: gamekeeper to gazelles. On one level, it humorously communicated the participants' view of their leader as a bureaucrat and themselves as graceful, self-managing professionals. It also captured a figure-ground reversal, in which our focus shifts from the leader-subordinate to a wider context in which they fit. In this framework, the leader's role is not to get results through others or supervise directly, but to manage a setting (Sarason, 1972), a social ecology (Emery and Trist, 1973). The leader regulates the boundary.

Leadership is not an exclusive property of the top of organizations; it is critically necessary at all levels. In each unit of an organization, the leader takes up a position on the boundary, mediating between outside and inside, articulating the purpose of the unit in the context of the larger whole, translating that purpose into action, and mediating conflicts both within the unit and between units.

In this sense we can regard leaders as shock absorbers, mediating between the wider environment and the organization, buffering and transforming external pressures into workable challenges for the internal divisions of the organization. If the pressures become too great, the leader may be removed, both as a symbolic action—the leader is held accountable for the organization's failure to perform—and as an instrumental action—will a change make a difference?

Leadership Transitions Are Critical Moments. Leadership transitions represent a "natural entry point" (Yin, 1976) for change. The situation is fluid or, in Lewin's framework of organizational change (1948), "unfrozen." The transition is an occasion to rethink the commitment to the present agenda, to reflect on roads not taken in the past, and to review future choices. Many significant changes—in policy, people, organizational structure, procedures— are more easily introduced simultaneously with a leadership change.

Waddington (1977) develops a lovely analogy for thinking about the timing of changes. He describes a surface with a deep valley that branches into two valleys with an intervening ridge. A ball begins to roll down the first valley, oscillating from side to side. A small push at just the right moment can easily direct the ball into the right or left valley. But once the ball has entered one of the two forks, it will take far more energy, several orders of magnitude greater, to get the ball over the intervening ridge into the other fork. Similarly, new ideas that easily enter an organization when one leader is chosen may encounter mountainous barriers when a different leader later takes over.

I recall vividly a forty-eight-hour flurry of activity by insiders and outsiders seeking to block the appointment of a new commissioner of corrections who was regarded as regressive. The decision was close, but he did get the job, and the choice was fateful for reform in the corrections system in that state for the four years of his tenure. There were few linkages from outside advocates to inside policy makers, and there was little internal interest in new programs. Once the ball was rolling down one valley, it was not possible to alter its course until a leadership change was made.

The most dramatic example of the opportunity of a new leader to set a new agenda is the political transition. In a political campaign, we explicitly link the debate about critical issues to the single choice of a new executive. New ideas are put forth, and priorities are reordered. Patterns of coalition are often realigned and new alliances are formed. Similarly, during a leadership struggle in an organization, dormant fault lines, such as between the old guard and young turks or among ethnic groups, may remerge; new alliances are forged as different factions jockey for influence (Zald, 1965). Different hopes and ideas are projected onto the leader. The status quo is shaken up. People who have been out of the dominant coalition get a chance to be influential in the new administration. People who have been stereotyped have a fresh opportunity to alter their images.

New leaders are Januslike: they must look both to the past and to the future. They affirm some aspects of the history of the organization; otherwise they would not likely have been hired. But they also carry into the organization new values. Hirschman (1967) has called these two dimensions trait taking and trait making. To be effective, a leader must accept some traits of the organization in order to create the relationship that will allow the making of new traits.

One reason leadership changes are such powerful moments of adaptation for organizations is that leaders always bring more to the situation than the appointing authorities can know. Supreme Court justices are legendary for surprising the presidents who appointed them. In selecting someone to head an organization, an appointing authority is betting on the fit between characteristics of the individual and of the situation, but both the individual and the situation contain uncertainties that can play out as unexpected benefits or as major costs.

Finally, leadership transitions are important because they involve periods of destabilization. Any new leader, whether an insider or an outsider, takes time to settle in and build a working team. Transitions may be times of reduced performance and vulnerability to outside forces. Historians have argued that the Bay of Pigs fiasco was very much a function of the Kennedy administration's newness and the underdeveloped relationships between the new leaders and the existing staff (Neustadt and May, 1986).

Leadership Transitions Are Underinvested. Despite the importance of leadership, far too many transitions are not well thought through or carefully managed. Organizations tolerate destructive leaders for much longer than they should, and when vacancies occur appointing authorities either act too hastily or delay too long. They do not think deeply enough about the new challenges or even consider whether that group of tasks should be organized in a single role. They fail to examine the requirements for the job, they consider too few candidates, and they do little checking on the candidates' prior performances. When the new leader arrives, they give little explicit attention to the processes of transition.

In government, changes in leadership are so built into the political system that leaders risk becoming uncoupled from the real work of the agency. At the going-away party of a public executive, the current commissioner was playfully introduced as "the temporary help." Leaders place little emphasis on succession planning; they realize that they did not get their jobs that way and it is equally unlikely that their successors will either. The result is often missed opportunities to shape the organization through more careful selection of the executive and a deliberate program to link the new leader and the existing staff.

A recent report on public-sector leadership (National Academy of Public Administration, 1985, p. 20) reached the following conclusions: "The capacity no longer exists—in the White House or in the Senate—to find and assess with care the qualifications of the large number of people needed to fill all appointed positions. . . . Difficult though it may be to comprehend, 79 percent of the presidential appointees we surveyed received no orientation of any kind at the time their appointments began. They went immediately into their jobs without any systematic guidance on the president's program, their role in implementing that program, the relationship between their agencies and the White House, the operations of the major management processes of the federal government, or effective ways to deal with the Congress and the press. Many of them learned these things the hard way, through inefficient and often painful experience."

The not-for-profit world often suffers from poor transitions. The change is unanticipated, there are no potential successors in the organization, and the board is ill equipped to undertake the selection task. The process begins with overreliance on an outdated description of the job. The board passively waits for people to apply and then picks the best among the resulting pool, with little consideration for how the entire process might be used as a strategic moment.

There are, however, hopeful signs. The executive recruiting industry is maturing, and the use of recruitment professionals is growing in the not-for-profit and government sectors. The private sector still leads in the attention it pays to the leadership succession process. Levinson and Rosenthal (1984), researching the six well-known companies for their book on the CEO, were surprised to learn how dominant the succession issue was. Friedman (1986) studied formal succession systems and found many *Fortune* 500 companies pay considerable attention to succession issues among top managers. Nevertheless, Lester Korn, founder of the largest executive recruiting agency, commenting on the top five to twenty positions in private-sector organizations, said, "Longevity, luck, and just being in the right place at the right time have been far too important in getting people into their positions" (Cowherd, 1986, p. 337).

Leadership transitions are thus volatile moments in the life cycles of organizations, occasions for renewal as well as for regression. Much hangs on how they are managed by all the parties involved: appointing authorities, incoming and outgoing leaders, and existing staff. The next chapter describes the stages in the overall transition process and focuses on why they so often are either overly ritualized or poorly attended to.

ᴄ⤸ *Chapter 2*

Initiating or Responding to Leadership Transitions

Given the rising rate of turnover of leaders, the role of appointing authorities has become increasingly crucial. Yet paradoxically, many boards and individual appointing authorities are ill prepared to manage a leadership transition. For many board members or for an individual leader (such as a governor) who assembles a staff and cabinet, it is a one-time experience, a task that must be learned on the job. Ironically, the board members of an organization with a long-tenured executive are the least likely to have experience with leadership succession, yet face one of the most difficult transitions. In government, the problem may be the reverse; politically appointed executives serve for such short tenures that there is little institutional memory of the processes of effective recruiting.

Key Stages in a Leadership Transition

The leadership transition consists of eight distinct but often overlapping stages.

1. *A decision to seek a change in leadership.* The present leader is resigning—either voluntarily or involuntarily. Because being without a leader provokes anxiety, too many boards are reluctant to face up to the prospect of asking for the leader's resignation. So they ignore early warning signs of performance problems. They also ignore signs of the leader's discontent, and may be caught by surprise, with no plan for an orderly succession, when the executive leaves. An effective board should be aware of the wider

opportunities that might lure its leader away as well as the personal life-cycle issues that can shape a decision to leave.

2. *The design of a search and selection process.* This is usually done when a leadership-change decision is made. The major risk in this area is that the machinery to support the succession process is not available on a standby basis. Too frequently the appointing authority rushes into the search for a replacement without adequately assessing the strategic considerations (see steps 3 and 4 below). When decisions are made hastily, the process may be either too participative or not participative enough, the deadlines may be unworkable, and the expectations of committee members or current staff may be unrealistic.

3. *An analysis of the strategic challenges facing the organization.* This requires a careful consideration of the organization's past and future, including the ways in which the wider environment is posing new problems or opportunities. The two greatest risks are carrying on business as usual when the organization needs to consider a dramatic shift and, conversely, overreacting to the current leadership by moving to an opposite type without a careful appraisal of the true strategic context.

4. *The translation of the strategic assessment into specific leadership needs and job qualifications.* The specifications should take into account the inevitable tradeoffs. A description of the desired executive may call for such an unlikely combination of skills and traits that it is of no help to those charged with looking for flesh-and-blood candidates. If the challenges have not been carefully considered, the search may focus on the wrong areas. For example, no amount of searching the universe of high-tech firms would have turned up an executive like Sculley from Pepsi-Cola for Apple Computer. Because the new challenges were identified in the marketing area, the right territories were searched.

5. *A search for prospective candidates.* The search may be extensive or limited depending upon whether a suitable internal candidate or a clear external choice is available. Too often the net is cast too narrowly, drawing in only candidates already known to the organization. Conversely, an organization can be overwhelmed with too many inappropriate resumes and be unable to discriminate thoughtfully among them.

6. *The screening and initial selection of finalists.* The first cut is based on an analysis of applicants' qualifications in relation to the needs of the organization. Aggressive selling of the challenges of the job is necessary to screen in enough genuine alternatives for the appointing authority to consider.

7. *The interviewing and final selection of candidates.* This action is based on a more thorough review of qualifications, intensive reference checks with previous employers and others, and a comparative analysis of each finalist's strengths and weaknesses. Too many search processes rely too heavily on the interview—which really tests only a candidate's skills in the interview situation—and too little on investigating prior performance in similar situations.

8. *A transition process.* Here the new leader, the current staff, and the board develop an understanding of one another's expectations and evolve working relationships. The orientation period may also be a time of working through the loss of the prior leader. The appointing authority often disengages too quickly once a search has landed a candidate, rather than making the additional investment necessary to ensure that the new leader builds effective working relationships upward, downward, and sideways.

This eight-part conceptual framework can capture only partially the variety and unpredictability inherent in a leadership transition. The process will vary depending on the circumstances surrounding the departure of the leader, the amount of advance notice, the strategic challenges facing the organization, the health of the enterprise, and the availability of qualified successors internally or externally. We can say the process is complete when no one, including the new leader, can use the transition as an explanation or excuse for why things are the way they are.

How the Process Begins

The stimulus for a change in leadership can take many forms: an anticipated retirement, a sudden death or serious health problem, the leader's unexpected move to another job, a merger or acquisition, interpersonal politics among the top management, or dissatisfaction with the leader's performance. Some of these are brutally sudden, requiring both the appointing authority and the staff to mobilize hastily. Others develop over time, with many signs along the way, some ignored, some attended to.

Recognizing Leadership Problems. It is difficult to reach the conclusion that an executive must be replaced. Boards have often been slow to respond to the need for a change because close links have developed with the CEO. "Most boards are not very tough on chief executives until there's a collapse," notes Kenneth R. Andrews, a former editor of the *Harvard Business Review* and director of several companies (Prokesch, 1986, p. F25). Alderfer (1986, p. 44) describes the process: "Directors reported that they sensed difficulties—often that the CEO was covering up problems— several years before the departure. . . . Despite their uneasiness, however, directors generally believed that they couldn't raise their concerns unless something was obviously wrong with financial indicators. . . . Two clear signs usually preceded the turning point: first, financial indicators would drop; second, directors would meet in subgroups outside board meetings without the knowledge of the chief executive. After these two things happened, the course of events seemed inevitable, yet it often took two or three years to unfold. Once the process of removing a CEO was underway, in no case I heard of did it reverse and the executive regain the board's confidence." As Alderfer notes, this process prevents a concerted exploration of the difficult issues while there is time to learn from the board's criticism.

The removal of an executive is always a difficult process. Judgments about performance are complex. To what extent do the critical problems lie in the leader, and to what extent are they symptoms of wider issues in the organization? The appointing authority may not be providing enough guidance and support. Assessing another person therefore inevitably involves self-appraisal. Some people react with denial, locating all the responsibility for nonperformance in the other. Others react with guilt, taking too much of the responsibility and not holding the other sufficiently accountable.

Deciding to request someone's resignation often involves wrestling with one's own complicity in the failing organization or leader. One board chair wrote to a private school head who had taken over from the school's founder, "With deep sorrow and regret I accept your letter of resignation. . . . My regret is heightened by my own sense of inadequacy in failing to give you the support over the past two years that hindsight indicated you needed to carry out the difficult job that we gave you. I had not realized, and I'm afraid most people connected with the school still do not realize or appreciate, the almost impossible task of replacing a founding headmaster who over twenty-three years had been the school's main economic support and indelibly imprinted the way he ran the school on the present faculty" (de Rham, 1983).

The letter writer's pain is clear. Yet the alternative of supporting a leader who has lost the ability to govern is potentially even more destructive for the organization, and possibly for the beleaguered leader as well.

Links to Strategic Plan. At senior levels, performance criteria are rarely cut and dried. They often flow from a strategic plan which the chief executive is responsible for developing and carrying out. Conversely, an executive may also be removed because no viable strategic plan exists. Sometimes a board will replace a leader who has a clear strategic vision that the board judges to be wrong. Until fairly recently, this was rarer, because a leader, by controlling the information presented to the board, could exert enormous influence on its views. With the rise in hostile takeovers, however, this kind of board–CEO struggle over strategy is happening with increasing frequency. The new dominant coalition usually comes to the board with an idea of how the assets of the corporation can be deployed more effectively. Usually the current CEO is opposed to its strategy, and a leadership change results.

When an absence of a strategic plan leads to a change in leadership, the appointing authority may move too hastily to fill the vacant role, charging the new person with developing a mission and strategic plan. But without some sense of where it is going, an organization cannot make a sound hiring decision. This dilemma cannot be solved, but it must be honored. An organization needs to think strategically before searching for a new leader and then use the new appointment as a spur to further elaborate and develop its strategy. Otherwise it will reenact the original dilemma and may select an executive who is incapable of getting it to where it really needs to be.

For example, some have argued that BankAmerica, when faced with a deteriorating situation, was too slow in removing Samuel Armacost and too hasty in reappointing A. W. Clausen, the former CEO who had recently retired from the World Bank. According to some, the difficulties the organization faced were the result of decisions and policies that had been set in the earlier Clausen era. By not stepping back and taking stock of the situation, the board may have forfeited the opportunity to bring in a new point of view. By contrast, when Mellon Bank faced similar difficulties (Fix, 1987a, 1987b), the board removed the existing CEO and created the space for a careful appraisal of the situation. After several weeks of thoughtful deliberations, they brought in the first non-Mellon, nonfamily CEO in the corporation's history, an executive experienced in bank turnaround situations. He in turn has attracted several seasoned executives to make up the new team. Similarly, an insurance company, facing a complex and changing environment for financial services institutions, hired a strategy firm to help a board committee assess its strategic situation and then hired a different executive search firm to look for a leader who fit with the new direction.

Because of the importance of leadership and the risks of being dependent on their leaders, boards should go through an annual exercise of imagining that for some reason they have to search for a new leader (Gilmore and Brown, 1985). Sensing what that task would be like can help the board think freshly about the fit of the current leader to the challenges and its dependency on the leader, and will help to keep alive the ability to conduct an effective leadership search.

Unexpected Resignations. When an executive chooses to leave at other than an expected time, such as retirement or the end of a specified term, the organization experiences repercussions different from those when the leader is asked to leave. Subordinates often rethink their commitments to the organization. Some may review earlier decisions not to accept outside offers and feel that they were stupid to have stayed. Those close to the departing leader may have fantasies of being recruited to the new organization. Some may actually leave to join the outgoing leader, causing a loss of critical talent just when the organization most needs stability.

The Limits of Formal Succession Systems. Formal succession systems are designed to keep an organization in a state of preparedness for leadership shifts. At middle-management levels, each executive might be asked annually to name one subordinate who is best suited to take over. When Larry Hinde, an executive in Schlumberger, tragically died in an unexplained incident, the organization moved quickly to fill his position with the person he had formally designated as his successor (Auletta, 1985). Presumably that person had in turn designated his successor. The risk with an excessively formalized system is that the occasion for really rethinking the role and the type of person best equipped to fill it will be missed. James W. Walker, a vice-president of Towers, Perrin, Forster and Crosby, a management consulting firm, notes, "Some chief executive officers identified their successors a few years ago but now find them unsuitable for the firm's new style. The more diversified a company is, the tougher it is to groom successors" (Fowler, 1984, p. D19).

Lester Korn suggests that boards focus less on the mechanics of the succession process and more on the assessment, in collaboration with the CEO, of the top five to seven executive positions (Cowherd, 1986). He notes that directors rate succession as the third most important issue, behind finance and strategy. Because of the importance of succession processes and the need to go outside in roughly 20 percent of the top jobs in *Fortune* 1,000 companies, Korn envisages organizations having retainer relationships with search firms that might advise on career paths and executive development as well as undertaking acutal recruitment assignments.

Internal Successor. In the 80 percent of the cases where succession does take place from within, organizations use a variety of methods. Vancil (1987) identifies three modes of organizing at the top that have implications for the succession process:

1. The *solo mode,* with only one executive at the top, is common for smaller companies. In this mode, no successor is clearly designated. An advantage is that the CEO and the board can look over the talent, testing the mettle of different executives against specific assignments. A disadvantage is that the competition for the

top job can interfere, and that once a winner is announced the losers may depart, taking considerable knowledge and expertise with them. When Jack Welch got the top job at General Electric, only one of the six who had also been in contention remained with the company.

2. The *duo mode* consists of two executives at the top, a chairman and a president. The CEO title can be shifted from one to the other at the right moment. Here the heir apparent, promoted from within or recruited from the outside, is clearly designated. If the relationship works well, the succession occurs smoothly, but when there are problems, the duo mode can be painful for the participants and unsettling for the organization. Harry Gray went through several heirs apparent at United Technologies before finally turning over the reins to Robert F. Daniell.

3. The *team mode* has a group at the top, often in an office of the chairman, with one individual as the lead executive or who holds the CEO/chair title. Vancil notes that this mode is found in about 25 percent of large organizations, up from fewer than 10 percent several decades ago. In these cases, the board takes the major responsibility for succession, with the option to go inside or outside. The depth of talent at the top allows the organization to cope with an unexpected change at the top. Like the solo mode, the team mode can create considerable competition for the top slot. Once the change is made, the shift in strategy can be much faster than it can in the duo mode, because the new executive takes both the CEO and chairman titles.

To be sure, sometimes continuity is in order, and the best executive to fill a role may be someone who matches the previous occupant. The point is that this course should be affirmatively chosen and not simply allowed to happen because of inertia. The duo mode is best suited to this type of continuity. All these succession processes occur over time. Reginald Jones of GE explicitly tested seven executives for three years. Robert Six of Continental Airlines delayed his own retirement several times because he did not think people were ready (Loving, 1979). As the rate of change increases, it is less and less likely that conditions will be sufficiently stable to test how several candidates fit with the strategic requirements, because the requirements themselves will be in flux, often dramatically.

Well-maintained succession systems do keep people talking about who is talented and how they might fit with the changing leadership tasks in the organization. But the most problematic situations—succession of long-tenured or founding executives and leadership changes in response to major strategic shifts or significant performance problems—are the ones that require the most creative thinking and most careful design on the part of the appointing authority. In these cases, ongoing formal systems are unlikely to be responsive.

Stumbling Blocks in Choosing a New Leader

Like generals who are always fighting the last war, appointing authorities may make appointments based on a thoughtful analysis of the problems of the previous leader, not the fresh challenges that a new leader will face. They fail to use the leadership change as an opportunity to rethink the role and mission. Often the board itself is part of the problem.

The Board. Part of the theory of having outside directors on a board is that they will be the fresh, independent voice that is necessary when an organization is in trouble and must make a change at the top. However, the fresh perspectives that new board members might offer are often lost because of an informal understanding that new members should listen and observe until they fully understand how the board operates (Alderfer, 1986). The fate of Ross Perot as a gadfly on the board of General Motors suggests that new perspectives are not always valued by those in power. His iconoclastic ideas were tolerated for a brief period before Roger Smith requested his resignation. Furthermore, friendships, the old-boy-network way board members are recruited, the development of "groupthink" (Janis, 1982), the difficulties of getting negative information about an organization—all these make it difficult for boards to be clear-sighted and objective when the crisis of leadership succession arises. Here is the *New York Times*'s description of the BankAmerica transition:

Mr. Clausen, who is 63 years old, presided over
BankAmerica in a time of rapid growth. But he is
viewed as responsible for many of the loans that have
now turned sour and are responsible for the huge
losses BankAmerica has suffered in the last year and
a half. Moreover, Mr. Clausen, to increase the bank's
profits in the short run, neglected to invest in automated teller machines and other automated equipment the bank has needed to keep up in a fast-
changing world of deregulated banking. . . . The
choice is likely to renew criticisms of the bank's board
of directors, which has been accused of not taking
action swiftly enough to remove Mr. Armacost as
trouble mounted. Now it is being criticized as bringing back to power one of its own, the man who
appointed many of its members. "It certainly is
bizarre," said one BankAmerica executive. Another
said, "It does not seem to be a logical choice."
However, the latter executive suggested that the board
could feel comfortable and trust Mr. Clausen, who has
been a friend of many of the board members for a long
time [Pollack, 1986, p. 36].

Organizational theorists have characterized this behavior
with a threat/rigidity hypothesis, suggesting that organizations
undergoing stress often act in constrained and uncreative ways just
when their external circumstances most require a breakthrough in
thinking (Staw and Ross, 1987). The board's anxiety leads it to
reach a quick decision in favor of someone with whom the directors
are comfortable, without thinking critically about how the candidate
matches their dramatically different strategic circumstances.

The weakness a board displays in managing a leadership
change may in fact be the organization's Achilles' heel. An example:
A charismatic priest had founded a not-for-profit group home for
delinquent and dependent boys. The organization had grown, had
weathered President Reagan's budget cuts, and now faced the issue
of Father Brown's departure. The central strategic issue for this
organization was overcoming its dependency on the founder. But

instead of being able to see this issue, the board members were incapacitated by that very dependency. During a critical meeting at which several candidates were being discussed, the board requested that Father Brown leave the room, sensing that they needed to stand alone. Yet when he was gone, they realized that without him they had no support for thinking about issues and following through on the necessary staff work. Only by redirecting their dependency onto an outside consultant were they able to reach decisions about both the substantive challenges and the process of recruitment (Gilmore and Brown, 1985).

Blind Spots. Cultural blind spots may also prevent a board from identifying key challenges. Schein (1985) reminds us that the culture of an organization is not the surface features that managers intentionally manipulate to create a climate, but rather the assumptions—unspoken, perhaps even unconscious assumptions— that the members make about the environment, the norms, and the purposes of the organization. It is enormously difficult for an insider to become aware of these features without assistance in getting some perspective. Far too often that assistance comes in the form of some crisis that shocks the organization into perceiving a dramatic shift in its context.

A nice example of organizational blind spots preventing those inside the organization from seeing what may be obvious to an outsider is described by executive recruiter John Isaacson. He had been asked by the director of the New York and New Jersey Port Authority to help recruit a new director of aviation. This job involves overseeing the four major airports in the metropolitan area, dealing with the terminals, slots for planes, ground transportation, and so on. As Isaacson began his work, he found himself in a world of aviation, peopled by alumni of the Air Force and the aircraft industry from the heroic aviation era of the postwar period. The dominant assumption was that the new director would be found in this world. When Isaacson began to probe the critical challenges that the director would actually face in the coming years, however, the list was dominated by ground transportation and luggage-handling systems, suggesting that candidates might be found in a completely different place than where people were looking (Tierney, 1985).

Lack of Time. One of the most pressing but mundane impediments to effective conceptualization of the key challenges facing an organization is simply lack of time. If the vacancy is at the top, organizations feel pressed to fill it quickly, even when an acting leader is in place. If a board or a committee must be mobilized, it takes time to get organized and sort out responsibilities. If the search task falls on a group, time pressures and other duties often prevent the intensive staff work that is required.

Extra Work Load. When a vacancy occurs at the division level, the work of the unfilled position spills upward to the appointing authority above, adding to the ongoing responsibilities of that role. Although supervising the unit offers a chance to experience some of the duties, it is no substitute for focused thinking about the past and future of the unit and the critical challenges it faces. Nor is it any substitute for obtaining the views of key outsiders. Therefore one of the early challenges to the appointing authority or search team is to delegate the responsibility for drawing up a clear picture of the job to be filled and for the other stages of recruiting in such a way that the requisite resources are put to the task.

Mixed Messages. Often the difficulty in an executive's performance stems from splits in the organization at higher levels. The board may be divided or several key executives may be pulling in different directions. Here, one of the central challenges is to work out those conflicts so that a new executive is not placed in the same situation that caused the previous one to fail. This will be particularly difficult if the board or appointing authorities place the blame for the failure on the previous occupant and do not confront the mixed messages that they may have been sending.

For example, the owners of a service business who happen to be brothers had been through several directors of operations. The problem was that the brothers were unable to agree on common strategic directions or on operational policies, yet both insisted on being involved in all areas of the business. Their interpersonal conflicts prevented them from clarifying the relationship of the operations director to the strategic plan. They would fill the job, scapegoat the individual, and then recycle through this process as a way of avoiding their deep interpersonal differences.

Sometimes these issues can be contained if they are recognized and translated into an explicit aspect of the search. I was involved in the recruitment of a county manager for a fast-growing county whose governing board historically split three to two on most issues. The job description clearly stated that a core skill would be the candidate's ability to cope with these splits. It also made clear that the board had an obligation "not to put the manager into an impossible position, and to respect the fact that on fundamental issues of values, the board should make the choice." Rather than distorting the search, the split in the appointing board was addressed head-on as a fact of life and its implications translated into performance characteristics for the successful candidate.

Leaders' Rivalry. One other factor that can contribute to an organization's failure to use a leadership transition strategically may be called into play if the current leader is actively participating in the selection. The retiring leader often struggles with rivalrous feelings toward a successor that result in significant unconscious distortions. Levinson (1974, p. 3) identifies ways that leaders make choices whose unconscious purpose is "to demonstrate that no one can run the organization like the retiring CEO."

The Dangers of a Passive Search

The search process is another stage at which an organization may fail to make the most of the opportunity offered by the leadership change. Organizations often fail to search widely and aggressively for potential candidates for openings. The appointing authorities may believe that they already have an adequate candidate and that the costs of a further search cannot be justified. They may advertise the position to satisfy affirmative action or prescribed procedures, but they fail to test their judgment of the known candidate by seriously seeking a stronger candidate. Some people believe that the job market is Darwinian and that the struggle of applicants to advocate themselves is an indicator of motivation and skill. This position may mask a desire to remain in the one-up role of rejecting applicants rather than risking rejection by candidates one has actively sought.

A passive search strategy may reflect a narcissistic confidence that the organization is the best in its field and will automatically attract the best personnel. For example, Harvard University long assumed that everyone's career aspiration was to be a tenured full professor at Harvard. But the implications of dual careers, the rise of other fine universities, higher salaries elsewhere, housing costs, and changes in attitudes toward mobility have all created a new situation that is spurring a critical rethinking of the hiring strategy (Butterfield, 1986).

Active executive recruitment strategies force an organization to confront difficult issues and hard choices in fitting the strengths and weaknesses of candidates to the structure of the organization. Active processes bring more players into the critical hiring decisions, making it harder for the appointing authority to keep control over the process. They take time and talent that may be needed for other critical issues. And they make it harder to keep secret the fact of the search from the current occupant, who may be in the dark because the approving authority fears political resistance or premature departure before a new candidate can be hired.

Despite the opportunity that leadership transitions offer, the anxiety and uncertainty that inevitably surround leadership changes often lead organizations to avoid capitalizing on these critical moments. They either act hastily as if to get the pain over with as quickly as possible and regain the comfort of having someone in the role, or get ensnared in procedures that bind the anxiety but prevent the necessary critical thinking and risk taking.

Yet successful recruitment strategies are among the highest leveraged actions that appointing authorities can take. If they get the right leadership in place, the authorities have discharged their responsibilities for stewarding the organization. The following section of the book presents the major elements in an active search: a strategic assessment, translating the challenges into characteristics of a desired executive, actively searching for potential candidates, and aggressively screening and checking out finalists.

↜ *Part Two*

The Key Steps in Replacing a Leader

As an organization faces the prospect of a leadership transition, anxieties and uncertainties increase dramatically. Unfortunately, many deal with this stress by not thinking ahead, coping a day at a time, just when the organization most needs their help in thinking deeply about the future and the type of leader necessary to meet the challenges. The process of an executive search, whether undertaken by an outside firm or by insiders, requires careful attention to each of the steps. Mistakes—such as failing to consult with important constituencies on strategic challenges, forgetting to think about potential pools of candidates from related areas, mishandling the delicate negotiations over a potential candidate's interest in the position, not checking thoroughly into the background of finalists—can affect the fate of the organization, propelling it down one path without consideration of other choices.

The sense of vulnerability during a leadership transition can cause people to move with excessive haste, ignoring the opportunity that leadership changes bring to import new values and behaviors into an organization. The use of interim, or acting, leadership can provide a scaffolding for both keeping the organization on track and attending to the search process. There will always be an element of luck in the selection of leaders, but careful attention to each of the steps in a thorough recruiting process can significantly minimize the risks.

29

Chapter 3

Determining the Organization's Challenges and Leadership Needs

Organizations, like people, grow and change. Like people, they sometimes experience significant developmental crises that call into question core assumptions about their culture, character, and identity. Merger, acquisition, or significant resizing may shift the boundaries between the organization and the environment. Relationships with stakeholders and markets might change dramatically. Like personal development crises, these are moments of uncertainty, confusion, regression to old patterns, and experimentation with new approaches.

At different moments along this life cycle, the leadership needs will change significantly. For example, when an entrepreneur starts a new business, the critical skills needed are the creativity and tenacity to develop a product and the persuasiveness to interest potential investors in both the idea and the company. As the fledgling firm gets an infusion of venture capital, significant outsiders enter the picture, and the entrepreneur must manage these critical relationships. Timetables become important. The core group must hire and develop new staff, bringing in executives with competencies in finance, marketing, and production. The original team members struggle for influence with the new executives.

Note: For the executive-search discussion in the following chapters, I am deeply in debt to John Isaacson (1977), who first introduced me to the art and science of executive search. I have drawn liberally from internal office materials that he has generously shared with me. I have also benefited greatly from Ted Ford Webb's coaching on all aspects of recruiting.

If the group works through these developmental tensions, the product is successfully developed in prototype, and yet another transition begins. Manufacturing capability must be developed, while marketing people develop the market and manage the uncertainties of release timing: when will the product be available at the performance level that has been promised? Again the critical tasks shift; the creativity that earlier was an asset may even become a liability if it prevents the development of an orderly manufacturing capability. The passing of the baton at Apple from Wozniak and Jobs to Jobs to Sculley, all in the space of four years, dramatically illustrates the shift in requisite leadership from creativity through production to marketing.

New Leaders Bring New Perspectives

Not every major strategic change has to be accompanied by a change in leadership, but changes in the composition of the dominant coalition are likely as different issues assume importance. One of the central challenges to an organization is to remain open to the outside, to detect and adapt to emerging trends that may pose threats or offer opportunities. The most powerful way for fresh, innovative perspectives to enter an organization is through new leadership. Nor is strategic change always sudden and obvious. Structures adapt slowly and often discontinuously. Slow, imperceptible shifts can accumulate until finally the sum of little changes reaches a magnitude that triggers a reorganization or major redefinition of role. The occasion of a change in leadership is always a useful moment to step back and examine these subtle transformations. There is reputed to be an experiment in biology in which a frog is placed in a shallow pan of pond water and the temperature is raised in small increments. The water can be brought to a boil, eventually causing the frog's death, without the frog ever leaping out because at no interval of time has the rate of change been sufficient to trigger a threshold of threat for the frog. Similarly, many of our organizations have experienced such continuous changes that only in looking back can they see just how significantly some basic feature of their environment has changed.

Every transition of a top executive, then, is an occasion for rethinking the mission of the unit and considering whether the transition represents a window for introducing new values or changes that would reaffirm the organization's competitive advantage or solve problems of performance. There are several ways in which appointing authorities can think strategically about a role as preparation for determining the specific characteristics to be sought in candidates for that role, which will be addressed in Chapter Four.

Testing the Mission. The classic strategic question, "What business are we in?" can powerfully reorient a search. Remember the earlier example of Isaacson's search for a director of aviation for the Port Authority. The Authority's view was that it was in the aviation business, oriented toward serving the major carriers. Yet the industry was in turmoil in the wake of deregulation. New airlines were making new demands on terminal space. The critical strategic issues, in fact, all focused on aspects of ground operations—the terminals, slots, baggage-handling systems, traffic congestion, parking, limousine service, and so on. Isaacson's redefinition of the job led to a very different conception of the search. More important, it served as the critical transition to a new way of thinking about the mission of the entire division.

Isaacson focuses on four key questions at the beginning of a search:

1. What is the product or value that the organization produces?
2. Why are they good at producing it? What is their relative advantage or distinctive competence?
3. Why do others value it?
4. How does the role in question contribute to the strategy?

A useful stimulus to fresh thinking on the mission is exploration of analogies. Asking the question "Where should we look to find people who do similar work?" sometimes leads to rethinking the mission significantly.

Trying to capture the mission in a fresh way can help focus the search. For example, when looking for a director of court services in a delinquency agency, Isaacson (1983, p. 9) suggested:

"Court services delivers a kid on time to eight courts and keeps him cool and engaged while he's there. We're in the transportation and entertainment business."

Reflecting on the History and Culture of the Unit. One technique for assessing the personality of an organization across time comes from the recent work of Neustadt and May in *Thinking in Time: The Uses of History for Decision Makers* (1986). After discussing placing individuals, by which they mean setting down a time line and a historical context for key individuals who are critical stakeholders to a particular policy problem, they develop a similar process for organizations. The underlying premise is the same: that both individuals and organizations have personalities that are relatively stable over time and that can be broadly understood from a careful examination of formative experiences. They write (p. 212): "Government agencies are in some respects like people. The organizations have public histories usually composed of 'big events' like statutes assigning them powers and money, changes in top personnel, and controversies over programs. . . . The details of institutional history include changes in internal organization, resource allocation, or operating procedures, including the procedures that constitute the organization's personnel system (incentives and training included)."

Neustadt and May offer as an example the Central Intelligence Agency and suggest that had President Kennedy been more aware of the institutional history of the agency, he might have asked better questions before approving the Bay of Pigs. In considering executive succession, thinking about institutional history is critical. Without carefully looking at the historical forces that have created the organization as it is presently configured, one runs the risk of perpetuating arrangements that might have made sense historically but no longer have any validity.

The technique for placing an organization is relatively simple. It involves filling out the items suggested in Figure 1.

For example, if a board is filling the top job in a hospital, a brief institutional history may remind the board members of the difficult merger ten years ago. They may recall that after the merger, the first leader of the combined entities bent over backward to avoid having one party feel swallowed, keeping certain services at both

Figure 1. Placing an Organization.

	Institution or Organization
Time line	Since start of key components.
Events (special events)	Laws, leaders, or controversies widely reported or widely known to distinct publics.
Details	Internal history: structures, procedures (especially incentives).

Source: Neustadt and May, 1986, p. 275. (Reprinted with permission of The Free Press, Copyright © 1986 by Richard E. Neustadt and Ernest R. May.)

facilities when economics might have suggested consolidation, carefully balancing the senior management team with people from the two different institutions, and so on. These issues are part of the culture of this organization. The first CEO may have managed the tensions successfully, but as the board thinks about the new challenges, some of these issues are likely to be reopened. A brief review of the institutional history may bring to mind some of the strategic challenges that a new leader may face. For example, if the capital campaign will be a central issue, it may well reawaken dormant issues about who gets what.

Neustadt and May note that the growth and use of the office of planning and evaluation at the secretary level in Health, Education, and Welfare (HEW), now HHS, was critically linked to the ability of a politically appointed secretary to match wits with career-dominated analytical groups assigned to major operating units. Even twenty years after the founding of this office, this history will be relevant to the appointment of its leadership, whether the secretary intends to continue this tradition or to change it in some significant way.

Identifying Critical Stakeholders. One useful process for rethinking the mission of an organization, a division, or a role is to identify the critical stakeholders who will interact with it (Freeman, 1984). A stakeholder is any one person or group of people who affects or is affected by the actions of the unit in question. One sign of a critical strategic shift in an organization is a shift in the stakeholders. For example, in health care organizations, the 1980s saw a critical shift from regulators to customers as key stakeholders. Whereas hospital presidents previously had to be able to negotiate the critical issues with state agencies, they now need different skills to relate to prepaid health maintenance organizations (HMOs), which control aggregated demand, and to oversee strategies for reaching the ultimate consumers—patients. During the early 1970s, many directors of factories in prison saw education and training as their dominant mission. The key stakeholders then were the department of education, federal agencies, and internal colleagues in inmate services. As innovative correctional agencies pursued the idea of focusing on profitable industries that could actually meet the competitive pressures in the marketplace, unions, outside markets, and competitors became stakeholders for the director.

One useful process is to brainstorm the stakeholders, identifying their power, their view of the unit under examination, and precisely what they want from it. This will give the appointing authority a vivid sense of how the role that they are hiring for interacts with the different people who surround it. The challenge may be to alter dramatically that pattern or interaction, but one should at least begin with what the starting situation is likely to be.

Mapping the Organization. It is helpful to develop an organization chart for the unit and to examine the rationale behind the chart. Does it make sense in terms of the current and future challenges? Many organizational oddities live on long after the circumstances that shaped them have changed. When one inquires, one often gets a complex story about how Harry never did get along with Fred and therefore information services and planning units were kept as separate entities. The risk is that long after Fred and Harry are gone, when new people are being recruited for either job, no one will remember the circumstances that separated the two units. Changes in leadership represent opportunities to rethink these relationships and to correct anomalies that no longer are required because the personalities or circumstances have changed.

Failure to use this opportunity may lead to regrets later on. A deputy secretary for children and youth in a large city controlled two major divisions, child welfare and detention. The detention division was a recent addition to the deputy's responsibilities. It had previously been under a board of directors and therefore had most of its own support functions, such as budget and personnel. Shortly after the deputy secretary's arrival, the position of detention director became open, and because of the urgency in getting it filled, he proceeded immediately with an active search and hired an excellent candidate. A year later, however, as he was reflecting on his overall organization, he regretted the missed opportunity to consolidate the administrative functions in a single support group at the time of the leadership transition.

Interviews with the important staff members who will be working with the new leader can also assist in understanding the job strategically. It can also be helpful to map the work flow that the leader will oversee. The appointing executive has to understand who does what and when in getting the product or service delivered. Understanding the critical decision points and who participates in those decisions with what discretion can help one understand the culture and climate of the unit. For example, is this a professional organization in which the leader role is predominantly related to management and support rather than intervening in case-by-case decisions, or will there likely be a substantial number of appeals to the top manager? As part of the flow charting, quantifying the goals with numbers adds to one's understanding of the key challenges, especially if there are any prospective shifts in magnitude that might require substantial redesign of the basic systems. For example, if one is hiring a leader who will oversee major expansion or contraction of the labor force, one needs to understand those shifts.

Checking the Fit of the Role to the Business Strategy. A job or role is often regarded as the solution to a particular problem, but the definition of the job may change more slowly than the problem to which it was originally responding. A leadership change is a useful time to rethink the relationship. For example, in an apparel business the chief financial officer (CFO) retired after years of long service. He had stepped into the job from the bookkeeping side. He was an excellent auditor and had developed both the systems and the reputation for very tight control of costs in an industry that generally runs on thin margins. Recently, however, the firm had found a new niche: supplying a major national retailer with small quantities on short notice, which allowed the retailer very low inventory costs and some hedge against the risk of large runs of products that might do poorly in the market. The firm was not competing with Far Eastern manufacturers on price but was selling quality and speed.

The last few years had been characterized by protracted struggles, with the chief financial officer holding the line on costs and the CEO and vice-president for production seeking extra machines to develop further their strategic assets of design and speed. Although the CFO was once the answer to the historic problem of getting control over costs and developing the basic systems, the company now faced a different set of challenges, and the CFO did not have the perspective to adapt to the current strategy. His retirement led to a rethinking of the role, and a search was launched to find a CFO with the orientation and background of a general manager and the capacity to understand and use financial resources to support the business strategy. The firm eventually hired a former general manager in the retail fish business who was oriented toward the market side with a product with a short shelf life.

Identifying Critical Shifts. Brainstorming critical shifts can rapidly create a picture of the emerging context of a unit or an organization. For example, the clothing manufacturer described above might have identified shifts from high to low inventories, from a broad market to a highly focused market, and so on. A useful ground rule for the brainstorming group is that anyone can list either a pair of items or just one half of the pair. It may be clear what one is moving away from but not yet so clear what one is moving toward; conversely, the new direction may be known but it may not be clear what aspect of the system will be given up.

A top nursing office in an academic health center developed the following list of shifts:

From	*To or Toward*
1. Loosely linked to nursing school	1. Integrated, synergistic
2. Uncompetitive	2. Extremely competitive
3. Reporting to COO	3. Reporting to CEO

4. Inward, department-focused   4. Externally oriented, focused
                                        on relationships to admin-
                                        istration and physicians

Often a small group can easily generate twenty to thirty key
shifts. As a second stage, ranking the top five can produce a clear
understanding of the transformations that the leader will be
creating and to which he or she will be reacting.

Who Should Be Involved?

Executive selection is often closely held by the appointing
authority because of the complexities of involving subordinates in
the selection of their future boss. A powerful compromise is to
involve stakeholders significantly in specifying the strategic
challenges and the scope of the job, but not in screening and selecting candidates. When searching for a state director of corrections for
a Democratic governor, for instance, the recruiter discussed with
legislators from both parties the challenges facing the department
and the particular skills required by a new director. As a result, the
new director found that his working relationships, especially with
Republicans, got off to a much stronger start than he had expected.

In another situation, a group recruiting a county manager
held a morning group interview with all those directly reporting to
the county manager, getting their input to the job description, the
critical tasks, and the necessary skills. In the afternoon the group
conducted a carefully designed workshop, involving some twenty-
five other managers at different levels in the bureaucracy. Each of
the participants interviewed each other and then reported to the full
group on the patterns in the responses to questions on qualifications and critical challenges. The result was that those in major
departments, whose acceptance of a new leader was critical, felt
substantially involved in the recruiting process and had the opportunity to wrestle with the complexities of finding the right person.
The process served to transform their naive fantasies into realistic
expectations.

The views of the former occupant of the role should always
be obtained. The former leader may well be consulted by prospec-

tive candidates, so a recruiter should know what he or she will say. If scapegoating is going on, the appointing authorities may be eager to put the messiness behind them, but past circumstances must be fully understood if the organization is to avoid repeating mistakes. The lessons of the previous administration should therefore be brought into focus. It is often natural for there to be inherent tensions between the outgoing and the incoming leader. However, these are most evident in the public sector. A top business executive who has studied all the presidential transitions since Roosevelt has noted that the willing cooperation offered by the outgoing administration is regarded with suspicion and contempt by the incoming team. The consequence is the loss of enormous amounts of organizational learning.

Too often searches are either overly participative, with no one person really staffing the effort, or overly closed, with little outside input. The design of the search process should be a well-conceived mix of focused staff work, wide consultation, and executive decision making. A useful discipline is to integrate the various contributions into a single, well-formulated mission statement and job description to be circulated to critical stakeholders for their reactions. Alternatively, this step can await the work of specifying the desired characteristics of the executive.

If the mission and strategy are incorrect, no amount of skill in the subsequent phases of the search will be able to compensate for the initial error. The next chapter discusses that step, and looks at how the mission and strategy shape the specifications of desirable candidates and how executives are matched to strategy.

~ Chapter 4

Developing a Profile and Expectations of the New Leader

Reginald H. Jones, former CEO of General Electric, has described GE's experience in matching leaders and strategic challenges this way: "When we classified . . . [our] businesses, and when we realized that they were going to have quite different missions, we also realized that we had to have quite different people running them. That was when we began to see the need to meld our human resource planning and management with the strategic planning we were doing" (Fombrun, 1982, p. 46). General Electric arrayed its businesses in terms of their growth rate and profitability in four major strategic categories: stars, dogs, cash cows, and question marks. These categories suggested different managerial types. For example, in managing a situation in which the issue is to extract profits for reinvestment in other parts of the business, the critical skill needed is the ability to monitor and control costs.

Gerstein and Reisman (1983) have developed a nice conceptualization of different strategic situations and how they translate into different job thrusts and specific characteristics of the ideal candidate (see Tables 2 and 3). Clearly, few business situations fit precisely into any one of the stages; furthermore, if a business is successful at hiring someone with turnaround skills, for example, it is not necessarily in the company's best interests to look for a different leader once the turnaround specialist has brought the organization back to health. However, being aware of some of these major differences in strategic situations and the implications for leadership qualities can be a useful antidote to the erroneous notion

Table 2. Characteristics of Various Strategic Situations.

I. Startup	High financial risk
	Limited management team cohesiveness
	No organization, systems, or procedures in place
	No operational experience base
	Endless workload: multiple priorities
	Generally insufficient resources to satisfy all demands
	Limited relationship with suppliers, customers, and environment
II. Turnaround	Time pressure for "results": need for rapid situational assessment and decision making
	Poor results, but business is worth saving
	Weak competitive position
	Eroded morale: low-esteem/cohesion
	Inadequate systems: possible weak or bureaucratic organizational infrastructure
	Strained and eroded relationships with suppliers, customers, and environment
	Lack of appropriate leadership: period of neglect
	Limited resources: skills shortages: some incompetent personnel
III. Extract profit/rationalize existing business	"Controlled" financial risk
	Unattractive industry in long term: possible need to invest selectively, but major new investments not likely to be worthwhile
	Internal organizational stability
	Moderate-to-high managerial/technical competence
	Adequate systems and administrative infrastructure
	Acceptable to excellent relationships with suppliers, customers, and environment
IV. Dynamic growth in existing business	Moderate-to-high financial risk
	New markets, products, technology
	Multiple demands and conflicting priorities
	Rapidly expanding organization in certain sectors
	Inadequate managerial/technical/financial resources to meet all demands
	Unequal growth across sectors of organization
	Likely shifting power bases as growth occurs
	Constant dilemma between doing current work and building support systems for the future
V. Redeployment of efforts in existing business	Low-moderate, short-term risk/high long-term risk
	Resistance to change: likely bureaucracy in some sections
	High mismatch between some organization skill sets,

Table 2. Characteristics of Various Strategic Situations, Cont'd.

	technology, people vs. needs created by redefined strategy Likelihood of lack of strategic planning for some historical period—highly operational orientation to executive team
VI. Liquidation/ divestiture of poorly performing business	Weak competitive position, unattractive industry, or both Likely continuance of poor returns Possible morale problems and skills shortages Little opportunity for turnaround or redeployment due to unsatisfactory "payback" Need to cut losses and make tough decisions
VII. New acquisitions	Acquisitions may be classified into one of the above situations. In addition, the following conditions characterize a recent acquisition situation: Pressure on new management to "prove themselves" Existing management ambivalent/defensive about change Fundamental need to integrate acquired company with parent at some levels

Source: Gerstein and Reisman, 1983. (Reprinted from *Sloan Management Review.* Copyright © 1983 by the Sloan Management Review Association. All rights reserved.)

of hiring a general manager who is capable in any organizational situation, across a wide variety of different businesses.

Kotter recently studied general managers (GMs) and concluded: "This belief [that a well-prepared and competent 'professional' manager can manage nearly anything] . . . is almost entirely wrong. . . . Almost all the GMs I have met in the course of this study, and elsewhere, are highly specialized. That is, they have an unusual set of personal characteristics that closely fit the specific demands of the contexts in which they work" (1982, p. 5). Kotter's research suggests that "the better performers started their GM jobs with characteristics that seem to have better fit the specific demands connected with these jobs" (p. 11). If the organization faces tremendous uncertainties and is genuinely unable to formulate an

Table 3. General Management Requirements for Various Strategic Situations.

Situation	Major Job Thrusts	Specific Characteristics of Ideal Candidates
I. Startup	Creating vision of business Establishing core technical and marketing expertise Building management team	Vision of finished business Hands-on orientation: a "doer" In-depth knowlege in critical technical areas Organizing ability Staffing skills Team-building capabilities High energy level and stamina Personal magnetism: charisma Broad knowledge of all key functions
II. Turnaround	Rapid, accurate problem diagnosis Fixing short-term and, ultimately, long-term problems	"Take charge" orientation: strong leader Strong analytical and diagnostic skills, especially financial Excellent business strategist High energy level Risk taker Handles pressure well Good crisis management skills Good negotiator
III. Extract profit/rationalize existing business	Efficiency Stability Succession Sensing signs of change	Technically knowledgeable: "knows the business" Sensitive to changes: "ear-to-the-ground" Anticipates problems: "problem finder" Strong administrative skills Oriented to "systems" Strong "relationship orientation" Recognizes need for management succession and development Oriented to getting out the most: efficiency, not growth

	Strategic Situation / Tasks	Skills and Characteristics
IV. Dynamic growth in existing business	Increasing market share in key sectors Managing rapid change Building long-term health toward clear vision of the future	Excellent strategic and financial planning skills Clear vision of the future Ability to balance priorities, i.e., stability vs. growth Organizational and team-building skills Good crisis management skills Moderate-high risk taker High energy level Excellent staffing skills
V. Redeployment of efforts in existing business	Establishing effectiveness in limited business sphere Managing change Supporting "dispossessed"	Good politician/manager of change Highly persuasive: high "interpersonal influence" Moderate risk taker Highly supportive, sensitive to people: not "bull in a china shop" Excellent "systems thinker": understands how complex systems work Good organizing and executive staffing skills
VI. Liquidation/divestiture of poorly performing business	Cutting losses Making tough decisions Making best deal	"Callousness": tough-minded, determined—willing to be the bad guy Highly analytical re: costs/benefits—does not easily accept current ways of doing things Risk taker Low-glory seeking: willing to do dirty jobs—does not want glamour Wants to be respected, not necessarily liked
VII. New acquisitions	Integration Establishing sources of information and control	Analytical ability Relationship building skills Interpersonal influence Good communication skills Personal magnetism—some basis to establish "instant credibility"

Source: Gerstein and Reisman, 1983. (Reprinted from *Sloan Management Review.* Copyright © 1983 by the Sloan Management Review Association. All rights reserved.)

effective approach, it may need a leader with high tolerance for ambiguity and considerable adaptiveness to alternative scenarios.

Occasionally an organization will be totally surprised. For example, Exxon Minerals was formed and developed its first strategic plan with the assumption that the business was going to grow rapidly, but within half a year the company found itself managing substantial cutbacks. Clearly the leadership team that had been selected to grow this business was poorly matched to the task of cutback management.

Another perspective on matching candidates to situations comes from looking at the pool of applicants and considering what the patterns tell about the ways the role has been conceptualized. Some jobs may require highly unlikely combinations of skills; if there are no candidates that meet the requirements the role may have to be rethought.

The very act of wooing a leader from the outside can be regarded as going to the market to see if the organization can attract someone with a specific bundle of skills at a specific salary level. Hirschman (1970) has proposed exit and voice as the two major modes from which organizations get feedback on their performance, the former being the market mechanism so beloved by economists, the latter the political process of interest to political scientists. Recruiting a leader is the reverse of exit as a signal to the organization. Who is interested in the job? What inducements must be offered? What alternatives did the candidate have? In sum, what is the meaning of this person's making this commitment to the organization at this moment in its history? If an organization experiences extreme difficulty in translating its strategy into a realistic image of a desired executive, or if its strategy is not credible and attractive to outsiders, then it has failed to meet the reality tests of the market for executive talent. Conversely, when it is able to make a good match—for example, when a company in trouble hires a well-known turnaround specialist to head it—the appointing authority's theory of the firm's need is made concrete. The simple act of selection can begin the process of realigning internal resources.

The remainder of this chapter presents some techniques for helping the appointing authority and key stakeholders specify richly and concretely the type of person being sought, and reviews some of the arguments for and against inside and outside candidates.

Techniques for Specifying Desired Characteristics of Candidates

All organizations and groups function at two levels: a work level, during which behavior is task related and reality oriented, and a basic assumption level, which is distorted by fantasy (Bion, 1961). During leadership transitions, anxiety is often high, and the risk of distorted thinking is great. Groups can shift easily from grossly overrating a former leader to the reverse. It is particularly easy to fall prey to imagining a perfect candidate "out there" who in some magical way will address all the needs of the organization. The process of specifying the desired characteristics of an executive for a particular role must both encourage creativity and stay close to reality.

Consider the Players

The Stakeholders. A first step in the process is to consider the stakeholders. Vividly imagining all the different players or stakeholders with whom the new leader will be in contact, and the often incompatible things that significant others will want from the leader, will assist in determining what type of person to seek.

For example, a large urban Blue Shield was looking for an executive to direct a health maintenance organization. It would be a late entrant in an extremely competitive market that had seen the number of competitors double within six months and was expected to double again in the coming year. One set of stakeholders was on the supply side—doctors, hospitals, clinics, and nursing homes. Another was on the demand side—corporations with a growing interest in containing skyrocketing health care costs. Considering these clusters of stakeholders, the new venture opted for the demand side, seeking someone with "access to corporate circles and a name that was already recognized in the area" (Gaul and Bivens, 1986, p. 8A). By imagining the work of a new chief executive and recognizing the critical priority of building links to the market side, the appointing organization was able to steer the recruiting firm to executives with a strong marketing orientation.

In another example, the search for a director for a difficult juvenile detention facility that had seen twenty-two directors or acting directors in twenty-nine years, credibility with the line staff was central. The desired executive had to be able to send a message of commitment and tenacity to the internal staff members in order for them to take reform messages seriously.

The Staff. A variant of the stakeholder process can be helpful in analyzing the distinctive competence or differential advantage of the desired executive. A leader should not necessarily do what he or she is best at but rather the tasks for which the leader has the highest differential advantage over the next best person for that task. When a vacancy for a new leader is being filled, many of the existing staff members can be expected to remain in the organization. It can be helpful to analyze their strengths and weaknesses. Consider the search for a director of prison industries, mentioned earlier, whose mission was reconceptualized from a training and education focus to a competitive orientation of making a quality product at a reasonable cost. The current industry organization had good production people, but no one with any marketing orientation, so the specifications for the new leader stressed the marketing aspects of the leadership role. If it had been clear that several key skills were missing and they were unlikely to come in a single person, then the recruiting task might have switched to looking for a team. Similarly, if an organization faced tremendous pressures from a labor union but had a strong and effective director of labor relations, the appointing authority would have more latitude in thinking about the skills needed in the top job than if the current internal capabilities in labor relations were terrible, in which case the new leader would have to play a leading role in that area personally or recruit a top labor negotiator.

One of the risks in doing this type of analysis is that a change of leadership inevitably leads to personnel movement of top executives, some by their own choice, others at the request of the new leader. Some of these exits will strengthen the organization, others may weaken it. Looking at which internal stakeholders the appointing authority will be willing and able to keep during the transition may help prevent inadvertent departures. (This issue is discussed further in Chapter Seven, in connection with acting leadership.)

Top Team. Increasingly it is becoming important to look at the skill requirements in a top team rather than expecting to find them in a single executive. The task for the recruiter in a turn-around situation may be to pull together an entire team. This often happens informally in the public sector when a highly regarded manager has built up a network of support people who follow him or her into new, challenging roles.

Consider the Qualities Needed

A second approach to developing a profile of the new leader is to draw up a list of key descriptors. One effective technique is to have a group of stakeholders brainstorm adjectives describing the ideal candidate. Once a full list has been developed, each person tries to create an image with just five key words. At this stage different conceptions of the necessary skills and behaviors surface. The discussion of various priorities reveals some of the tensions that may surround the translation of the mission into operations.

For example, in specifying the desired characteristics of the head of the juvenile detention center mentioned above, the top staff of the agency listed more than thirty adjectives. As each staff member was forced to choose five, different bundles emerged, but with considerable overlap. One person saw the key characteristics as "tough, minority, political, responsive to headquarters, kid oriented." Another listed "kid oriented, street smart, imaginative, systems builder, tenacious." The group then was able to discuss the different bundles, the likelihood of their being found in a single person, and how they tied in with the overall strategy and mission. These discussions are better held before actual candidates have been identified so that criteria can be aired without political jockeying for particular candidates.

Another useful exercise is for individuals—or, more creative-ly, groups—to imagine that a person has been hired and that in a planning meeting with that person they are setting objectives. What objectives and timetables would they set for the executive, looking out over the next few years? The group then constructs what might be regarded as a draft performance contract, drawing on each person's own theories of the sequence of tasks and the amount of time that would be needed to reach each milestone. Again, differing expectations can be worked through and discussed.

Another method for thinking about specific people is what Isaacson (1983, p. 10) terms the "irrational, unfair, unarticulatable sixty-day test." Knowledgeable people are asked to assume that, within the first sixty days, their intuition tells them that the new person is right for the job. What might be some of the early clues— long before one can reasonably expect solid accomplishments—that might lead to such an intuition? What small behaviors, often beneath notice, offer real insights into the characteristics being sought? Vivid, hypothetical examples are needed, rather than platitudes like "win the trust of line staff." For example, someone might say "dance with staff at the Christmas party" as a way of highlighting a contrast with a former leader who was very reserved and disengaged from staff. Asking people to think back to prior transitions and what early signals made them think that the choice was going to work can help them think concretely.

I recall the moment I became confident of one newly appointed leader. He had taken over after a succession of different leaders of a corrections agency facing a major court battle. As part of a consent decree, five other consultants and I had been brought in as evaluators. When the newly appointed leader sent each evaluator a thank-you note after a conference, I knew that he was going to be effective at the critical task of rebuilding alliances with outsiders. That one tiny detail showed that he was aware of the need to co-opt the outsiders and had the follow-through to do it, characteristics that had been absent in the prior regime.

A somewhat different and quite powerful approach to identifying desirable characteristics is to think of actual people as examples, especially people who would not be candidates for the job. For example, in discussing leadership issues with the National Jail Center someone suggested Jesse Jackson because he could both be very tough on his audiences of black teenagers and at the same time inspire them to higher achievement. This analogy beautifully captured the tension in the center's mission to join with its customers (sheriffs and jail managers) and yet to be completely honest about the often deplorable conditions of local jails.

Put the Job in Context

The various approaches to specifying desired characteristics of candidates can be pulled together into a set of questions that will help set the job into a strategic framework:

1. What are the strategic challenges facing this leader in the coming six months? Year? Two to three years?
2. How would you know or begin to suspect within the first three months whether your choice was going to be successful? What would be some early indicators?
3. Who are the people and roles that this person needs to interact with? What specific behaviors does each want from this leader? What conflicts might there be with him or her?
4. What behaviors, attitudes, and skills are required to be effective in relating to each of the major stakeholder groups?
5. What are the day-to-day tasks and responsibilities? How does the overall flow of work occur in this unit? What particular skills would add value? Which ones are essential?
6. What are the magnitudes of the major internal tasks, such as budget size and complexity, numbers of employees supervised, total employees, and annual sales?
7. What are some key adjectives that would describe the ideal candidate? If you had to pick only five to seven of these to capture this person's essential qualities, what would they be?
8. What skills and past experiences does the leader need to work effectively?
9. What are the typical daily, weekly, monthly, and yearly activities of the job?

Inside or Outside?

Many people erroneously assume that a strategic examination of mission and leadership characteristics is needed only when a job is to be filled from outside the organization. When *any* major executive post becomes vacant, the appointing authority should cycle through the mission and strategy questions that were discussed in Chapter Three and do the work of translating them into desired characteristics of the leader. Only by doing so can one test the fit of an internal successor. In a sense, it is only fair to internal candidates to compare them against a wider potential pool, so that they feel they have been affirmatively chosen. Within an organization an aggressive search can often be productive; candidates from other divisions may offer special strengths, especially when the job has been reassessed strategically. For example, as companies face the quality challenge, people with hands-on knowledge of production may be more attractive than those who have come up through finance.

One leader in a public agency strongly believes in the use of transitions for both personal development and organizational renewal. He has a firm policy of never promoting within the same line but rather giving people new assignments in different divisions. In this way, the new leaders get to take their new roles without the usual problems of supervising former peers. He has the new appointees spend a retreat session with the agency director, developing their transition strategy, and then go on a learning journey, interviewing key others with whom they will be working in their new roles. Within this scheme, he is always actively searching to match people and roles (Friedman, 1986).

Similarly, large organizations such as General Electric have developed internal executive placement groups. GE is constantly culling the top six hundred executives, thinking about who is ready for what roles, reassessing the challenges in different jobs, and building the human capital at the top of the company (Friedman and LeVino, 1984).

The greater the shift in strategy, the more likely it is that the search will need to go outside. People and organizations adapt to one another over time, forming a culture that shapes the behavior of the group. People who have grown up during the old code, even those who are high performers by past performance criteria, may have difficulty in the new orientation. When AT&T needed to nurture a marketing orientation, it discovered that it could not do it by retraining executives, who had grown up during the regulated era, but rather had to import executives from marketing-oriented companies to champion and model the new values. Even then, some of these outsiders failed because of the culture clashes.

Going outside has its risks. In the case of general managers, Kotter (1982) argues that even the most talented outsiders have two liabilities: they rarely bring the detailed knowledge of the business and industry that he sees as essential to high performance, and they lack the necessary network of personal contacts, both inside and outside the organization. He concludes that outsiders should be considered only when relevant relationships can be developed quickly, when many key relationships are transferable (for example, within an industry in which many external relationships are the same for all companies), and when the inside choices are so weak that taking a risk makes sense.

One study suggests that insider appointments in business outperform outsiders. Of 110 companies studied, 25 percent of those with insider chief executives had returns on invested capital that exceeded 10 percent, whereas only 10 percent of those with outsiders achieved those rates of return (Bernstein, 1980). Of course, the classic reason for going outside is financial difficulties, so on average outsiders would have faced more difficult circumstances. Nevertheless, it is clear that learning must take place before an outsider is up to speed and has developed the necessary networks to implement a new program.

Outsiders need to be able to read and adapt to the culture in which they find themselves. One fast-growing high-tech company hired a highly regarded executive who failed, in part because he was used to working with excellent support that did not exist in this company. He was constantly being surprised by mistakes in analyses that his department produced and that he had not checked over closely enough. He never was able to make the transition from a setting with a talented support staff to an organization stretched very thin from its high rate of growth.

Often the question of insider versus outsider involves a tradeoff: freshness of perspective (outsider) against the ability to implement effectively (insider). Some organizations have been lucky in getting an insider who brings both a fresh vision (usually from having been outside the dominant coalition) and the insider knowledge to move rapidly. The Philadelphia school district conducted a year-long search and ended up with an excellent inside choice who has been a major force in revitalizing the school district. Paradoxically, external search firms can play a useful role in helping appointing authorities see the value of some of the inside candidates, especially in comparison with real rather than fantasy outsiders.

Once the characteristics of the desired leader have been determined, the search for that leader begins. The next chapter discusses the techniques that are used to produce a pool of high-quality candidates.

∼ Chapter 5

Conducting an Effective Executive Search

Effective selection of a new leader takes time. Table 4 gives a rough estimate of the ranges of effort (in person days) and elapsed time that each of the four steps can take. Important as the first two steps are (identifying the key challenges and developing a profile of the desired candidate), it is the active search phase of identifying potential candidates—step 3—that involves the most effort and takes the most time. Executive recruiting firms suggest that 150 to 200 hours of telephone networking may be required to build an adequate pool of high-quality finalists for a key executive role. In one search for a health commissioner, for example—a search with serious time pressures—106 people were contacted either as sources or as potential candidates. This effort took 23 days and 164 hours of effort and yielded a pool of 30 potential candidates.

It is at this stage that many organizations get bogged down. A board is often ill equipped to put in the full-time effort that is required; when top executives are doing the hiring, the search competes with other pressing business. Often an appointing executive gets caught up in a vicious circle. In one organization, the new leader reorganized early in his tenure, creating two new deputy positions, one for operations and one for administration. He filled the operations position quickly from within but felt that no viable insider was available for the administrative opening.

He began an active search to fill this job, using his executive assistant as a key staffer. Because all the units at the next level—such as personnel, budget, planning, and labor relations—were now re-

Table 4. Time Involved in Overall Search Process.

Stages	Person Days		Total Elapsed Time in Weeks	
	By Top Authority	By Staff or Recruiter	Low	High
1. Rethinking the strategic challenges	½ to 1	3 to 8	1	2
2. Specifying the desired characteristics	½ to 1	3 to 5	2	4
3. Building a rich pool of candidates	1 to 3	20 to 30	6	16
4. Screening and selection	3	2 to 5	7	18

porting directly to him, however, he and his executive assistant found it very difficult to spend adequate time on recruiting. Hence, he delayed filling the position and perpetuated the overload. In this instance, the labor relations role, critical because of upcoming first-time negotiations, was also vacant, yet the leader was understandably reluctant to fill that spot without consulting the person who would be supervising that role and would be held accountable for the performance of that unit.

A delay in filling a deputy role also has other repercussions: the longer the lower-level units get accustomed to reporting directly to the higher level, the more difficult the transition becomes when the deputy arrives and takes over directing them.

Hiring key executives is a critical task that, if done well and in a timely fashion, generates benefits far beyond the time that is invested in it. In this chapter, I examine the major components of an active search: identifying the areas in which candidates might be found, helping sources think about potential candidates, actively selling the opportunity, and managing information on the search. I close with a discussion of the advantages and disadvantages of using an executive recruiter versus developing the capability internally. For the internal option, I identify the specific characteristics necessary to be a good recruiter and describe how that role can fit into an executive development strategy for an organization.

Developing an Active Approach

Much of the variance in the performance of organizations is linked to the quality of the people, which in turn depends on effective recruiting. For a new leader, therefore, it is important to stay on the task of hiring key managers and not get seduced into the fascinating substantive challenges of the job. For example, Joseph Califano was appointed to President-elect Carter's cabinet as Secretary of Health, Education, and Welfare on December 21, 1980. Califano (1981, p. 34) writes, "From the moment Carter asked me to be Secretary, I began making lists of candidates for jobs. . . . From Christmas until mid-March I spent at least five and often ten hours a day, discussing, interviewing, and selecting personnel. If necessary, I talked to candidates' spouses, . . . bosses, and friends, assisted in making housing arrangements or getting free legal advice on conflict of interest problems, and even negotiated leaves of absence from their private jobs and bonuses to help them move."

Califano realized that despite the many pressing substantive issues, he would be powerless to offer sustained leadership without attracting top talent to the department. A change in the presidency clearly represents an extreme in the turnover in top policy posts, but it exemplifies the two-stage process that is frequently seen when leadership change is used as a critical revitalization approach. The first stage is getting the top person (for the organization, division, or unit), who in turn attracts the next layer of talent required to bring about the change. Gabarro's research (1985) suggests that personnel actions come in two waves, an initial set immediately when the leader takes over and a second wave when the leader has a clearer sense of how to undertake the reshaping.

Assume that the appointing authority has identified the strategic challenges and has translated those into the types of skills and behaviors that a new leader should bring to the job. Assume further that the appointing authority has overcome all the blocks to an active recruiting approach and has been able to get the recruitment process organized and staffed with trusted personnel. The next steps in the search process are to identify areas where interesting candidates might be found and to begin an extensive telephone hunt to identify specific people.

Identifying Promising Areas

Talent runs in strings. Talented people often surround themselves with other thoughtful, talented people. These pockets of talent come about because good leaders recruit good people, and good young people actively seek places where exciting things are happening. The Lindsay administration in New York City had many difficulties, but it was clearly an exciting place that attracted many talented young people to their initial jobs in public service. Over the years since then, many graduates of that particular administration have gone on to make distinguished contributions in administrations all over the country. Henry Kissinger's National Security staff has served as a rich pool in foreign affairs. In the corporate world, Procter & Gamble has a reputation for developing talent in the world of marketing. Alumni of Digital Equipment Corporation have staffed many of the successful new high-tech ventures around Boston.

Identifying areas where talent may be found is key, because no amount of active searching will rectify an error in choice of area. Like the drunk under the street light who was looking for the keys he lost in a dark alley, many organizations search areas that they know well rather than the ones that might actually have high-quality candidates. Ideas for areas flow both from the mission of the role and from the specific challenges that are identified for the job. Recall the earlier example in which John Isaacson recognized that a new director of aviation might be found in the *ground* transportation business.

Similarly, in the case of the new HMO, the key challenge was getting access to top managers of corporations, so the project head looked for executives with that access already in place rather than for health care executives with a knowledge of the business.

Identification of potential areas can begin with the same people who drew up the specifications for the job. In a group setting, each person can be asked, "Where (in what location, profession, or jurisdiction) might interesting candidates for this job have worked?" A facilitator can then take one suggestion from each participant in a round-robin fashion until the group has a rich list of potential areas. The kinds of areas that might be explored include competitors; organizations that share the same clients but offer different services; services to the organization, such as accountants, lawyers, and consultants; observers of the field, such as journalists and academics; trade associations and national groups; subcontractors; and government regulators.

It is useful to push the group to think divergently about as many places as possible. One technique is to look at some of the major tasks facing the role and then think about where one might find the person for each role. For example, if a city is looking for a director of a computer center and one strategic task is to build a unified organization from three or four groups that had been in different organizations, one might think of people who had been through recent mergers. Another task for that job might be predominantly technical, in which case the areas might be consultants, major computer companies, or information services executives at major corporations.

Even when the area seems fairly straightforward, it is useful to probe, focusing the search on the experiences that are most likely to have produced the desired candidate. A highly successful high-tech company decided to create an internal venture capital group. In discussions with a search firm, the company realized it did not want the traditional type of venture capitalist: usually a Harvard MBA, from one of the right colleges, who was very bright and had done well working for an investment or finance firm or had done strategy and financial analysis for a major strategy consulting group. Instead, they asked the search firm to look for an operating type who had taken more than one successful venture from concept to market. They wanted someone who could add value, not just on the financial analysis, but also on the people, the operations, and the difficult developmental stages involved in nurturing the venture to maturity, "someone who has made their mistakes on someone else's time." This type of up-front discussion saves considerable time during the search and prevents misunderstandings when candidates are presented for consideration in the final pool.

In another situation, a commissioner of health was searching for a deputy. The search team began to think of places where such a person might be found and turned to other state governments. The team realized that thirty-six governorships were up for election; of those, fifteen were sure to turn over because of retirements and limitations of terms. The search team therefore targeted states whose health departments had a good reputation and that were likely to have a turnover.

An area may also be shaped by the relative risks in the job. For example, in one city with an embattled mayor and a rash of scandals, someone considering the recruiting challenges suggested focusing on two categories: people toward the end of their careers, with secure pensions and professional reputations, who might be recruited as a capstone challenge; and young, untried types who would be willing to take the risks because they would get a much larger operation at an earlier career stage. Targeting a search on a particular stage of a career can be effective. Governor Blanchard of Michigan, facing critical fiscal issues, told recruiters for the state treasurer role that he wanted someone "who would worry about ruining his reputation on Wall Street . . . someone who would care about how our bond issues did, because his future income would be on the line." They found someone from a Wall Street firm who has taken the state bonds from a Baa rating—the lowest in the nation—to top grade ("Alum Fights in Trenches of State Government," 1986, p. 5).

Using Sources

As one begins to map out the territory within which the hunt will take place, it is useful to distinguish between sources and candidates. Sources are lodestones of talent, people well positioned to know the field and the likely candidates. Sources can be consultants, academic experts, professional associations, perhaps newspaper or magazine reporters who have recently done some work in the area of interest. They have perspectives and careers that are oriented more to the field than to any single organization. Their work brings them into contact with many different organizations, so they have a wide circle of acquaintances and can make comparisons. A legislative staff member may have such a vantage point, especially if the job will require careful collaboration with legislative bodies. A recent program of the relevant national professional association can provide a list of speakers who may be good sources, as can the author list of a journal in the area of interest. People at the end of careers related to the role are excellent sources, as they often have in their own backgrounds ideas about unlikely places where potential candidates might be found.

Sources play two roles, at different stages of the search. In the early stages, they help the recruiter understand the lay of the land. They can assist in testing out the job description and can react to and add to the initial hunches about the best places to look. Sources help the recruiter sound credible in subsequent contacts with other sources and with candidates, by adding to his or her knowledge of the industry and its career dynamics. At the end of the search, sources are critical for getting initial reactions to specific candidates or the types of skills that they bring.

It is often good strategy, therefore, to make the first twenty calls to sources rather than to candidates. The recruiter must communicate the excitement and challenge in the job, so that the source is motivated to think about the problem. In fact a source can be a major asset in refining the pitch, both by serving as an audience for a trial run and by explicitly questioning whether the job is likely to attract people and how it can best be sold. A source is like a focus group in a marketing survey; the recruiter is getting some reactions to a proposed package: the challenge, the salary, the location, the job security, the substantive opportunities, and so on. Information from the source can lead to revisions in the package or can shape how the recruiter makes the pitch to actual candidates.

One of the critical skills of a recruiter is getting sources to stay on the telephone long enough to offer initial suggestions for candidates. Despite good intentions, many who say that they want time to think and will call back fail to do so. A particularly well-positioned source may be worth a second call, but only after the recruiter has gotten some initial suggestions to check out (as a pretext for the call). In probing for names, one can sometimes free up a source by suggesting that they name people who would *not* be likely to take the job but represent some of the desired characteristics. This technique can get sources thinking and can lead to some good positive suggestions. Asking specific questions—for example, about sources' participation in national association activities or experience with particular consulting firms—can also help jog memories. It takes time for people to begin to access their knowledge about potential candidates.

During the initial stages of a search, a higher percentage of calls goes to sources than to candidates. As the search proceeds, the ratio of sources to candidates shifts. The line between source and candidate is fuzzy, however; the role of source can be an ego-protecting position from which to think about the job. As a source, one can inquire further about the job and its prospects without explicitly declaring an interest in being a candidate. The role of source can serve both candidate and recruiter as a transition in either direction. An unlikely candidate can be treated as a source, and a source can develop into a candidate.

Actively Selling the Job

Whether the recruiter is calling a potential candidate who is already happily and productively employed or an eminent source who is extremely busy, there is a limited opportunity to get that person's attention via what Isaacson has termed "the pitch." Because selling the opportunity is so critical, the recruiter and the team should, before going to the market, spend time developing, refining, and actively practicing the pitch. An actual script is useful, but it must be modified for each different context. In developing the pitch, the task is to identify the aspects of the job that will be regarded as assets—the organization, the colleagues, the salary, the careers the job could lead into, the skills that could be developed, the physical location, and so on. It is also useful to imagine possible reasons why the job might be hard to sell and ways to reframe those aspects positively. The pitch also includes concrete information—facts and figures, historical trends, current strategic plans for the unit—that establishes that the recruiter is knowledgeable about the context.

These presentations must be honest; nothing destroys a working relationship so much as a feeling of being misled. The appointing executive must carefully review the pitch and authorize the assertions that are to be made. The team should also anticipate questions that candidates and sources may ask: How many new people could I hire? Could the role report in at a higher level? What would be my budget? How much can current policies and procedures be altered?

In framing the pitch, however, the appointing executive must take care not to make commitments that are organizationally unsound. At a time of transition in a governor's office, the three most important people to the overall financial management of the state were hired in the reverse order of importance. Each extracted from the governor a promise of "direct access" to the governor. When the team finally took shape, the governor wanted the budget secretary (the last hired) to oversee the entire operation, and thus had to renegotiate his promise of "direct access."

Persuading a happy job-holder in one setting to become a candidate for a job in another setting often stimulates deep anxieties. The candidate is in a one-down position, involving judgments of fitness; to compete raises issues of losing. To consider changing jobs also raises deep identity issues, requiring one to rethink one's career, both as it has unfolded up to the present and images for the future. If a physical relocation is involved, a change will raise issues with spouse and family. The recruiter during this phase is therefore not just a technocrat building a list of names. He or she must be aware of the psychological needs of potential candidates as they reflect on these issues and be prepared to help them make this mental transition.

Keeping the Books

An accurate record of conversations with all sources and candidates is critical. Issues of considerable importance are involved, and the recruiter needs to be able to review quickly previous conversations so that any additional information can be couched in the context of prior discussions. The simplest device for keeping track is a notebook with alphabetical dividers and a page for each person. The source of the reference goes in the upper left, and the name of the person being called goes in the upper right, along with a code to indicate whether the person is regarded initially as a candidate (C), potential candidate (PC), or source (S). Key facts such as title and phone number are listed.

The remainder of the sheet is used for a log of contacts with that person and for entries about that person. For example, if Ms. Jones names five people she thinks would be good for a job, those five names are noted on her sheet, and each becomes a page with Ms. Jones listed as the reference. If Mr. Smith then offers information on one of those five, it appears both on Mr. Smith's page and on that person's page.

At the front of the book, it is helpful to keep a running list of actual candidates, noting those that have agreed to send a resume. A system of logging in the resumes and building candidate files will ensure that they are acknowledged. A short printed document containing a description of the recruiting process as well as a job description and background information on the organization, to be sent when a candidate has expressed interest, is a big time saver.

During the intense periods of a search, it is not easy to keep the books up to date. Most critical is to capture the new names and phone numbers. A paper clip on a page can signal that there are cross references to be transferred at the end of the day. The book is effective only when it is up to date, so great care should be taken not to let it get too far behind. If the organization is of any significant size, the books that are developed become ongoing working assets of the recruiter and can often be a useful starting place for subsequent job searches.

If two or more people are making calls, the team needs to develop ground rules, or they are likely to get in each other's way. One strategy is to begin in different networks, so that the overlap is minimal. As the search proceeds, they will be getting into similar pools and will need to update each other regularly about who has been called. Nothing makes a worse impression on a potential candidate or source than being called by two different staffers. Conversely, the organization presents itself positively when someone else can take a return telephone call and be knowledgeable about the prior contacts.

In addition to the notebook documenting the telephone networking, the recruiter must handle carefully all resumes that come in from a public job posting or from others who hear about the job and apply. Sometimes organizations become so taken with an active search that they unconsciously belittle people who apply for the job on their own. A protocol for such applications should be established so that each is logged in and acknowledged, with information on the overall time frame and when the applicant is likely to be contacted further. If the recruiter fails to tell an applicant the schedule, phone calls requesting the information are sure to follow. Since many candidates may not want a current employer to know that they are applying, letters addressed to business addresses should be marked "personal."

Staffing the Search: Internal or External?

There are three options for getting the necessary support for effective recruiting. First, hire an executive recruiting firm. Second, build an internal capability by developing the skills of a staff member. Finally, one can sometimes get outside assistance in the form of an advisory committee, with one member taking the lead in the sustained recruiting. This last method usually works only in the public sector when the role being recruited for is important enough that some of the key external stakeholders are willing to put in significant time.

External Consultants. Recruiting is difficult work. It calls for clinical skills as well as perseverance and stamina. Building an internal capability is not easy, and often an external recruiter can be the best way to ensure that the necessary time and talent are put against the job. If one decides to use an executive recruiting firm, however, it is critical to take sufficient time to interview and check out the firm, since success depends on trust and compatibility.

Because of the increased mobility of executives, the executive recruiting industry is growing rapidly, but it still suffers from its earlier reputation of being shady and surreptitious, hence the slang "headhunter." In a *Wall Street Journal* and Gallup poll ("Survey of Business Executives," 1980), top executives reported that executive recruiters were the provider of services they were least satisfied with, in comparison with lawyers, investment bankers, accountants, and others. Only 11 percent were "very" satisfied, 42 percent "fairly satisfied."

Executive recruiters follow a process close to that outlined here. They begin with a description of the job to be filled, build lists of potential candidates from active searching and from preexistent data banks (if they are specialized in the area), help to screen candidates, and check out credentials. Two norms of the industry are important. Most firms will redo an executive search if the candidate hired fails within the first year for reasons related to the recruiting process. Second, firms will not recruit for two years from a firm in which they have placed an executive. This second standard cuts two ways. On the one hand, it protects an organization that opens itself up to a recruiter from having its talented executives recruited away. If a recruiting firm is big and specialized, however, it may be barred from recruiting in many organizations and may not be able to search as rich a pool as the appointing authority may want. Most firms will give a list of organizations that are off limits to them, so that a client can assess the costs to the search.

The work of recruiting should not be overdelegated to an executive recruiter. Collaboration and trust with the appointing authority are as important as the competence of the recruiter. For this reason, the hiring organization should know both the firm and the particular recruiter who will be assigned to the search. It is wise to check with colleagues who have used the firm previously.

Some of the issues to reflect on in hiring an outside recruiter are size, specialization, and costs. Big firms may have richer data bases and more national or international contacts, but they may give less customized service than small firms. There are both generalist and specialist firms, each with strengths and weaknesses, depending on the type of executive being recruited. Fees are usually about one third of the starting salary of the position, sometimes paid on a contingency basis.

The great advantage of a skilled outsider is that he or she can challenge the organization's "groupthink" (Janis, 1982) about the strategic challenges and the kind of executive that is needed. But not all search firms have the skills to advise on strategy, and too many accept uncritically the job requirements as given by the client and view their contribution as simply finding and assessing talent. Isaacson suggests that the major variance in performance of search firms is in the front end of the work: "The most overrated part of headhunting is the search. It's not hard to come up with lots of names for a job. The trick is to figure out what the job requires. Any job is a solution to a problem, but most people who hire don't stop to think what the problem is. They just look for someone who has the same credentials as the last person who had the job, when in fact the job has changed in the meantime. So they're always fighting the last war. In most cases, the real solution is to change the problem" (Tierney, 1985, p. 358).

Internal Search Team. Grooming and matching talent to top jobs are often an ongoing process for organizations, and there are many arguments in favor of developing an internal recruiting capability. In some organizations this is highly organized. General Electric, as we saw in Chapter Four, has a group that functions as an internal search firm, judging talent and recommending developmental moves (Friedman and LeVino, 1984). Other organizations have one or two people who specialize in recruiting but take on other staff assignments when no active searches are under way. This role can make a major contribution to a staff member's executive development, because it involves working with the organization's leadership in a close and confidential way as well as talking with many executives both inside and outside the organization.

Many organizations fail to recognize that senior management recruitment is a continuous process. Especially in the public sector, the myth is that the major recruiting occurs at the beginning of an administration and that once the team is in place, the work of the organization begins. A close look at many administrations, however, reveals a fairly constant flow of executives in and out, many of them requiring some outside searching.

If a search is to be handled internally, one of the most important tasks is to identify the right person to run it. The work is difficult and time-consuming. Developing a deep pool, as we saw earlier in this chapter, requires intensive telephone work to both sources and candidates. The work calls for considerable clinical skill: judging when to push potential candidates, assessing people on the basis of limited context, and listening, as it were, between the lines. It also requires the persistence of a direct sales representative making cold calls. Isaacson has suggested that a good recruiter is part salesperson, part social worker, part detective, and part investigative reporter.

Because the process of networking takes place among several of the stakeholder groups of the organization, it has to be done with a quality that will reflect well on the organization. Few things are as damaging to the reputation of an organization as mishandling recruiting by failing to acknowledge resumes, failing to inform people of the steps in the hiring process, losing files, announcing who has been hired without telling those not selected, and other such breaches of etiquette. Conversely, a well-executed search builds the reputation of the organization and signals its values. In some respects, running an effective search is like running a political campaign, keeping tabs on a large and growing network of people, each with different motivations that must be attended to.

It is fatal to overdelegate this work to someone in the personnel department who hardly knows the appointing authority. The recruiter, whether inside or outside, is an agent of the appointing executive and needs easy access to that executive to check out situations rapidly when they arise. This person must effectively represent the interests of the hiring executive and communicate this relationship to potential candidates. The closer and more valued the aide is to the appointing authority, the clearer it is to others that the search for quality personnel has high priority.

Attributes of a Good Recruiter

To be effective, the recruiter must be:

- *Assertive:* Able to get past executive secretaries without being unduly aggressive, to keep busy people on the telephone and persuade them to think of candidates, to push until they have made a contribution to the search.
- *Articulate and persuasive:* Able to communicate the mission, the excitement of the job, the degree of challenge, and the opportunity for someone's career, and to tailor the pitch to different people.
- *Persistent and not easily frustrated:* Networking takes time. Like panning for gold, it involves much sifting through dirt and rejecting fool's gold until one gets to the high-grade ore.
- *Organized:* Capable of staying on top of the growing complexity, keeping good records of each encounter, knowing who said what about whom on what date. A search develops a lot of

information and engages, albeit briefly, many people, some of them very important to the organization.

- *Attentive to detail:* Able to keep track of many different commitments and follow through, sending a full description of the job, providing a map to a candidate coming in for an interview, and so on.

- *Trustworthy and discreet:* Many people do not want their current employer to know that they are interested in a job. Many others want some signal that the hiring organization is interested in them before they will express their intent to be a serious candidate. Rumors abound in both the public and the private sectors. An effective recruiter has to be discreet and has to come across to candidates as someone who can be trusted with confidential and potentially damaging information. One state commissioner agreed to talk with another state about an opening there and was outraged when a local radio station announced what he had thought was a confidential meeting. These gaffes not only damage the situation with a particular candidate but, if known, keep others from indicating a serious interest.

- *Capable of effectively representing the appointing authority:* The way questions are handled and the speed with which the recruiter gets back to the candidate indicate whether or not the recruiter has good access to and a high-quality relationship with the appointing authority.

- *Fascinated by the issues of authority and management:* Because the interchange between a recruiter and candidates is about managing, organizing, and changing, a staff member in this role needs to be familiar with the true difficulties of running complex organizations.

- *Knowledgeable about the industry or business in which the job is located:* This, too, indicates seriousness and allows the recruiter to make persuasive arguments and relay important information.

Peter Bell, a foundation executive who served as recruiter for former HEW Secretary Joseph Califano, has noted that he would informally measure the success of a recruiting effort by looking at the subsequent career paths of the finalists who were *not* hired by Califano. If these candidates went on to important jobs, it demonstrated that the final pool of applicants had all been people of substance and that as a recruiter he had given his boss meaningful choices.

An ironclad law of recruiting is that the final choice cannot be better than the best person in the pool. Once a rich pool is developed, the appointing authority faces the processes of choosing a final candidate, which is described in the next chapter.

↩ Chapter 6

Selecting and Hiring
the Best Candidate

Few skills are more critical—or harder to develop—than the ability to assess talent in people. Some executives seem to be good at surrounding themselves with talented people, and others are not. To be really successful in building a high-quality staff, a senior executive must have that talent and be able to detect it in others, because often the first challenge for newly chosen subordinates is to build their own team.

The selection process involves two rival bases of comparison. First, candidates are stacked up against one another: Who has more of the relevant experience and skills? Second, each candidate is compared against the ideal that inevitably has formed during the process of specifying the challenges and necessary skills. The ideal candidate can sometimes cast a shadow over the actual pool. If the search team suspects that someone is substantially better than anyone they have been able to draw into the pool, they may defer making a judgment and reopen the search.

One of the contributions of a well-run search, however, is that it increases the appointing authority's confidence that no good candidates have been overlooked. If the pool does not contain a desirable candidate, the specifications of the job will have to be reconsidered—perhaps the salary, the combination of tasks, or the level of support. In a sense, going to market with a well-specified job can be viewed as market research into the organizational design, job content, and the wording of job titles. If there is a serious anomaly, it will show in the lack of viable candidates.

If a pool of potential candidates has been developed, however, the process of final selection begins. In an initial sort, the list of twenty to forty names is reduced to the six to ten who deserve a closer look. A second, more difficult cut produces a short list of finalists, and finally a choice is made. This chapter examines these steps, which are based on different ways of thinking about the candidates and call for different procedures.

Narrowing the Field

In its early stages, the winnowing process should be explicitly divergent, to maximize the choices the selector will have. For example, even if bringing in someone from outside is clearly indicated, it may be helpful to carry one inside candidate into later stages of deliberation. Similarly, an interesting applicant who does not precisely fit the specifications might be kept in the pool to stimulate further thinking.

Assume that the active search process described in Chapter Five has developed an initial list of ten to thirty names, culled from perhaps several hundred names. The recruiter has already sorted the large group into categories: "clearly unacceptable," "unlikely," and "possible." Already the recruiter has some information on those "possible" names and has formed impressions from contacts with them: how they responded to the description of the challenges, the questions they asked, their interest in the job, and their willingness to be considered.

First Interview. The next step is a brief initial interview with the most promising candidates, usually focusing on the candidate's current organizational context (what the organization does, its niche, its clients, budget, funding, income, size of the department, size of the total organization), the prospect's role in the organization (what he or she does, where the job fits, how it is linked to key strategic issues, reporting relationships, key working alliances up, down, and laterally), and the nature of the candidate's work (a day-to-day overview of work, most important project, biggest challenge, toughest problem, story line of a key assignment from idea to implementation, whose idea it was, key stakeholders, critical barriers, outcomes, and lessons learned).

During these twenty-minute interviews the recruiter focuses the discussion on the aspects of the candidate's experience that are relevant to the job. For example, if the executive is going to have to work with entrenched bureaucrats over whom he or she has relatively little control, then the conversation might focus on a past experience in which the candidate has had to negotiate commitment to a new policy.

The screening process is best accomplished when the recruiter is constantly thinking, What type of person do I have in front of me? How does this person's career fit what one might expect? Isaacson (n.d., p. 91) has developed a shorthand list of critical skills he considers necessary for an effective executive; he terms them *hunger, speed,* and *weight.*

> 1. *Hunger.* Hunger is the marriage of imagination to ambition. Hunger is having a rich fantasy about what one wants to accomplish and the will to struggle to realize it in the world. Hunger is the drive to leave a mark, to build a monument, to make something out of nothing. It is the capacity of a mature mind to tap the irrational and intuitive depths of personality and to harness those darker powers to moral pursuits. T. E. Lawrence described this quality as follows: "All men dream . . . but not equally. They who dream by night in the dusty recesses of their minds wake in the day to find that all is vanity; but the dreamers of the day are dangerous men, for they act their dream with open eyes, to make it possible."
>
> 2. *Speed.* Speed is the capacity to learn quickly, mastering and retaining technical material that is relevant to one's work, pushing ahead courageously to new territories that one is uncomfortable with. Creativity or breaking set, the ability to see the same set of facts in a different framework, is another critical element. Most critical is the ability to learn from one's own experience, especially from mistakes, the ability to step back and reflect on a painful failure and draw

the right lessons about one's own behavior rather than blaming others.

3. *Weight.* Weight concerns how someone carries his or her authority. It is the combination of solid judgments that marry legal authority and personal capacity to command respect and obedience. Weight means the marriage of truth telling and command in a single person. It concerns the ability to learn and speak the truth to superiors fearlessly, but the ability to accept and execute their decisions. Looking downward, it is the ability to hear the truth from subordinates without defensiveness and take action that will command respect and follow through. The exercise of authority is experienced as weight when it is in the service of a mission or task, not simply interpersonal bullying.

At this stage the recruiter should not feel pressure to have a zero-defect pool. There will likely be candidates who on closer inspection turn out to be completely out of the question. There is never enough time to do even a preliminary check on *all* the candidates. Someone may be in the pool simply on the recommendation of a usually reliable source.

The First Cut. A meeting should then be held in which the appointing executive and the recruiter winnow down the "possible" list. The executive should also quickly screen the "unacceptable" and "unlikely" lists, in case any require special treatment. Other managers or staff members may participate in the discussions at this stage, but the ground rule of confidentiality must be well understood. The recruiter presents names and any information that is available on the candidates in the pool—resumes, brief comments from sources, and information from the screening interviews. The appointing authority sorts the group, screening out some and noting key information that would be needed on others if they were to become serious candidates. Clark Kerr, former president of the University of California, who feels that trustees are becoming too risk-aversive in searches for college presidents, suggests that appointing authorities might want to look affirmatively for "good trouble" in the backgrounds of potential candidates (Hechinger, 1984, p. 6). For example, an applicant may have been fired by a previous employer for reasons that indicate integrity rather than incompetence.

The meeting should result in six to ten candidates for further inspection. As with the earlier screenings, the organization will benefit by explicitly keeping different types of candidates in the pool. For example, if the critical choice is between someone with excellent health care credentials and someone with excellent access to the corporations in the area, the final pool might contain the best in each category. One might even keep in the pool a candidate who ranked lower than someone screened out, precisely because that person represents a different conception of the leadership role. Especially if the search has turned up candidates with one or two of the desired characteristics but few with all, the appointing executive is well served by a recruiter who says, "Let's look at three different candidates to explore what strengths each would bring and what weaknesses we would have to manage around."

With the pool reduced to six to ten candidates, the recruiter can invest more in checking out the credentials of each. A critical issue is how to assess the person against the challenges. People are more complex than their resumes or their performance in an interview can show. Clearly the best measure of potential is current performance in a job that resembles the one being recruited for.

In jobs in which there are many qualified applicants, some organizations have successfully used assessment centers, structured workshops in which managers simulate key tasks, take question-naires, interact with peers, and receive feedback on their managerial potential from assessors. Such centers have rarely been used for the top job, but I have heard of one successful use in selecting a city police chief. A half dozen or so finalists were invited to an assessment and selection session that ran for several days. The candidates were put through a battery of tests and group exercises to assess their competencies along the many dimensions that were deemed relevant for an effective police executive. In one part of the selection process the finalists were videotaped as they dealt with an angry city council member (an actor). All candidates felt that they learned a great deal about their own executive performance and that the method of selection was fair. Clearly this is an extremely costly method of selection, however, and rarely would one be able to assemble all the finalists in such an open assessment process (Hale, 1979).

Interviewing

Interviewing is one of the major methods of assessment in executive selection, yet the empirical research (mostly conducted on lower-level jobs) is not encouraging about interviews' effectiveness for accurate screening (Arvey and Campion, 1982). Interviewers often disagree significantly in their appraisals of candidates. First impressions often dominate; initial decisions are sometimes reached in the first quarter of the interview. Unfavorable impressions can be created quickly on the basis of very few negative items, yet favorable impressions build slowly. Recall of information from interviews is often extremely poor. Many assessments are implicitly driven by comparing the candidates to two clusters of attributes that are used across vast ranges of different jobs: personal-relations attributes, and attributes of the good corporate citizen—trustworthy, dependable, conscientious, and so on (Morgan, n.d.).

In the executive search, interviews add one more source of information to the image of a candidate, although most seasoned recruiters place more stock in past performance than in the interview. Moreover, interviewing—especially early interviewing by the appointing authority—has benefits that go beyond learning about the candidate.

The Earlier, the Better. Appointing authorities should do some initial interviewing before the end of the networking process. This keeps the search reality-oriented and prevents fantasy candidates from dominating their thinking. The process resembles buying a house. A couple has in mind a set of desired specifications—cost, neighborhood, schools, layout, and image. As they look at each house, they compare it against their ideal, and they also alter their ideal, sometimes adding a desirable feature they saw in one house, more often revising the ideal in light of the realities of the market. Frequently home buyers know right away when a house fits with their revised ideal. Rarely do they go back to houses that they visited and rejected earlier.

Like houses, people come in complex bundles of strengths and weaknesses relative to a particular role. Bringing in candidates early on, on a regular basis, is a powerful, concrete way to keep the appointing executive engaged in the overall process. Clearly, the recruiter needs to guard against the eagerness of the appointing executive to hire someone, but occasionally one will uncover an exceptional candidate early in a search and be able to close much sooner than anticipated.

A second value of early interviews is that they can sharpen the thinking about the job. For example, in one public-sector recruiting effort, the importance of experience with critical political figures within the state became apparent only when the interviewing began. Had that been realized sooner, the search could have been more effective by making clear that out-of-state candidates would have to be extraordinary on some other dimension to offset that weakness.

Early interviewing also builds the appointing authority's skill at interviewing candidates. Like job applicants who do better at interviews when they are ambivalent about the job, the appointing authority may build interviewing skills and learn more about what aspects of the candidate are really important.

Finally, interviewing talented people about a key role is an opportunity to learn more about the challenges of the job. It could almost be viewed as a free source of consultation. One hears several different perspectives on how the job would be tackled and gets into the network of talent that surrounds the role to explore other thoughts about the critical challenges. Califano writes in his memoirs of his tenure as secretary of HEW, "Just about every one of the two dozen top health professionals I considered for posts in the Office of the Assistant Secretary for Health urged me to mount an anti-smoking campaign. Each insisted that such a campaign was essential to any serious preventive health care program" (Califano, 1981, p. 183).

Main Approaches. Two major approaches are used in interviews designed to round out the emerging picture of the serious candidate: the historical approach and the future-oriented, evaluative approach (Isaacson, 1977). In the latter, candidates are asked how they might handle key situations or problems. The answers are then evaluated for thoroughness, creativity, and clarity of thinking.

The risk with the future-oriented approach is that, especially in stressful situations, people often act quite differently from how they say they act, and they are most often unaware of the difference. Argyris and Schon (1978) have used the terms *espoused theory* to describe what individuals say their management practices are, and *theory in use* for how they actually behave. For example, if an executive is asked how she would handle a crisis with an external constituency group, she might describe a plan that involves careful consulting both within and outside the organization before acting. Under the stress of an actual situation, however, she might act unilaterally.

The historical school starts with the assumption that the best predictor of one's future behavior in some specific situation is one's past behavior under similar conditions. People are remarkably consistent, and the task of the interview is therefore to stimulate the candidate to tell his or her story, guiding the discussion to those past situations that offer the closest match to the future situations or to the areas in which there are questions about the candidate's qualifications. For example, an executive was asked to reflect on her previous work experience and talk about one or two crises. After a few moments of thinking, she responded with a detailed description of a situation when she had to respond within forty-eight hours to a sudden budget crisis. "Who did you involve?" she was asked. "How?" "Why were civil service staff willing to work after hours?" These questions never asked the candidate herself to make a judgment about her skill, but elicited a concrete story on which the interviewers could judge her ability to handle stress. Furthermore, this was a story that could be explored during checkouts by calling some of the others who were party to this crisis.

Even when there is no exact counterpart to the characteristic being explored, the interviewer usually can find some similar episode. For example, suppose the job requires testifying before the legislature. One could ask the candidates to discuss experiences they have had that most resemble legislative testifying. Then this experience can be explored in detail.

Conducting the Interview. A typical executive-level historical interview might take from two to three hours. The executive
recruiter might be conducting the interview, with the appointing
authority present and perhaps a few other key executives listening
in. The group would have been briefed before the candidate is
brought in. The interview typically opens with introductory remarks about the job, the critical issues, the criteria, and the context
of the job. A good recruiter has helped the candidate become more
knowledgeable about the position. This session should not be like
a legal cross examination but rather a collaborative exploration of
the person's previous career to determine the fit with the job.

The interview is best organized around a biographical frame.
Isaacson (n.d., p. 98) has compiled a list of career milestones, items
to look for at various stages of a career.

1. *Early history*
   a. The home, the neighborhood, and stories about class and
       motivation.
   b. Parents' careers: good news and bad, analogies to current
       career.
   c. Parents' accessibility and the models of authority.
2. *College and graduate education*
   a. Evidence of technical ability.
   b. Early leadership stories, evidence of hunger, crossing class
       lines, breaking out of expectations.
   c. The rare story: a young synthetic imagination.
3. *First jobs: Apprenticeship jobs*
   a. Learning to salute authority: demonstrating followership.
   b. Technical-language mastery as a professional.
   c. Role expansion.
4. *Second jobs: Aiding and abetting: Project management or
   executive assistant roles*
   a. Evidence of set-breaking, creativity.
   b. Evidence of set-setting: framing truth, selling sideways,
       and occasionally commanding down.
   c. Hearing the truth, even when painful or confrontational.
5. *Third jobs: The opportunity to self-destruct*

a. A line job: a role with control over product, production, and finance.
b. Framing truth: set-breaking and set-setting on the basic product and market. Answering the fundamental question: What business are you in?
c. Selling the truth in three directions: up, down, and sideways.
d. Weight as a synthesis of hunger and speed. The spiritual dimension of authority.

People love to tell their stories. Questions about family of origin, neighborhood, and family culture will often bring out a great deal of the candidate's orientation and core values. This is not a psychoanalytical probe but an exploration of themes and ideas, within the candidate's awareness, that have influenced his or her current values and choices. For example, one manager talked of his inventor father, who made electrical farm equipment in the basement in the evening and on weekends. As a child, he often had to work for his father assembling products. His father would quickly become impatient and oversupervise the boy's work. This person had a clear sense of how this pattern had shaped his passion for autonomy; when he reached top management positions in the Department of Labor, he collected and studied national survey data on autonomy as a major component of job satisfaction.

Exploring the family—patterns with siblings, parents, and extended family members—can throw light on two critical aspects of leading: values and authority. Childhood influences have a major effect on how work is viewed. One woman executive spoke about the strong message she received that she could do anything she wanted. She spoke of discussing critical issues with her father, and his emphasis on the importance of service. These stories are important to how she understands herself now and are significant to others who are selecting her for a critical assignment. Our first experiences with authority are in our family of origin. Isaacson (1983, p. 21) writes, "The most important thing to learn about any candidate is how comfortable he or she is with authority. Can they act decisively without demanding personal submission? Can they report up decisively, staking out their convictions without the hint of rebellion? Can they sell in the market without the fear of rejection? Can they win and lose, both and readily, and retain composure and friends?" Questions that can elicit these themes include: What line of work were your parents in? What was your father's career like? Was he hard to get along with? Easy to talk with? What messages did the kids get about work? Who did what around the house?

The Appendix outlines an effective biographical interview. The key is to follow the historical threads, to probe gently for more specific material, and to lend support by feeding back themes and patterns as they emerge. Review Isaacson's list of career milestones. A candidate's school experiences measure ability to master technical information quickly and may offer early signs of leadership potential, a willingness to move against the grain. First jobs often contain stories about accepting someone else's authority. Second jobs show early signs of wanting to take on independent projects and to have space in which to succeed or fail; the candidate may have subordinates to direct. Throughout the entire unfolding of the story, one is looking as much for the capacity to learn from mistakes as for achievements and skills. Isaacson notes that people are creatures of their experience. Each new job has some significantly different features. How skilled is the candidate at learning from experience? How well can he or she confront new areas, make mistakes, and readjust the approach?

Who should conduct the interview? The usual options are the appointing authority, a committee, or a recruiter, either in, or out of the presence of the appointing authority. Group interviews require careful preparation and management as the different interests of the members can create an incoherent experience with little deep probing of the core issues. If the group meets beforehand to review what is known and decide on key issues, it can agree upon a strategy for the session.

One interesting aspect of using the historical method of interviewing is that one may come to know outsiders much more deeply than insiders. One agency had used the method of in-depth historical interviews for a key job, with a half dozen of the top staff sitting in on the interviews. They became aware that they knew far more about the childhood, early work experience, and critical turning points of the three final candidates than they did about each other. This led to a series of lunch meetings at which they informally interviewed each other to build richer knowledge about their colleagues.

Checkouts

Reference checks are increasingly important as recruiting becomes more active, because one is more likely to be considering candidates who are not well known to the hiring organization. Furthermore, a recent survey of over five hundred executives revealed that almost one in five new employees misrepresents qualifications or salary information. The president of a Massachusetts reference checking firm (the emergence of such specialized services is indicative of the problem) noted a 20 percent increase in fraudulent resumes in the past three years (Yu, 1985, p. 3). On the other hand, concerns about privacy and lawsuits over misrepresentation by former employers are on the rise. One senior executive expressed concern that his responses to queries about his executives might be taped and used in a lawsuit related to an employee's career.

Well-known stories such as presidential candidates and their running mates—Mondale/Ferraro and McGovern/Eagleton, for example—attest to the risks of an unknown skeleton turning up in someone's closet. New York's Mayor Koch experienced a major crisis in the management of the city's Health and Hospital Corporation when it was revealed that its chairman, Victor Botnick, had lied about his college credentials. Botnick had been a close aide and trusted adviser to Koch, so the risks are not limited to appointments of strangers.

In executive selection, one is concerned less with detecting outright misrepresentation and more with understanding the strengths and weaknesses of the final candidates in the pool. The best sources of evidence about the candidates are people who have worked with them, in particular people who were able to see them

Note: Throughout the "Checkouts" section, I have benefited from internal training materials prepared by Ned Rightor of Issacson, Miller, Gilvar, and Boulware.

in action during some of the critical episodes discussed during the biographical interview. During the interview, the recruiter or appointing authority can ask the candidate for names of people who might be useful to talk with about the episode. Candidates are often asked to name people who could serve as references, and these are likely to be people who are favorably disposed. However, one can always request permission from candidates to interview others who would have valuable perspectives. One can also ask the candidate for people in specific categories, for example, "Would you give us the names of several legislators with whom you have had significant disagreements so that we can talk with someone who has opposed your reforms?" Alternatively, one can request a letter from the candidate giving blanket permission to make reference checks.

Written appraisals by former employers are common, but increasingly they are more guarded, even when the candidate has stipulated that they may be held in confidence. Legal concerns are leading companies to set policies of giving only dates and job titles, without opinions about performance (Johnson, 1985). Telephone checkouts are faster and more likely to allow the discussion necessary to develop a full understanding of the candidate. In any case, the recruiter's skill and the types of questions will be key to getting useful information.

The appointing authority and the recruiter prepare for the checkouts by reviewing the finalists. The recruiter presents the final candidates and reviews the strengths and weaknesses of each in light of the critical challenges of the job. If the search has been successful, there may be several finalists who present strong but different approaches to the job. Some of the critical issues will have been explored in the interviews, and often the appointing authority is ready to make a preliminary selection based on the information in hand, pending final checkouts. More often two or three people are still of interest, and the recruiter will need to do full checkouts on all of them. For each candidate, the appointing authority should determine the critical issues that need further attention, so that the checkout can focus strategically rather than comprehensively. It is often helpful, before beginning the calls, to rank the major questions that still need to be answered and the hunches or nuances that need further testing.

Like the biographical interview, the checkout is designed to deepen one's understanding of the candidate's previous career and to compare the candidate's self-assessment with the views of others. In preparing for it, look for blanks in the story, patterns of strengths and weaknesses, and incidents that might need further verification.

One of the advantages of the thorough checkout is that one gets to know outside candidates as deeply as those inside. Everyone has strengths and weaknesses. The core issue is the particular fit with the challenges. Candidates with no trouble in their background may have taken too few risks. Churchill, in urging the reappointment of a general whose career had been sidetracked, wrote, "Remember . . . it isn't only the good boys who help to win wars. It is the sneaks and stinkers as well. . . . I am not at all impressed by the prejudices that exist against him in certain quarters. Such prejudices attach frequently to persons of strong personality and original view. . . . We are now at war, fighting for our lives, and we cannot afford to confine Army appointments to persons who have excited no hostile comment in their career. . . . [This is a time] to try men of force and vision and not to be exclusively confined to those who are judged thoroughly safe by conventional standards" (Gilbert, 1985, pp. 861–863).

At the beginning of any checkout interview, it is important to set the context with the informant. Especially with people suggested by the candidate, the presumptive alliance is between the candidate and the informant. An effective recruiter is able to get the informant to ally himself or herself with the appointing authority and give a full account of the candidate's strengths and weaknesses. It is amazing what people will tell if they are asked the right questions in an effective manner, but if those questions do not come up, people feel comfortable withholding relevant negative information. The quality of the information depends on the climate created between the caller and the source. For this reason, some calls are more effectively made by the hiring executive. For example, a call from one state commissioner to another about an institutional director will most likely elicit identification between the two executives and a fairly candid appraisal. On the other hand, a search firm can often explore some relationships more candidly by serving as a trusted intermediary with difficult information.

The usual assumption is that checkouts are designed to "get the dirt" or "flush out any hidden skeletons" in the candidate's background. This casts the caller in the role of an investigative reporter or a prosecutor. More effective is a goal of getting an accurate portrait. The process resembles the movie *Rashomon,* in which each character has a different, and in its own way truthful, perspective on the story. A good opening is to give the recruiter's name and organization, the reason for the call, and an estimate of how long the call will take. A checkout usually takes about an hour (thirty minutes for the interview and thirty minutes for reviewing the notes and filling in missing bits of the conversation). If the candidate has suggested the informant's name, that should be indicated; if not, the informant should be told the source and assured of confidentiality. An effective line of questioning might go like this: "How did you know X? What was the nature of his or her work? How did you relate? What were X's and your responsibilities? We need a real story; it is important to X's candidacy. We want to know the challenges, difficulties faced, the fights, the victories and defeats, the way X has changed, grown, developed." Get dates, titles, organizational settings, relationships, overall and everyday responsibilities. Lead the informant into recalling and telling stories. A good checkout conversation shifts from the inevitable initial guardedness to a collegial tone indicating that the informant has joined with the task of building an accurate portrait.

Here are some useful questions:

Would you rehire this person? If so, in what capacity?

If you owned a business, would you let this person run it for you? (or if that doesn't make sense, "run the marketing or planning for you?")

How does this person deal with conflict?

What would the impact on business have been if someone else had had the job?

Can you give me an example of how this person displayed a particular strength or weakness?

Since none of us is perfect, what are those little things that
he or she needs to work on?

What did the candidate get done that really made a difference
to your company?

How does the candidate make decisions? What kind have you
known him to make? Why were they successful?

Sometimes offering hunches is useful: one can get valuable
information from the reference's reaction to and modification of the
hunch. Phrases like "I get the impression" or "others have
mentioned" can introduce these hunches. The source experiences
the recruiter as taking a risk and responds in kind. When working
with negative information, it can help to indicate the belief that
candidates who have never made mistakes may never have taken
risks. Point out aspects that do not jibe, and probe around seeming
inconsistencies. Remind the source that no one will be served by a
bad match.

Often the best probes are simple requests for more specifics,
such as a general phrase like "say more" or even a long pause. The
more vivid the details to support broader evaluative characteriza-
tions, the more useful the information will be to the selectors. They
can look behind the attribution to the data on which it was based
and potentially see a different implication in the story. Sometimes
analogies can help people loosen up and explore someone's
character in an offbeat way. For example, "This job sounds as if it
were like walking on a tightrope. Is X the type who likes a net or
the type who cuts the net down dramatically?"

Much of the skill in doing effective checkouts is being able
to listen beyond the words. As people approach talking about
negative aspects, they often speak more quietly, struggle more to get
the words just right, or approach them indirectly through humor.

Some useful concluding questions for closing the checkout
are:

What advice would you give to X's next boss to get the
maximum contribution?

Given what I have described about the key challenges in the

role we are looking at X for, what questions should I have
asked you that I haven't?

Is there anyone else with a different or better perspective that
you think I should talk to?

The recruiter should take full notes on the conversation,
including key phrases that reveal the character of the reference or
key aspects of the candidate. Some people take notes on a word
processor during the interview; others dictate notes afterward.
Either way, it is important to fill in notes and set down impressions
both of the reference and of the candidate as soon as the conversation is over. Often one's feelings immediately after the conversation
are the best guide to whether or not the reference was indirectly
selling the candidate, seemed to be delighted to be getting rid of the
person, was honestly telling the facts, or seemed to be strangely
aloof from someone he or she supposedly knew well. No single
checkout is determinative. One keeps going until the portrait is
consistent. It is particularly important to move away from the
candidate's list of references; this will show whether they were
artfully chosen to give only one side of a complex story. Reflect on
the quality of the references. As we have said, talent runs in strings,
and if the references seem like solid performers themselves, it bodes
well for the candidate.

Closing

After the final selection, there may still remain considerable
negotiation to bring a talented executive into the organization.
Often an organization goes through an exhaustive search and selects
someone who in the end decides not to accept the offer. In a well-
run search, the recruiter would usually have worked through many
of the potential problems before the final closing discussions, but
there are still difficult issues of salary, reporting relationships,
moving costs, assistance with spouse and family relocation, all of
which must be handled sensitively. If a full search has been
undertaken and there are genuinely good alternative candidates in
the final pool, the appointing authority will be in a substantially

better negotiating position than if there is only one viable candidate
at the end.

Candor is critical. During the inevitable dark hours in the
transition, people reflect on their motives for accepting a job;
feeling that they were misled will negatively affect their commitment. Furthermore, candor often can be decisive in selling a
difficult situation. When Vartan Gregorian was being recruited to
lead the New York Public Library, he had to take a telephone call
concerning another opening for which he was being considered.
Richard Salomon, a board member involved in the search for a new
director, tells the story as follows:

> Our minds were made up at this point, but his wasn't,
> so we were trying to sell him on the library. We tried
> to sell him on the intangibles of the job. He was being
> extremely affable . . . but beneath the affability he was
> being distinctly noncommittal. He told us that he had
> to take a phone call at nine o'clock. . . . There was
> something dramatic about the proceedings. Promptly
> at nine, the call came, and he took it in another room.
> The call lasted twenty minutes, and then Gregorian
> was back. . . . He was beaming. "I'm your man," he
> said. "I'm your man." He told us that he had been
> talking to the chairman of a university in an area of
> the country flooded with sunlight. "I like sunlight,"
> he said. They had offered him a car, a chauffeur, a
> house, and a stipend fifty percent higher than we
> could meet. But he said he was our man. I wondered
> why. "Well," said Gregorian, "if this fellow had been
> smart enough to tell me that he had a third-rate place
> and wanted me to come down and make it second-rate,
> elevate it to a second position, I might have considered
> it. But they pretended they were first-rate, and with
> people like that you simply cannot do business."
> From that moment on, we held nothing back from
> Gregorian [Hamburger, 1986b, p. 58].

In some situations, the appointing organization has reached
a decision about a desirable candidate (often someone with a public

record) before receiving any commitment from that person. In these instances, timing can play a critical role. For example, when New York State was looking for a new chairman of the Metropolitan Transit Authority, Robert Kiley, formerly head of the Boston Transit Authority, headed everyone's list. But at that moment he was in a primary race for mayor of Boston. The search group assessed his chances in the primary as nil and waited for him to drop out or lose. Right after his withdrawal, the recruiter made the call and began a courting process that eventually landed the executive that everyone wanted for the job (Gargan, 1983). Peter Ueberroth turned down the U.S. Olympic Committee presidency several times over a two-month period. Korn and Ferry, the recruiting firm conducting the search, talked with him several times, capitalized on the knowledge that his wife was a great sports fan, and arranged to have several prominent people call him with appeals to his patriotism. Eventually he yielded and accepted the job (Kleinfield, 1983).

In the closing process, often the appointing executive takes the lead—negotiating directly, but drawing on what the recruiter has seen of the candidate's motivations. Lyndon Johnson was reputed to be a remarkably persuasive recruiter, as evidenced by his talking Arthur Goldberg into leaving a lifetime Supreme Court seat for a limited assignment as ambassador to the United Nations. Califano tells a lovely story of Johnson's strategy to get Joseph Fowler to return to government as Treasury secretary:

> When Fowler had left as Treasury Under Secretary in the Johnson Administration to return to law practice, he told LBJ that he would not return to any post; his wife Trudye had suffered enough of the pressure of public service. In less than a year, Douglas Dillon resigned as Secretary. Fowler, knowing Johnson well and anticipating a call from him, carefully prepared a list of characteristics the Treasury Secretary needed, emphasizing those he lacked, and the names of candidates for the post. As expected, Johnson called. When Fowler arrived at Johnson's outer office, the President escorted him to the Cabinet Room, sat him

down in the President's chair. Fowler took out his
notes and went through the characteristics Johnson
should seek in a Treasury Secretary. When he was
halfway through and before he had identified any of
the candidates, Johnson, who had been pointedly
distracted, looked right at Fowler and said, "All right,
Joe, let's cut the bullshit. What are we going to tell
Trudye?" [Califano, 1981, p. 34].

In briefing the appointing executive during the closing, the
recruiter reviews why the candidate is willing to leave the present
post and what the person finds attractive about this position. The
recruiter is also prepared with the salary history and the raises the
candidate would have received in the old job. Possible financial
packages are reviewed that might make the difference in the
candidate's accepting the offer.

Some candidates may go to the final stages in a search as
leverage either in their current positions or for other offers they are
seeking. In these cases, the appointing executive should be prepared
for the counteroffers that might come and develop a strategy to
defend against them.

The active approach to executive search presented in
Chapters Three, Four, Five, and Six should substantially improve
the odds of making an effective choice of new leadership from 50
to 90 percent. A thorough checkout should make the areas of risk
known and capable of being addressed. Although getting the right
executive in the properly defined role is well over half the battle, the
critical joining of the new executive with the organization poses
another set of opportunities and dangers.

The next chapter deals with the issues of interim or lame-
duck leaders. Often an organization is surprised by the sudden
departure of an executive or discharges its leader in the wake of a
sudden crisis and must install some form of interim leadership to
allow time for a systematic recruitment process.

~ Chapter 7

Coping with the Interim Situation: Acting Leaders and Lame Ducks

Organizations often face the need to replace a key executive with little lead time, either because the executive leaves voluntarily or because a crisis has made it necessary to remove the executive quickly. In such hurried situations, the appointing authority faces the choice of appointing a replacement immediately or designating an acting leader for the role. All too often the decision is made hastily and without much attention to longer-term issues. Often the next person in the chain of command is asked to assume the acting role. If this person is not adequate to the task, however, the pressure to fill the job permanently may be too great to allow adequate time for a quality search. Making acting appointments without thoughtful consideration of the longer term can also mean the acting leader needlessly leaves the organization when the new leader is finally appointed.

In another scenario, the current leader is scheduled to step down when a new leader is found and a search gets under way. In these situations, the authority of the current leader can be undermined as subordinates begin to focus on the upcoming transition. Lame-duck leadership creates a period of ambiguity that has some similar features to acting leadership.

Yet all leadership is limited in both time and scope. All leaders come between a predecessor and successor and are therefore in some sense interim or acting. Legally, being acting or interim is no defense against being accountable for one's actions in the roles. That we draw the distinction so sharply between leaders and acting leaders may suggest our psychological need to avoid thinking about the time-limited nature of people's tenure. In roles in which transition is programmed, such as the presidency, we see the powers inherent in the role immediately transferred to each new occupant. Our desire for leadership to protect and support us makes us reluctant to imagine not having leaders or having leaders with diminished capabilities.

The Climate of Acting Leadership

Webster (1946) defines *acting*, in this context, as "doing duty for another; officiating; holding a temporary rank or position or performing services temporarily." Yet in this use it is difficult to escape some of the other definitions of acting, such as "impersonating, simulating." The term *acting*, and its associations with theater, evoke images of someone else writing the script, of actions made on behalf of another. Some organizations designate these temporary situations as "interim," suggesting that their distinctive function is to bridge the time between the departure of the old leader and the arrival of the new. All these associations suggest the complexity of the acting role: that one is not a free agent, that one's authority is limited both in scope and in time, often in ways that are not well defined.

Organizations often experience a period of acting or interim leadership as disturbing. A heightened sense of uncertainty fosters rumors and speculation about who will be chosen as the new leader. Time horizons shorten dramatically; participants become increasingly unable to commit to long-term projects that may go nowhere if the new leader changes direction. People adopt a one-day-at-a-time attitude. Because an acting leader is not viewed as having the authority to resolve strategic questions, the organization shifts into routine gear, staying clear of significant challenges. In several such organizations that I have worked with, people have been unable to discriminate realistically between issues that were genuinely linked to the new leader and issues that were not. They seemed to identify all constructive activities as linked to the choice of new leadership.

A key role of a leader is to mediate between the organization and the wider environment. Kanter (1983) has found that workers like powerful supervisors, who they feel can negotiate successfully on behalf of the group for the resources (money, sanction, discretion) needed to do work. Groups with acting leadership therefore feel disadvantaged, at risk of losing out to groups with leaders who can represent them successfully. These boundary issues are often shaped by the person chosen to serve in the interim role. An acting leader put over former peers may be regarded as too much of a peer to represent the group effectively. If the acting leader is still responsible for the former division as well as the whole unit, there are problems of dual loyalties. A leader brought in from the outside or above, however, may not be regarded as knowledgeable or loyal to the division.

Why Did the Original Leader Leave? The difficulties surrounding the acting role are affected by the reason the vacancy exists in the first place. On the face of it, an executive's departure for a personal reason, unrelated to the business—perhaps a spouse's career move or a life-style issue—should produce less stress than many other reasons. Even when the reason is genuinely personal, however, the claim of "personal reasons" has been used so often as a face-saving device to cover over some organizationally related trouble that it probably will not be believed. Furthermore, people in the organization may feel abandoned by a leader who has asked them to make commitments to the organization and is now putting a higher loyalty to external commitments. The remaining executives may begin to reconsider their own commitments.

If the executive has been fired either for a major crisis or as a result of a long-festering dissatisfaction with performance, the dynamics vary enormously depending on the reactions of the staff. If staff members feel that the leader has been scapegoated, many talented people may decide to leave. There may be great group cohesion, or the group may split into two camps, depending on how the firing is viewed. Those who favor the firing may have reactions of manic triumph and unrealistic hopes for the future because they attribute all problems to the scapegoated leader. Yet even in triumph there may be feelings of guilt and fear of one's power in destroying the leader.

A precipitous exit because of a major policy difference produces a similar split, some of the staff agreeing with the leader, others siding with the appointing authority. In this instance, the staff may feel abandoned and vulnerable. Some will experience guilt feelings that they should follow the leader but cannot because they do not have the options or need the security from the job. The former leader will be more of a martyr under these circumstances.

Sudden vacancies from death and illness are particularly upsetting. Staff are often in shock, working through the loss and perhaps feeling irrationally guilty for their role in the pressure that was on the leader. Here any acting leader struggles with the difficulty of stepping into a role that may be psychologically held vacant in tribute to the leader. Early initiatives seem unseemly.

When the executive leaves for a new job, followers often have complex reactions. If they feel that the leader has left too early, before completing tasks that they and the leader had mutually agreed to do, they will feel abandoned. For example, when a forceful leader of the New York City public school system left to accept an attractive offer, he was asked why he was leaving at so critical a juncture. He replied, "We've had lots of difficult times. There really is no 'right' time to leave" (Maeroff, 1985, p. B3). Staff members may consider leaving or have hopes of being recruited by the departing leader at the exciting new situation. There may be feelings of being jilted or used, the sense that perhaps the leader used the job as a steppingstone to a better position. Gabriel and Savage (1978, p. 88) note that nothing is more disturbing in a stressful military situation than the feeling that a leader is using his troops to further his career. Resentment is particularly pronounced if people think that they have taken risks with the leader, who has now left them vulnerable because of their identification with the leader.

A change in the appointing authority—during political transition, for instance, when a change in party at the top means changes down the line—creates anxieties about how deep the personnel changes will go. Here one often finds acting leaders reporting to acting leaders, compounding the overall sense of uncertainty. In these situations, people who are close to the former leader will often be initially distrusted.

Even a scheduled departure such as a retirement can be occasion for appointing an acting leader, if the search and selection have been prolonged and no successor has become available. This situation can be damaging because the organization has already experienced a weak period, with a lame-duck leader expected to leave on a given date. People have been oriented to that date as a planning horizon, and if they then must face an acting-leadership situation, they feel thrust into another limbo.

What Kind of Leader Is Needed? Circumstances that trigger the leader's departure also affect the type of interim leadership that will be needed. If the organization is relatively stable, the acting or lame-duck leadership can take a predominantly caretaking stance, preventing regression and maintaining the existing course during a strategic search that might raise directional shifts over the horizon. If, on the other hand, the vacancy is both a symptom of and a result of a major crisis in direction, such as a scandal or major retrench-ment or failure in current strategy, then the acting leader may need to be viewed as a medical trauma team, able to come in and stabilize the situation so that the long-term issues can be addressed. Within the crisis-driven situation, there may be opportunities for the acting leader to take painful measures and incur the wrath of key constituencies so that the permanent leader can start out on a more positive note. In these instances, an acting leader can be a very short-term turnaround specialist.

A dramatic recent case is that of Laurence Tisch's leadership at CBS, which began as a short-term assignment and has ended up with Tisch taking the permanent job. Tisch, a board member and major stockholder of CBS, joined a dominant coalition on the board to oust Thomas A. Wyman as chairman and CEO and install Tisch as acting chief executive for an unspecified period to redirect the organization. The strategy was to initiate some major changes and at the same time to search for a candidate who would fit the style and direction of the changes begun by Tisch. A news account describes the first three months: "After just three months at the helm of CBS Inc., Laurence A. Tisch has made change commonplace at the once-unshakable network. Cost cutting has become routine, layoffs are the norm and entire departments have been eliminated. . . . As acting chief executive, Mr. Tisch set out to streamline the company and reduce its $1 billion debt—much of it resulting from Mr. Wyman's 1985 stock repurchase plan. Mr. Tisch engineered the sale of CBS's book publishing unit to Harcourt Brace Jovanovich

Inc. for $500 million and its music publishing arm to SBK Entertainment World Inc. for $125 million" ("Tisch's Regimen Built Trimmer CBS," 1986, p. D2).

A variant of this high-profile interim leadership is the situation in which the appointing authority is clear that what is going on now is unacceptable and must be immediately addressed but is not clear on the right long-term direction. For example, the mayor of Philadelphia had a potentially explosive situation in a juvenile detention facility. He hired an outside consultant to come in for three months both to take charge of daily operations and to "assess the overall functioning of the center and develop a plan for its future." The consultant, Paul DeMuro, ruled himself out of contention for the permanent job, believing that he could be more objective in making recommendations if he were not a candidate. DeMuro, reflecting on his experience, noted that sometimes an acting leader can have even more authority than the permanent leader. He reported directly to the managing director of the city, outside of the actual chain of command within the welfare department. Furthermore, it was known that he had been brought in by the mayor, so he benefited from that connection as well.

The biggest tension DeMuro experienced was the conflict between the internal operating work and the long-term work of planning and rebuilding external support. In the end, he felt that such turnaround assignments would be much more successful if a team of three were brought in: one in the lead oriented toward planning, another for communications and media relations, and a third for operations. During his short tenure, he faced several crises surrounding an investigation of child abuse, union walkouts in sympathy with five workers who were arrested, and overcrowding. He was able to make strong decisions that left major constituencies, such as the union, hating him. The successor was then able to come in and begin to rebuild staff competence and morale, while DeMuro continued to take the heat for the unpopular decisions.

On the negative side of such cases, staff members often believe interim leaders do not take personal risks because they do not have to live with the consequences of their decisions. This feeling may create long-term morale problems. Interim leaders probably work best on changes that are more tangible, such as refinancing debt, selling off major assets, or restructuring, than in areas in which the needed changes are inevitably long-term developments, such as professionalizing a social service staff.

The Selection Process

Selecting an acting leader is a time-compressed version of the process of selecting a permanent leader. Here the focus is on the key tasks of the interim period and fitting a leader with those challenges. A turnaround situation calls for a powerful person who knows the organization well and has a vision of what needs to be done. In preventing an unraveling situation, there may be a richer array of choices, but whoever is chosen must be calm, confident, skillful with people, and able to make difficult decisions. In a maintenance situation the number of choices is greater still. The latter two situations can tap insiders; the first one often requires someone from the outside.

Common sources of acting leaders are present or former board members, consultants who know the agency or industry well, subordinates of the role, staff to the role or to the superior of the role, the superior of the role, and former occupants of the role, often out of retirement. Except in a deliberate turnaround situation, the normal procedure is to have the second in command, if there is one, assume the acting position. This is so much the expected choice that some explanation is due if that person is not appointed.

When staff members become acting leaders, the major issue is their readiness and ability to carry line responsibilities, even temporarily. Some staff people develop an organizational personality that can be understood only in relation to a line manager—the tough guy to a line manager versus good guy, for example, or the reverse— and may be very different in an acting line role without the leader who gave meaning to their prior behavior (Jaques, [1955] 1978).

In many situations, a choice must be made among several people. Usually there has been no formal description of who is regarded as the first among equals. In such a case, if the acting leader retains responsibility for a division, others may suspect him or her of favoring that division. These multiple roles can be complex. One deputy secretary who was also serving as acting secretary remarked that he had approved a request for training support from one of his subordinates when working on his divisional paperwork, but when he reviewed it as the acting secretary, he denied it because of wider constraints over the budget.

In some situations the acting role moves upward rather than downward in the hierarchy, with the superior of the vacant role taking over. This situation often dramatically increases the executive's span of control. It can also mean that the staff assistant of that executive becomes in effect the acting head or at least a significant liaison with the nominal leader. This plan can cause problems after the role is filled, because people may have enjoyed reporting in at the higher level and may manipulate to maintain those links even after a permanent replacement is found.

How Long? The predicted duration of the acting leadership has several implications for the organization. If the duration is known and fairly short, the possibility of an outsider becomes more remote since it would take an outsider some time to get on top of the job. Moreover, people often adapt more successfully, since we all adapt more easily when we know how long and why. The specific span of time can also indicate some of the key tasks of the acting leader. For example, in a county that was searching for a new county manager, the county executives knew that they needed an interim manager who could oversee the current year's budget cycle. Frequently, however, the length of time is underestimated, or unexpected difficulties are encountered in the search, so appointing authorities are well advised to be conservative in their estimates of how long someone will serve in an acting capacity.

A Full Candidate? An important question is whether the acting head is a candidate for the permanent position. Discussions at the time the acting leader is designated can deliberately rule this out or explicitly include it. More often it is left unclear, creating uncertainty for both the acting leader and others. One strategy of ensuring that the acting head will not be viewed as a candidate is to bring someone out of retirement who clearly does not fit the image of the permanent candidate. When the New York City Transit Authority found itself without an executive director, seventy-year-old Daniel Scannell, who had retired as COO eight years earlier, was tapped. The board felt the need for someone who would address some of the major trouble spots concerning train reliability but could also be a calming influence. One transit official commented, "He knows how to diffuse the passion and keep the dialogue going. When he sees someone out on a limb, he doesn't get out the saw, but tries to strengthen the limb." The board also assigned Scannell to chair the search committee (Goldman, 1983).

Many organizations do discuss explicitly whether the acting leader will be a candidate but rarely think through the career consequences for that person. An acting leader who is seen as a candidate and does not get the job may be uncomfortable resuming his or her former role in the organization and begin to look outside. Therefore part of a decision to take an acting role should be to explore other reentry paths. It often can be useful to discuss the acting leader's career after the new executive is found. The new leader may resent having someone around who has run the division previously, or alternatively may value and develop a special relationship with this person. Being included in the search process can also be an important element in helping an acting leader make the transition back to being a subordinate.

Appointing authorities often think that the acting role can serve as a test of a potential leader's performance. This does not often work out in fact. Designating a leader as acting communicates ambivalence on the part of the appointing authority, and subordinates and key outsiders tend to respond to an acting leader differently than they would if the same person were in the role permanently. Furthermore, the uncertainty of support from above often leads to impaired performance by the acting leader. Many executives in these situations think that they behave as they would if they had the job permanently, but their colleagues rarely agree. In several cases acting leaders were judged poorly during their interim tenure and then went on to head up similar organizations elsewhere with considerable effectiveness.

Tasks for Acting Leaders

If the acting leader's job is seen as "keeping the lid on, babysitting," as one acting secretary described his charge from the governor, the interim leader can lose momentum and paradoxically create the conditions for more difficulties. As a basketball team that switches to a run-out-the-clock strategy sometimes learns, this approach can often backfire. Interim leaders must strike a balance between authentically leading and acknowledging that their successors are critical stakeholders in their actions. One acting leader described his philosophy: "Frankly I feel that there is only so much you can just watch without taking action on it, whether you are in a temporary position or not. I do not think the term 'acting' should be used. You are either in the position with the full responsibility that someone would have who was not termed acting or you are truly a pawn. . . . I cannot anticipate who will be here after I leave in February. If I sit here and second guess what the next director will do, I will not be effective" (confidential interview).

Yet the shortness of tenure does suggest that it is appropriate to see the primary task more in terms of a transition. This means that an acting leader has to focus on the critical changes that are under way and frame the issues for the subsequent appointment. The acting leader can also play a critical role in the recruiting process by ensuring that it is aggressively managed.

Such a focus helps prevent the lame-duck quality. Consider the following example: A new CEO of a major hospital found that the leadership of the nursing department was under a complicated arrangement sanctioned by the prior acting CEO. The group of clinical directors had collectively designated one of their members as a spokesperson for nursing but did not view her as exercising the full authority of the vacant role of head of the nursing division. The new CEO, shortly after arriving, appointed her acting head of nursing and elevated the role to the top executive staff from its previous position under a chief operating officer. This woman faced a number of dilemmas. First, her authority with her peers was problematic, as they had unsuccessfully pushed for a peer model that would have made her only the spokesperson for the policies that the group arrived at collectively. Furthermore, there were several major vacancies in the nursing department as well as critical operating and strategic issues that could not very well wait until the search committee found a permanent leader.

She felt it was critical to capitalize on the CEO's decision to elevate nursing to the executive team. Not to respond to this opportunity would set back the overall development of nursing when the new leader was finally selected. So she had to exercise sufficient authority over the group of clinical directors to prevent them from appearing divided and immature to the CEO. She also moved ahead on hiring for two of the vacancies—one in budget and one in recruiting—because these functions were critical and would greatly overload the new leader if left vacant. However, she chose to leave vacant two roles that had been unfilled for some time, because these roles were essential in the overall development of the alliance with the nursing school, a strategic issue of considerable importance. To foreclose options in this area would do the new leader a disservice.

Involving Staff in Transition Planning

One task that the interim leader can easily undertake to bind anxiety and channel it in productive ways is to organize the staff around preparing for the transition. The proposed process might work as follows:

Briefing Materials. First, the acting director calls a meeting of all the major division heads and requests that each begin to prepare transition material to brief the new leader. A common format may be provided or the directors may be left to decide how best to present the issues and information for their division. The usual materials contained in a transition briefing include the background and experience of division head, a table of organization, resumes of key people, a brief description of the major areas of responsibilities for the unit, including the statutory responsibilities, key initiatives in the current budget year, major items in the budget year, a history of the division, current legislative matters, and critical issues in the coming six months. It may be helpful for the group to develop the format and topic headings at the staff meeting, imagining that they were taking over as the new leader and considering what critical information they would want. This process helps existing staff to identify with the incoming leader. At this initial meeting, time lines should be laid out and the ground rules for preparing the documents should be discussed. For example, how much should the staff members in a unit participate in developing the briefing book?

An alternative version of this process, much less structured but also serving to keep people oriented on the transition, is to suggest that each staff member keep a file of copies of items that would be useful for the new leader to understand. When the transition actually occurs, the raw materials from which to assemble relevant briefing materials are ready.

If the first procedure is followed, the acting leader carefully reviews each of the submissions and critiques them. Alternatively, a round-robin review is held; each division head reviews a peer's report for its potential helpfulness to a new leader. This approach has several advantages. It exposes all division directors to two other divisions, one that they critique and one that is critiquing their report. Moreover, someone who is less close to a division can often suggest where there is too much or too little information. Finally, peer review may keep the documents more honest, less focused on selling the new leader on a division and its leader.

On the basis of the reviews, the division directors redraft their reports. The acting director might then lead the group in developing an overview of issues that do not fit neatly within any single division. For each critical issue a small subgroup might be assigned to staff out the background of the issue and develop a factual presentation of the problem at present and how it has changed over time. These documents would then be merged into a cover memorandum for the overall briefing book.

Pluses and Minuses. Preparing such a briefing book has several potential benefits. During a period of great uncertainty, the presence of a real, purposeful task can constructively bind some of the anxiety that the search for a new leader often creates. If the briefing book is prepared before the new leader is known, it may be more factual, less slanted to a particular philosophical orientation.

Assembling this background information also saves the new leader time. Obviously the new leader will have particular requests and want to shape some of the presentation of past work, but that can take place on the foundation that this process has established. Finally, whether the division executives who prepare this material stay or leave, the summing up of their tenure is a healthy exercise to go through. If the reports are not prepared until after the new leader is designated, many of the division heads may not be available to work on them.

The process also has drawbacks. It could bring about a strong collective judgment about the key issues that might make it harder for the incoming leader to introduce a new vision. Conversely, it could trigger substantial conflict among divisions and lead to bickering and fighting that the acting leader may not be authoritative enough to resolve. If the process fails to flag the issues that the new leader is really interested in, people may feel that they did considerable work for nothing. Drafting a briefing book may also be more developmental when guided by fresh questions and perspectives from the new leader.

Finally, if the materials are very well prepared, the new leader may be forced to make decisions before he or she is comfortable with the culture or climate of the new setting. The process of assembling these materials can give a new leader some breathing room and an excuse to put off some initial decisions.

This kind of leadership by an acting or lame-duck leader probably makes the most sense when a structured search for the successor is under way and the time of the interregnum is roughly known. In these cases, the initial search work of identifying key issues can also contribute to the development of the briefing books. As the critical issues that the department is facing become better defined through this process, potential candidates can be screened against a well-grounded understanding of the major issues they will face in the early months of a new administration.

Identifying Robust Issues

Another important task for any interim leader is to decide which major issues to act on and which to leave open for the successor. Because of the uncertainty about the new leadership, groups often become stuck and feel that anything that they do might be wasted. This is particularly true during close elections, when agency staff find it difficult to imagine activities and priorities that will be equally valid no matter which candidate is elected. However, relatively few issues are so tightly linked to the person and values of the new leader that it makes sense to defer them until the outcome is known. Identifying robust issues can make clear what needs to be done regardless of which future comes about.

The process involves first listing the key issues that the organization is facing. Next the group imagines different outcomes of the leadership search, either using the names of known alternatives or using likely types of candidates who might be selected. For each issue, the group assesses how much they would regret (low, medium, high) if they had invested heavily in working on that issue for each of the alternative future leaders. Robust actions are those items that score low on regret across all the possible leadership options.

For example, top civil servants in city government found themselves in a quandary when the sitting mayor suddenly resigned and the three most likely candidates to be the next mayor had widely differing philosophies. The group developed the chart illustrated in Table 5. From this analysis, they determined that they could safely work on productivity, management training, and economic development. How each leader would deal with those issues might vary, but one could proceed with confidence that the work would in some way be relevant. On the other hand, continuing to work intensively on a controversial issue like trash to steam or the use of private contractors might, depending on the outcome of the election, be of no value.

Table 5. Identifying Robust Issues.

Issues	Scenario A: Wilson Goode	Scenario B: Frank Rizzo	Scenario C: John Egan
1. Productivity	Low	Low	Low
2. Use of private contractors	High	Medium	Low
3. Management training	Low	Low	Low
4. Improved labor-management climate	Low	High	High
5. Economic development	Low	Low	Low
6. Trash to steam	Low	High	Medium
7. Civil service reform	Medium	Medium	Low

A variant of this process is for the interim leader to pose to the group several scenarios about the actual person or type of person who might be selected as the new leader. Then, for each scenario, people are asked to imagine the tasks that they would work on now if they knew for sure that this person would be the next leader. Usually, it is found that the lists, one for each potential leader or type of leader, overlap considerably. For example, in a nursing division, this process was used successfully to move beyond a stalemate brought on by two completely different options for the leadership of the hospital. They agreed that the division would have a recruitment crisis regardless of the leader and that the development of computer competence in their area would need to continue under either scenario. Note that the items to move forward on may not be the top priority for any of the particular scenarios, but the strategy will be robust in that it will be viable across a range of futures.

A lame-duck director used this process to think through which items to move ahead on and which to defer for the new leader. There were two possible candidates that the board might select, an insider whom she knew well and an outsider whom she knew less well. She faced three major issues: development of a management information system (MIS), hiring a public relations director, and costing out options for building renovations. When she looked at how these issues related to the two candidates, she was able to take three different approaches. Because the board was pressuring her to develop the MIS area, and because the system was essential for cost containment, she moved ahead on this initiative. The public relations role, however, would be dramatically different depending on the leader selected. The insider would need a spokesperson for legislative and media affairs, whereas the outside candidate was comfortable in that role and would want a back-room support person. Therefore, she put that issue on hold. For the building renovations, she pushed ahead for the data but did not make any commitments.

The appropriate use of acting leadership can thus be a major component in capitalizing on the opportunities that surround a change in command. It can sometimes play an important role in the turnaround or development of the unit or organization, and it can facilitate the transition by preparing the organization for new leadership. In Part Three, the focus shifts to the new leader and the strategies he or she can use in joining with the organization and building a team to meet the challenges.

How New Leaders Can Take Charge Effectively

As leadership changes occur more frequently, new leaders need to pay more attention to the organization's history and continuity of values. How does a new leader choose which organizational characteristics to retain and which to change? What themes, systems, and people are inextricably linked to the former leader so that changing them involves battling with the shadow of one's predecessor? The three chapters in this section discuss the dynamics of how the new leader connects with the existing organization—how he or she works through the shadows of previous leaders, connects with existing staff, and builds the new team. Although seemingly sequential, beginnings are layered with multiple meanings. The first decisions both resolve the issue at hand and send messages about the values and style of the new leader. Meetings are forums to do work and at the same time appraisal sessions of the participants. Who is on and off the new team is closely dependent on previous relationships with the former leader. It is both difficult and important to stay close to the difference in perspectives that the new leader and the existing staff have during the honeymoon period. Unlike real honeymoons, often it is only at the end of this period that the leader and some of the existing staff acknowledge their joining in the new team.

Chapter 8

Dealing with the Shadows of Previous Leadership

There is a well-known parable in which several blind men try to describe an elephant. One feels the trunk and says that an elephant is like a snake, another feels a leg and declares an elephant is like a tree, and so on. In the same way, the various parties to a leadership transition have different vantage points that create dramatically different perceptions. When a leader joins an organization from the outside, these different perspectives often shape initial encounters between the leader and the existing staff.

Table 6 suggests some of these major differences. In most settings, not all these differences would be pronounced, but they often lie beneath the surface. The new leader may have a longer planning horizon strategically yet be impatient to get changes under way. Existing staff, on the other hand, may have a foreshortened planning horizon but see a long time over which to bring any changes into being. If there has been an interim period with acting leadership, staff members may be especially focused on the present. They may have adapted to the uncertainty by living a day at a time, eschewing any new projects until the new leader is named.

There are differences, as well, in the duration of commitment to the organization, which existing staff may sense and resent if they believe the new leader is using the organization as a steppingstone in a career.

The new leader may feel pressure from the board for immediate actions, while the staff is less sensitive to these external forces. The new leader may regard existing policies and staff as open

**Table 6. Differences in Perspective Between New Leaders
and Existing Staff.**

Focus	New Leader	Existing Staff
Duration of commitment	Short, until the next promotion.	Long, expect to stay until retirement.
Attitude to prior job of new leader	Established credentials, gave experience needed to do this job.	Different from here, same approaches may not work here.
Initial assumption about existing staff	Guilty, untrustworthy until proven otherwise.	Basically competent and willing to help.
Priorities	New agendas, needed changes.	Unfinished current agendas.
Status of existing policies/programs	All to be reconsidered.	Have withstood test of time and constituency review. Keep until new ideas prove their worth.
Attitude toward organizational structure	Predisposed to reorganize to fit new style.	Familiar with current structure, reduces uncertainty while trying to understand new leader.
Orientation	Often external, toward customers and constituencies.	Internal; often sense new leader takes them for granted.

to review, needing to be tested against the outlines of a new strategy. Existing staff, meanwhile, see less need for changes in personnel or procedures. Similarly, the new leader may view the organizational structure as likely to need change, while the existing staff are comfortable with it. Finally, the new leader's orientation is often on the critical external constituencies of the organization, on the bottom-line results, while internal staff are often inward-looking. These differing perceptions can result in serious disagreements in which neither party recognizes the underlying reasons.

Triangles in Leadership Transitions

Too often we think of leadership transitions in a dyadic framework, examining the dynamics between leader and existing staff. The metaphor of a "honeymoon" suggests just such a pairing "till death do us part," denying the reality of previous leaders and eventual successors and reifying the organization into a single corporate entity rather than recognizing the complexity of the different interests that make it up. In fact, however, leadership transitions are better thought of in terms of a *ménage à trois*, with all the complexities that such three-way relationships entail. Nor is it an accident that the triangle is so prevalent in leadership transitions. Bowen (1974a, 1974b) argues that any two-person relationship in stress will involve a third party in a triangle as a way of stabilizing that relationship, and leadership transitions are fraught with stress and anxiety. These are times when boundaries and roles are redrawn, and inevitably people are anxious: about their careers, their priorities, their relative influence.

During a governor's first year in office, several colleagues and I worked with him on the quality of working relationships among his cabinet and staff. We discovered that almost all the hot issues had a triangular structure. In part this was because the governor contracted with each cabinet secretary and staff member separately. All felt that they had individual agreements and understandings with the governor but had not taken part in agreements that he made with others and that inevitably would affect them. When a difficulty arose, he would often attempt to resolve the problem with a series of meetings with the individuals rather than confronting the issue directly with all the parties present. His unconscious motivation was to preserve some absent third party who could be blamed for the difficulty—although the blame might shift during the series of encounters.

For example, the governor might be irritated with some action of a cabinet member that came to his attention indirectly. He would express his displeasure to his chief of staff, thus forming an alliance with the chief and making the secretary the blamed outsider. The staff member would bring the issue up with the secretary. The secretary, not sure whether the staffer was really communicating the governor's concerns or his own, would mention the issue casually to the governor on some opportune occasion. The governor would reply that he was concerned but would make some mollifying comment to the effect that the chief of staff sometimes overreacted. As a result, the chief of staff's credibility as a barometer was reduced, the chief of staff and secretary each believed his version of what happened and felt he knew the governor's true feelings on the matter, and everyone lost the opportunity for learning, so that they were likely to repeat the process.

In such a case, the triangle results from the ordinary unconscious motivation to avoid an anxiety-producing confrontation. In other instances, triangles are used more consciously as a political strategy. For example, the secretary in interaction with a powerful interest group may blame the budget secretary for a painful budget cut, yet in meeting with the budget secretary would support the decision.

Triangles also come up in the relationships of people to strategic issues. Newcomb (1953) has explored the dynamics of two people (A and B) interacting about a third issue or person (X). He describes the tension that results when A respects B and B respects A but each has a different orientation toward X. The tensions can be reduced, by changing B's view of X, by changing A's view of X, by changing B's view of A, by changing A's view of B, or by agreeing to disagree.

In leadership transitions, the new leader often falls prey to the dynamic that "the friend of my enemy is my enemy." Almost by definition, anyone who was too close to the prior leader is suspect, even if the new leader is favorably disposed to the prior leader, because the new leader is trying to establish himself or herself distinctively. One staffer commented that he felt he could have been welcomed into the inner circle of a new leader but that the price of admission was to join in devaluing the former leader. He refused to do so and shortly left the organization.

Four Kinds of Triangles. The major triangles that inevitably occur during a leadership transition are illustrated in Figure 2. They lie like land mines beneath the surface of the terrain that a new leader must traverse to enter the organization effectively. Chapter Nine will discuss the early tasks of a new leader and several of these triangular dilemmas in greater depth.

The first triangular relationship is actually a pair of triangles that work the same way, between the old and new leaders and either the appointing authority or the existing staff. Here the dynamics

Figure 2. Key Triangles in Leadership Transitions.

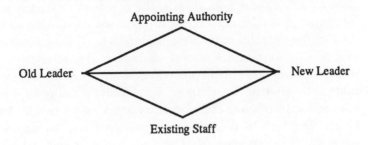

Appointing Authority

Old Leader   New Leader

Existing Staff

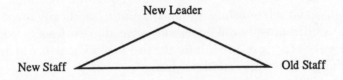

New Leader

New Staff   Old Staff

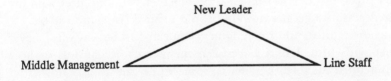

New Leader

Middle Management   Line Staff

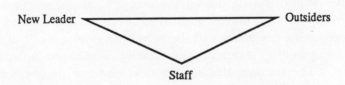

New Leader   Outsiders

Staff

revolve around the reasons for the changes, both expressed and imagined. For example, if the old leader was beloved and extremely close to the appointing authority, the new leader may feel like an interloper in developing a relationship to the appointing authority and to the current staff. New leaders who follow charismatic founders or long-tenure leaders often find themselves struggling with the shadows of their predecessors, an issue that is discussed more fully later in this chapter. Conversely, if the prior leader is blamed for the troubles of the organization, then the new leader may be idealized both by the appointing authority and the staff, setting up unrealistic expectations. The importance of such triangles is that each pair in the relationship is inevitably shaped by the dynamics of the other two pairs. Assume that the two leaders are both professionals and want to have a thoughtful transition. If their individual relationships to the appointing authority are dramatically different—the old leader's negative, the new leader's positive—it will be far more difficult for the two to work together than if they are both in positive relationships.

With amazing frequency these dynamics prevent new and old leaders from having in-depth discussions of the issues or the organization. One leader spoke of her ambivalence about meeting her predecessor: "I wasn't clear on whether I should meet with my predecessor to get his view on people, critical issues, and so on. He was discredited, and his judgment appeared to be way off. I never met with him. I may have been mistaken." Regardless of how discredited the former leader is, some value can usually flow from such a meeting, if only to substitute reality for the fantasy figures that dominate during transitions. In addition, the predecessor may have helpful intelligence on key people, may suggest items that require follow-through, and finally may be a useful reminder that someday the new leader will also be exiting, raising vividly the issue of what will be the central preoccupations and hoped-for legacy.

The triangle linking the new leader with new staff (or rehabilitated old staff) and old staff is the dynamic of in-groups and out-groups, a central tension in the early days of a new team. Sometimes a new leader immediately brings other outsiders into key posts such as finance, because trust can be taken for granted. The risk is the creation of a dominant coalition predominantly new to the agency and not in psychological contact with the hearts and minds of the majority of the organization. Often an old staff member will become part of this inner circle and be viewed as selling out to the new coalition, stripped of his or her credentials as an old-timer in the organization. Such a new, outside coalition may sit atop an organization but be unable to implement the new strategy because of its failure to establish working alliances with the operating core of the agency.

When new staff members are brought in, existing staff members may overallocate their negative feelings to the newcomers, because it is safer to be angry at the new staff than at the new leader, on whom they are dependent. Therefore, when one sees generalized good feelings toward the new leader but unreasonable hostility toward someone identified with the new leader, it often is a safe bet that there is some displacement at work. It can be helpful for the working relationships among the top team to bring this issue to the surface and to help people match their feelings with the appropriate relationships.

A very frequent pattern in leadership transitions is for new leaders to visit, talk, and develop connections with the line level of the organization without attending to the development of the relationships to middle managers. This triangle is particularly common today because of the prevalent idea that organizations are sluggish, bureaucratic, excessively layered, and overstaffed, and such popular themes as semiautonomous work groups, quality circles, and quality of working life. Leaders are drawn to the directness and tangibility of the line worker's role. The consequence is that the middle managers feel (and actually are) left out; long-term results may suffer, as the middle managers are sure to outlast the new leader.

Alternatively, a leader can become cut off from the line and excessively preoccupied with higher immediate subordinates. In this pattern, the line staff become the outsiders, despite their importance in the ultimate changes that need to take place.

A new leader with a good relationship with middle managers will be effectively represented at the line via the chain of command. I recall riding in a state car driven by a middle manager and inquiring why we were going so slowly on a rural road with no one around. She replied that the director was adamant about not getting speeding tickets in state cars because of the potential adverse publicity. I felt the presence of the director in this subordinate, not because she was afraid of punishment, but because she had internalized his concerns and understood the reasons. She could therefore make line staff also feel his presence in a constructive way. When an organization achieves this level of commitment, the leader is in contact with both the middle and the line, and the middle is potentiated, not bypassed. At the same time as the middle managers become confident of their relationship to the top, the top can be in direct contact with the line without stirring up primitive feelings among the managers that they are being spied on.

In another triangular pattern, many new leaders develop excellent relationships outside of the organization but fail to do so with those inside. In one organization, shortly after a new leader had taken over I attended a strategic planning meeting in which there were almost as many outside consultants as internal staff. Fortunately, the group was able to wrestle with the dynamic in which the leader was using interesting outsiders as a substitute for developing the necessary relationships internally. Consulting firms are often employed in the aftermath of a transition. Especially if they have a prior relationship to the new leader, they may be deployed as a palace guard whose loyalty is purchased. They may then be experienced by the organization as questioning the internal competence of existing staff, and they may keep the leader from building relationships inside. In another version of this triangle, the new leader joins with the customers in ways that the organization experiences as attacks. Obviously the leader needs to be in contact with key outsiders but in ways that link the staff to them as well. Conversely, the new leader may get so enmeshed in the internal organizational dynamics that the customers are ignored. Both are prescriptions for failure. This dilemma is treated in greater detail in Chapter Nine.

Sometimes inside staff have strong links with outside groups that can be used internally as potential threats to the leader. If the leader develops effective relationships with those staff members, however, then those same links become working assets.

Managing Triangles. The general strategy for managing

triangles is to remain related to both parties without discussing the absent third party in destructive ways. By constantly keeping issues in the right channels and blocking detouring maneuvers, a leader can bring considerable health to an organization's relationship system. For example, a managing partner handled a detoured complaint from one partner about another by cutting short the one complaining, immediately telephoning the third party, and saying, "Mr. Brown is in my office with some concerns about your behavior and I thought you should come up here right away so that you can work them out." In addition to working on the immediate presenting issue, the managing partner sent a clear signal about how he would respond to future attempts to complain to him unconstructively.

Given the importance of triangles in leadership transitions, let me summarize what to watch for.

1. Identify the main players in the triangle and in particular the hot leg of the triangle, the one that is carrying a disproportionate amount of the conflict.

2. If you experience an intense dyadic encounter, looking for a potentially underinvolved third party may shed some light on the dynamics that you are experiencing.

3. Identify the third person who is often in the cool or distant position and benefiting from the deflection of affect. Are there ways to involve that person so that he or she takes a fair share of the issue?

4. Watch for over- and underfunctioning. Who is doing whose work for whom? How is the work of worry distributed? Who carries more than a fair share of worry? It is often easier to throttle down an overfunctioner than to get an underfunctioner moving. Often an underfunctioner will not be motivated until the overfunctioner stops protecting the other (often unwittingly).

5. Look for ways to stay in contact with the person with whom you are having the most trouble in the triangle. For example, might an out-of-town business trip provide opportunities to relate in a significantly different way?

6. Look for conflicts that are being detoured. Are people getting

angry at someone who is less powerful (and therefore less risky to hate) than the real target of their anger?

When triangled by someone complaining about an absent third party, an effective response is to ask, "What did he say when you discussed this with him?" Deliver it in a tone that makes clear it is absolutely expected that the issue has been dealt with directly. When it is acknowledged that no such discussion has occurred, as is usually the case, one can then shift to work with the complainer on finding a way to take up the matter constructively with the appropriate person.

In the end, the most important work in triangles is always the work on the self. Salvador Minuchin, the well-known family therapist, reacted to a meeting with a foundation executive by saying, "I didn't like myself when I was with Mr. Smith," rather than simply locating the problem in Mr. Smith as a person. If one is alive to the ways in which one contributes actively to the process of triangulation, one can gain the necessary perspective and communicate a broader understanding to the other two parties, who in turn will begin to address and resolve their issues between them.

The Shadow of the New Leader's Past

Leaders think of the moment of their entry into an organization as a beginning, a clean slate, with no historical constraints or shadows of former leaders (Sarason, 1972). There is a fantasy of fathering oneself, not having to work through the obligations and relationships that flow backward in time. In one organization, the new director of a division repeatedly referred to the specific date of her arrival as if it were some watershed in the organization's history, missing completely the fact that it was mainly a personal watershed. Another leader moved quickly to rotate all the regional deputies, saying that he wanted to give everyone a "fresh start," an action experienced by the staff as avoidance of the inevitable complexity of evaluating their performance. The new leader is often disengaging from his or her role in a previous setting, finishing up some final obligations, working through endings with staff, making sense of the successes and disappointments. At the same time, staff in the new setting are working through their disengagements with the former leader and the anxieties about the coalitions forming around the new leader.

Just as the organization has a history that has preceded the leader, so too does the leader have a history that affects his or her entry into the organization. One important historical aspect that shapes the climate of entry is the process by which the leader was selected for the post. For example, coming in as part of a long, well-planned internal transition differs dramatically from coming in as the result of an exhaustive external executive search. The perceptions about which interest groups dominated the selection process will inform the early views of coalitions, especially if a thoughtful search has made the choice a clear statement about the desired directions for the organization. If there has been a search, it will matter whether the new leader is believed to have been the first choice or second or third. Moreover, the new leader will be held up for comparison against other real or imagined candidates. For example, in a controversial selection process at the University of Pennsylvania, the trustees went outside to choose Sheldon Hackney as president against the favorite inside candidate of many students and faculty, Vartan Gregorian. Newspaper accounts of the selection politics suggested that "Gregorian would be too strong as the chief executive" versus the trustees (Fancher, 1980, p. 4b), thereby making Hackney's handling of the board an early drama in his transition. Hackney has had to struggle with the comparison, especially as Gregorian has gone on to enjoy a highly visible success at the helm of the New York Public Library.

If the appointing authority has selected an outsider when viable inside candidates were in the pool, there will inevitably be feelings that the talent inside the organization has been ignored. Existing staff are likely to test the new leader to see if he or she measures up to the inside candidate. When a new owner of the tradition-rich *New Yorker* appointed a new editor from outside, rejecting the internal candidate who had long been groomed for the post, the staff reacted angrily. One member commented that "the shouldering aside" of the presumed successor and the insistence on the new editor in the face of staff protests "tear up the unwritten charter that until now has guided the *New Yorker*. They annul its crucial editorial independence . . . they compromise its integrity. They overthrow the magazine that I and so many others have loved and believed in and worked for over the years" (Span, 1987, p. 8C). In such a case, the new leader will inevitably be compared with the insider and will be a target, along with the appointing authority, for the staff anger.

The new leader's prior career and experiences relevant to the current job also send messages. For example, a leader's background in marketing will shape the interactions with that function and other groups. People's perceptions may be based on less tangible evidence as well. When a new president was appointed to a division of a top *Fortune* 500 company from a subsidiary where he had achieved a significant turnaround, one particular story about him circulated widely prior to his arrival. A consultant had been working with some of this executive's top staff and felt there were serious problems that were not being effectively communicated upward. The consultant proposed that the staff videotape presentations on these issues for the boss's review. They did, and he was reportedly taken aback both by the seriousness of the issues and more important by his lack of awareness of those issues. From that moment on, according to the story, he launched a revitalization effort and dramatically altered his own leadership and communication style.

The effect of such a story preceding one's entry is enormously powerful. Nor does this process end when the new leader arrives. A full year after this executive had taken over the division, staff members were still using his prior record in the subsidiary as evidence for his chances of success in implementing a new procedure that went against the corporatewide process. The meaning that is extracted from a leader's prior experience is always subject to reinterpretation and reexamination, depending on how it links to current issues within the organization.

Because of this, people from a leader's prior setting will be disproportionately influential. One organizational development consultant, anxious about influencing a new leader in an organization where he was doing an extensive amount of consulting, looked up who was on the Harvard Business School faculty in organizational behavior when the new leader was a student there to find out what people and theories he had been exposed to. People seldom go that far, but existing staff members often use their professional networks into the prior organizations of a new leader. The consequence is that the "fresh start" may be asymmetric; the existing staff already know things that shape their approaches to the new leader, while the new leader has relatively little information on existing staff.

At the same time, the new leader is managing the ending of his or her relationship with the prior organization. Sonnenfeld's discussion (1986) of the ambivalence that arises as leaders exit and look back on their accomplishments is one of the rare treatments of this topic. I believe that unresolved issues regarding exit can interfere with the new leader's taking charge in the new setting.

Existing staff often look for clues as to whether a leader is loyal to the new setting over previous associations. One new leader discovered, after some of the staff were comfortable enough to give him honest feedback, that his frequent use of the phrase "this place" had irritated people, conveying a sense that he was an outsider evaluating the "place" rather than a new leader joining them. A simple phrase played into the core anxiety about whether he and they shared a future. Similarly, leaders often use stories about their prior organizations as a way of establishing their credibility but the stories are heard less as testimony to their competence than as evidence that they are still tied to their old organizations.

Especially in turnaround or major revitalization situations, the leader is often recruited from a setting more developed or successful than the organization in crisis. In such a situation, it is very easy for the leader's prior organization to live on as a normative basis for comparison. One commissioner of police, recruited from the Secret Service, constantly compared some negative feature of his current organization with the superior processes in the Secret Service. A spouse in a second marriage trying to change the current relationship by making constant comparisons with the first marriage would have a similar effect.

These multiple forces play out concretely in such decisions as whether to bring staff from the prior setting. In many corporate successions, an outsider coming to a top leadership position will bring several associates from the prior organization. Exxon Office

Systems became an enclave of former IBM executives. When Frank Cohouet took over Mellon Bank, he reached back to a former organization to recruit his chief financial officer, with whom he had undertaken a similar turnaround assignment (Fix, 1987b, p. 8b). A leader cannibalizing talent from a former setting must wrestle with the risk of undoing whatever accomplishments were a source of pride at that organization. On the other side, former employees may eagerly seek to join their departed leader, creating difficult choices for the new leader. As we saw earlier, such importations create a triangular framework for the leader and new and old staff. Staff recruited from the former organization are particularly problematic when they do not report directly to the new leader; people assume they have special access because of their prior relationship.

Most new leaders experience moments of doubt about whether they should have taken the new job and feel nostalgia for the old setting. One leader who had undertaken a turnaround assignment in a professional school found himself so discouraged after his initial weeks that he actually asked the provost why they had decided to keep the school open. A critical part of the success of making the transition to a new organization is for the leader to accept the real differences between new and old settings and to make decisions that reflect those differences. As in all transitions, the more effectively one can work through the losses from the change, the more one will deal straightforwardly with the new situation, without allowing the disappointments and successes from the previous setting to distort current judgments.

The Shadow of the Former Leader

In one of the most frequently told jokes surrounding the issue of leadership succession, a departing leader gives his successor two sealed envelopes, with instructions to use them during organizational crises. Several months later, the new leader encounters his first truly difficult crisis and remembers the two envelopes. He opens the first and finds the message "Blame me." The strategy works like a charm. More time passes, and the leader encounters his next crisis. Eagerly he seeks guidance from the second envelope. The message reads "Prepare two envelopes."

This humorous story throws light on a number of the critical relationships in the triangle of the old leader/new leader/existing staff. At one level, it suggests the bond between the leaders, who both know that in some circumstances leaders are called upon to be blamed even when it is not their fault. This scapegoating theory of leadership (Gamson and Scotch, 1964) says that leaders are held symbolically responsible, beyond their actual control over critical performance criteria.

The story also suggests that the old leader is available as a target for the bad so that the new leader can be regarded as good. Often the easiest and quickest source of identity for a new team is the most obvious differences with the prior administration. In one retreat that I facilitated for a new leader (Brown) and his top team, made up of some newcomers and some existing staff, I was struck by how frequently the prior leader (Smith) was mentioned. In this instance, the new Brown administration was most clearly identified as the not-Smith administration, in the way that a term such as *postindustrial* indicates that we know better what era we are leaving than what era we are entering. The new leader was informal, open, trusting, and participative, in contrast to the former leader, who was viewed as formal, suspicious, controlling, and intimidating.

The group at the retreat included Flynn, who had headed up a major operating division and had been Brown's rival for the top job. Brown had elevated Flynn to deputy, with some specific assignments but without supervision over the two major operating divisions, which reported directly to Brown. He had taken this step because in his early weeks of service he felt that Flynn's strengths could be harnessed effectively. Furthermore, Flynn's retention would send a signal that the work he had done as a division director was valued. By moving up, Flynn would gain valuable experience toward eventually getting the top job. Moreover, the promotion would take him out of the major operating division, so that he could not use that as a power base. Brown and Flynn had traveled together to all the major plants in the state and had developed a good working alliance. Both had served as Marines in Vietnam, and Brown was confident of Flynn's loyalty.

In preretreat interviews, the hot issue was the relationship of Flynn to Brown. Several people spoke of an emerging alliance between them. The image that was put into my mind was of a Svengali, manipulating the leader into acting against his own nature. People implied that Brown was no longer the person with "a good intellect and a heart, a bright glow, honest, open," but was becoming more like Flynn, more "unfeeling, intellectual, unilateral, less open to team work." Flynn, one person said, "has a negative, distrustful attitude, and Brown is beginning to take it in. [Flynn] is beginning to shape the way Brown sees the department. . . . His view is being distorted . . . he is being heavily influenced, now making little jokes and snide remarks about people when I know he is very respectful of people and always looks for the best in them."

At the retreat, it became clear that since Flynn had played a key role in the prior administration, he was a repository for leftover feelings. He was being used as the carrier of both what was good and what was bad about the prior system; Brown was oriented to the good in Flynn, the rest of the staff to the bad. The group used Flynn in part to protect their idealization of Brown, the outside leader who would lead them in new directions. When Brown made decisions that they did not like, they would see Flynn's influence. Frequently one sees a holdover staff member carrying the shadow of the former leader.

The central drama was over the mix of history and hope. Surrounding the new leader is the hope of a new vision, and there is fear that it will be blunted or co-opted by the existing staff. On the other side, old staff represent both historic achievements and working capital—knowledge about the problems, the politics, the key actors that will be invaluable if it can be tapped safely.

At one point in the retreat, Flynn discussed his view of the circumstances that prevented the group from dealing with some of the value issues it was facing. He used the metaphor of a military assault: "We were the first wave that had captured the beachhead, there was no time to talk values then. The troops had performed admirably. You (or we) are here now and have the opportunity to think about new directions only because of the blood, sweat, toil and tears of my grunts." For him, the central issue was whether or not his achievements (and those of the former leader) would be acknowledged and valued rather than judged from a new and potentially unfair vantage point of hindsight.

Much later in the retreat, another member of the team, new to the organization but from within the state, said to a new member from out of state, "You *need* to hear the legislative history of that initiative." The out-of-stater replied sharply, "I don't *need* to hear anything. I would like to hear that background, but will make my own decisions." It was as if history could be used only in the service of conservative agendas rather than in support of change agendas. Listening was confused with being co-opted, as if one feared one's own resolve in the face of historical facts.

One of the critical issues during the retreat was Brown's relationship to Flynn. Teams can often get caught up in patterns that no one wants, and this was the case here. Figure 3 sketches the dynamic, potentially self-reinforcing and stalemating, in which they were caught. Brown kept Flynn because he valued his competence and his historical knowledge about issues and people, both inside and outside the department. Others feared Flynn's strength and mistrusted him, so they would not use him. As others used him less, Brown overcompensated and used him more. Flynn responded by disengaging from the rest of the team and not offering his advice in team meetings. Others began to view this as evidence that Flynn was just biding his time until he could manipulatively get his way when meeting alone with Brown. They projected their paranoia onto him as a way of preserving good relationships among themselves and with the leader.

Flynn felt trapped. The competence for which he had been retained was hard to give in ways that were accepted. During a session to address this issue he noted, "My views are tainted by the past." He felt burdened by the baggage. He noted that he had "backed off . . . given others a wide berth . . . the room they need." Once this pattern was visible and discussable, a division director was able to say to him, "I feel cheated if you do not participate fully." Another commented, "Don't mute your strength." The group then was able to explore specific issues in which this dynamic had resulted in poor decisions, with people feeling blindsided because of the series of two-way communications when three parties were needed. The group was eventually able to discuss playfully the

Figure 3. Vicious Cycle of Interaction.

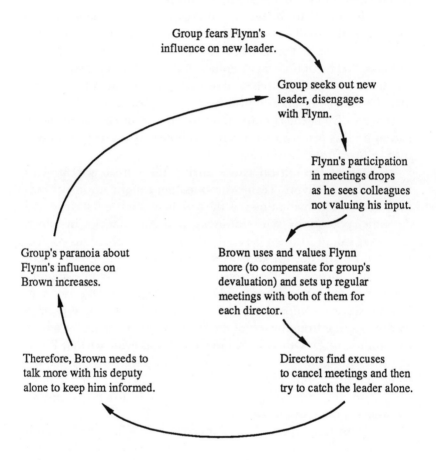

need to "exorcise Flynn," to free him from the ghosts that were interfering with their ability to use his competence.

The afternoon discussion ended with the new leader, Brown, giving his view of his and Flynn's different strengths and weaknesses and urging staff members to use their own judgments about whom to consult, depending on the issue. People had been able to step back from the trap and to see the dysfunctional, self-maintaining aspects of the cycle that they had fallen into. They could take back some of the projections and deal with each other on a more reality-oriented basis.

Different perceptions of the new leader and existing staff create tension during the transition. Two people in an anxious relationship will inevitably triangle with a third to redistribute the anxiety, in ways that often distort and inhibit learning. Often the third position in dynamics between the current leader and the current staff is the leader's past, or the past leader. The next chapter looks at the process of joining between the new leader and staff, the early initiatives that critically shape the initial climate, and some of the major traps or dilemmas into which new leaders can fall.

Chapter 9

Connecting with Existing Staff: Three Typical Traps

One of the central tensions in the early months of a new leader's tenure is the two-way nature of dependency. At first glance, the new leader would seem to be one up on the staff, sitting in judgment on the policies, programs, and people in the organization. However, the new leader is also extremely dependent on the staff for providing relevant information and handling ongoing business during the transition. An outsider appointed to a state department of revenue commented:

> There wasn't a wise old man who I could obviously go to who was about to reveal the contents of his briefcase or put his arm around me and say: "Okay kid, I know it's a tough job. I know you are the first non-lawyer, non–tax expert to ever walk in the door. And I know there's no way for you to decipher the extent of corruption, or to figure out what's really important that needs doing—and who the doers are. But breathe deeply, bite your lower lip, and here's how it's done." There was none of that. The most frustrating aspect of the first six weeks—six to ten weeks—was the stark realization that no one was going to tell me anything. . . . You can't fully appreciate the stark terror that results from knowing that you're in a position of enormous authority and that you have not one clue as to what is really going on around you. No

one would tell me if my coat was on fire or if the
computer had completely broken down [Behn, 1985,
p. 19].

A large public bureaucracy with civil service protection for
many employees may be an extreme case, but in all transitions the
new leader is highly dependent on existing staff for information.
Staff members can injure a new leader as much by what they do not
do or say as by what they do, and thereby avoid direct resistance.
David Mechanic (1964) has written insightfully on the power of
"lower participants," who control information about what is really
going on in the remote recesses of complex organizations. More
recently, the Iran-Contra affair brought to light an example of this
power in the National Security Council: "These sources said that
Colonel North . . . was able to expedite plans for secret programs
because he knew every office in the foreign affairs sectors of the
Government whose officials had to be briefed, and he had personal
relationships with their directors. Colonel North also served under
four national security advisors in five years and found that the almost
annual change in leadership and continual turnover in the staff was
an advantage to him. Former and current members of the council's
staff say he served as the institutional memory of the National
Security Council, providing a continuity that made him almost
indispensable" (Schneider, 1987, p. 4). One can well imagine the
reluctance of existing staff to give up their strategic informational
advantage by telling a new leader everything they know, even if it
were possible.

One strategy for dealing with such dependency is to embrace
it by taking a deliberate student role. By channeling the anxiety of
being dependent into a structured encounter, new leaders can
effectively join with existing staff and develop valuable working
alliances as they obtain the necessary information. With thoughtful
questions and skillful inquiry, they establish credibility.

People who have difficulty acknowledging their dependency
on others sometimes employ what British psychoanalyst Melanie
Klein (Segal, 1974, chapter 7) terms a manic defense, in which they
experience feelings of omnipotence and control over others and the
situation. They frequently punish others, treat staff members as

pawns rather than as people, and enjoy their triumphs in order to feel secure in what is in reality a threatening and risky environment. As with all defenses, they distort the reality of the situation, and the quality of thinking that goes into their decision making suffers. These feelings of independence and self-importance can be especially aggrandized when the leader is also the subject of grand fantasies of hope and salvation from existing staff.

Given the complexities of the relationship of a leader to existing staff and the triangles that crop up in the early months, a critical task for the new leader is to connect authentically with existing staff, to join the organization. This chapter discusses this process and the early initiatives that set the tone of the new leader's tenure, describes three potential traps that result from the dynamics of transition, and concludes with strategies for coping with these traps.

The Psychological Process of Joining

If the new leader fails to connect effectively with existing staff, then all the skill and insight in the world will be of no avail, because the leader will have no channel into the organization through which to work change. Effective joining involves (1) focusing on and working with the positive, healthy parts of the system while confirming the reality of the system, often by empathizing with some painful aspect of it; (2) helping people tell their stories so that they feel heard and begin to hope that the leader can help resolve some of the critical challenges; (3) acknowledging the existing structure and leadership before beginning to change it; and (4) avoiding getting caught permanently in a coalition with one party or another, but rather moving to connect with the different groups and making each feel understood (Minuchin and Fishman, 1981).

One of the most difficult tasks for a new leader is to talk about change without making existing staff feel they are being blamed for the situation that needs changing. This problem can be particularly acute when performance has been an issue. In an industrial basic research lab, a corporately mandated cut of nearly half the scientists and technologists had just preceded the new leader's arrival. The ostensible reason was lack of bottom-line results and a belief that the lab's work had become unrelated to the businesses, but the scientists perceived the cuts as vindictive, going far beyond what would have been justified from a business-driven decision. The new leader of the research facility, trying to get the lab moving again, faced the difficult issue of pressing the need to change, but without blaming the existing staff, who already felt attacked by the corporate level. The leader articulated a theme of partnership while praising the scientific excellence in the lab.

A test of whether the new leader has effectively joined is whether current staff feel that their dilemmas have been understood by the new leader. A powerful example of effective joining occurred in a troubled juvenile detention center, which had been in the news repeatedly and had a terrible reputation (Gilmore and Schall, 1986). In its twenty-six years of existence, it had had twenty-three leaders.

A new director was then recruited via an active national search. The staff members awaited her with some anxiety, fearful of an uninformed housecleaning and feeling that they had often been unfairly blamed for problems that lay beyond their control. Many had joined the staff in order to do good things for children but experienced "the system" as getting in their way. Shortly after her selection and before beginning the job, the new leader addressed the staff at the institution and told a story that rapidly circulated within the agency: "A pilot and co-pilot had just taken off when the co-pilot told the pilot that they should return immediately because a rat was gnawing at the fuel line. The pilot not only continued his ascent but increased the rate of climbing. The co-pilot grew agitated and repeated his warning. The pilot reassured him. 'Don't worry,' he said. 'We're going to fly so high no rat will be able to live'" (Gilmore and Schall, 1986, p. 267–274).

The story acknowledged that there were serious problems yet suggested that a new vision would address them. The story also nicely suggested a switch in the organization's focus from children's negative behavior to their strengths and to the positive things that could be done for them during detention. The story also suggested support for the healthy, goal-oriented aspects of the staff.

Note that the story did not give any specific content to the change vision. To do so in ignorance of the culture of the institution and the history of previous failures would have been risky. Instead it sent a general message of hope, while acknowledging that there were serious problems. It announced the strategy of moving toward health rather than fixing each problem in a defensive, negative way. A testament to the success of this joining is the vitality of the symbol and story. Buttons showing a rat with a large red line through it were made up and worn as symbols of people's commitment to the change effort. The story is now handed down to new staff as part of the institution's informal orientation.

In another case, a new leader came into an organization that he felt was preoccupied with its past. Rather than confront that issue directly, he spoke of "building on the rich history" and actually began to collaborate with a key insider to write down the history. He felt it could become an asset if it shifted a backward-looking oral tradition to a forward-looking written examination of the values relevant to the future. His explicit strategy was to join and move rather than confront.

The leader must never forget that joining with an organization is necessary to create the working alliances needed to change it. Some leaders fear they will be co-opted and lose their vision; they remain remote, keeping the vision fresh but unimplementable. Others go to the opposite extreme, wanting to be liked, focusing all their attention on being accepted; they can then no longer pose a challenge to the organization. What is required is a complex balance.

Hirschman (1967) examines a similar dilemma in the design of projects in underdeveloped countries. He argues that designers need to balance "trait-making" aspects—those features of a project that make it an engine of development—with "trait taking"—those features that have to be accepted in order for the project to be implemented. He offers the fascinating example of a Nigerian railroad project, which aspired to make new traits of a professional civil service that transcended tribalism. It failed because the competitive mode of trucking was so well adapted to small, tribally based, nonprofessional operations. He advises project planners to allow for the traits that must be accepted as the price for the opportunity to introduce new traits. Similarly, leaders must think developmentally about introducing new competencies to their organizations. For example, in one organization a leader had to accept and even strengthen the centralization of the organization before he could implement his long-term goal of decentralization.

The Symbolic Importance of Early Actions

The first impressions made by a new leader powerfully shape key working relationships both internally and externally. Paradoxically, because there are so many pressing concerns, a leader's earliest actions are those least likely to be well thought through. These early actions have a dual nature: not only do they deal with the matter at hand—a decision, a personnel matter, a press release—but they serve as data for people's early theories about the new leader. The actions are interpreted, and these interpretations in turn shape the meanings of subsequent actions until the "personality" or "character" of the new administration emerges. When a new president takes office and makes the first decision on farm supports, for example, people not only make inferences based on the substance of the decision but also attend to the process. Did he listen more to political inputs than technical? Was the process open? How was Congress involved? When the next similar issue comes up, people act on their hunches about the leader's approach to these kinds of issues. In this way, the initial decisions can inadvertently shape a process.

In a new leader's first days, even trivial issues will be spun into theories. For instance, a lawyer took over a state consumer advocate office. At the end of his first week, the central receptionist was sick. The new leader asked that the full names of each attorney be written on the receptionist's phone instead of just the first names so that a temporary receptionist could answer the phones competently. As a result of this innocent request, a rumor swept through the office that he was going to insist on all personnel being called by Mr. and Ms. rather than by first names, which had been been the practice.

Early actions also symbolize what the new executive thinks is important. Who the leader sees, in what order, and for how long take on great meaning to outsiders. In reality, of course, initial meetings often are determined by mere accidents of scheduling.

A few examples will illustrate how a new leader can take advantage of the importance of early actions.

- A new leader of a professional school was given a copy of the school bulletin, which had just come from the printer. He felt it was unattractive and reflected the low self-esteem of the institution. Without knowing where he would get the money, he threw out the 15,000 copies and initiated a crash replacement. He got fresh advice on the graphics, for the first time including photographs of the faculty, and revised the descriptions of key features of the school. The action communicated far more powerfully than words his commitment to a new image and his belief that the faculty was a critical asset to the school.
- A new director of detention moved her office down from an executive floor to a major circulation point in the institution and began coming into the institution on evening and night shifts.
- David Gunn, shortly after taking over the New York City Transit Authority, pulled controversial Grumman buses from the fleet as a dramatic way of establishing his commitment to safety and his willingness to act in the face of complex problems.
- A new director of state corrections sponsored a two-day retreat to address many long-festering issues in the state's relationship with local correctional officials. Rather than just giving an opening speech and then leaving, he stayed for the entire two days, working aggressively to rebuild some trust that the two levels could be partners.

By contrast, the new director of a major teaching hospital constructed a glass partition where the corridor leading to the executive suites met the main hall and remodeled the executive offices with carpeting and new furnishings. The first night the glass broke—"the hand of God," noted one staff member. The director's intent may have been to signal a need for respected executive leadership, but some staff took it as a separating gesture that suggested lack of trust.

Similarly, political leaders when they request everyone's pro forma resignation create the impression that they are unable or unwilling to acknowledge individual differences in past performance.

Because of the symbolic importance of early initiatives, new leaders may be well advised to reflect on how those initiatives might look from the followers' point of view. In service businesses, organizations place great emphasis on initial encounters, because they know how difficult it is to win customers back after some initial irritation. Similarly, new leaders can save considerable anguish later on in their tenure by attending to first impressions with existing staff. Peters (1978) calls attention to the mundane aspects of leadership that often shape followers' perceptions: the calendar, the types of questions, the location of meetings. For example, a new leader who moves around to the different offices of current executives sets a different tone from one who calls them into his or her office.

Three Potential Traps for New Leaders and Subordinates

The initial culture created by a new leader and followers results from an interplay of intended and unintended consequences. Eric Brettschneider, deputy administrator of Special Services for Children in New York City, tells a story that illustrates the interplay of serendipity and intent (Brettschneider, 1985, pp. 3-4). Two days after Brettschneider took over his position, a child tragically died in foster care. A television reporter asked him who should be held accountable. He gave a complex bureaucratic response, touching on the need for confidentiality and so on. The reporter pressed by changing to a hypothetical question: "In general, if a child falls through the cracks and dies, who should be held responsible?" Brettschneider replied, "I am responsible" and elaborated on his strategies for changing the agency. That evening, he was somewhat taken aback to hear the reporter say on television, "We looked into the death of this child and we tried to find out who was responsible," followed by a cut to Brettschneider saying, "I am responsible." His initial dismay changed as many workers and stakeholders in the voluntary system fervently congratulated him for not passing the buck. "That was really wonderful, what you did last night, Eric.

You assumed responsibility, and that's something that has not happened enough." One often does not know the meaning of one's actions in a new setting until one listens to the backtalk.

Leaders, especially early in their tenure, do not get fully developed options from which they select a path. Rather, a direction begins to emerge from a sequence of choices—about people, issues, resources (Peters, 1979)—and from serendipity. The timing may be as much affected by external events as set by the leader. One risk is of being captured by crises and operating routines so that there is too little time for the thinking necessary for setting new directions. Bennis (1976) has termed this the "unconscious conspiracy" and has written eloquently of discovering that his time as a new university president was being filled with allocating parking spaces and approving decisions competently made elsewhere. This overuse of the new leader on details serves to contain the uncertainty that would be felt if the new leader were to focus truly on the substantive challenges. Bennis calls this conspiracy "unconscious" because it is neither the explicit intent of the subordinates nor the desire of the new leader, yet they interact to bring it about. Just as many organizations flee from using leadership transitions strategically, many times both leaders and followers draw back from ruthlessly focusing on the critical issues that may have been defined during the executive search.

In my work with transitions, I have encountered three patterns of misunderstanding that often arise in the early months of new leadership, with unintended negative consequences. They resemble what Harvey (1974) called "the Abilene paradox," named when he found himself and his family a hundred miles from home on a hot day in Abilene, only to discover that none of them really wanted to be there. Their trip resulted from each misunderstanding the wishes of the other and not being able to inquire freely to uncover their mistake. Similarly, these traps arise from misunderstandings and the inability to discuss the situation freely.

1. Patterns of Delegation. New leaders often find a bottleneck of issues waiting for their attention. Until the new leader can deal with these issues, others in the organization are left waiting to do their end of the work. Two groups emerge, an overworked inner circle and an underused out-group. Therefore one of the central initial tasks is to develop a better pattern of delegation (Onken and Wass, 1974).

In the work discussed earlier with a governor, his staff, and his cabinet, we uncovered a seemingly contradictory set of complaints. The governor complained that he was overwhelmed with operational issues that he did not think needed to be brought to him. Meanwhile, the cabinet secretaries complained that they were not given enough authority to run their departments.

Figure 4 diagrams the process we discovered. In the give and take of early working relationships, subordinates make two types of mistakes: they consult when they should handle the issue on their own, and they fail to consult when they should. If they make the first type of mistake, it is rarely brought to their attention. When we asked the governor what he did when someone brought him an issue unnecessarily, he acknowledged that he rarely confronted the secretary, not wanting to appear unresponsive. In such a case, the subordinate can easily misinterpret the leader's responsiveness to mean that the leader wants involvement on that sort of issue.

If on the other hand the subordinates fail to consult when they should have, they get rapid and vigorous feedback. They develop a maxim (risk-aversive, to be sure) of "If in doubt, check it out." Since the latter type of error is systematically corrected while the former is not and may even be encouraged, the overall pattern is for more and more issues to reach the leader, when neither party wishes them to. The leader feels overloaded and diverted from more important tasks; the subordinate feels lack of trust and elbow room to do the job. And the new leader, swamped in trivia, has less time to set the overall direction to guide staff, so that more issues are experienced by staff as ambiguous and having to be checked out.

The most powerful antidote to this pattern is a joint learning stance. After a piece of substantive work is completed, a small amount of time is taken to reflect on the work and the appropriateness of the patterns of participation. The reflection may reveal the desire of both parties to have more work delegated and lead them to explore concretely what issues this delegation can be applied to.

Often in the early days of a new working relationship, people are not comfortable with reflective feedback. It may be necessary to have a workshop session that explicitly focuses on emerging pat-

Figure 4. Cycle of Overloading the Leader.

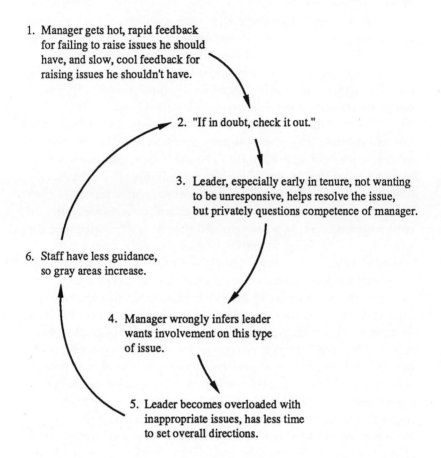

1. Manager gets hot, rapid feedback
   for failing to raise issues he should
   have, and slow, cool feedback for
   raising issues he shouldn't have.

2. "If in doubt, check it out."

3. Leader, especially early in tenure, not wanting
   to be unresponsive, helps resolve the issue,
   but privately questions competence of manager.

6. Staff have less guidance,
   so gray areas increase.

4. Manager wrongly infers leader
   wants involvement on this type
   of issue.

5. Leader becomes overloaded with
   inappropriate issues, has less time
   to set overall directions.

terns. In the work with the governor, many of the cabinet officers said that they were reluctant to raise the issue over any one item because it did not seem important enough to complain about, but they did feel able to raise it when asked to reflect on the patterns of the new administration, because in aggregate they felt that the stakes were significant.

2. Patterns of Attention to Internal Versus External Issues. Leadership is by definition a boundary role, mediating between the inside and the external environment. Therefore, all new leaders face immediate choices about the relative time and attention they devote to internal versus external issues. Chapter Eight discussed briefly how a new leader can get caught in a dysfunctional triangle in allocating attention between inside and outside stakeholders. It is worth exploring this dilemma more fully, because paradoxically, a desire to rebuild external support can backfire if the leader does not simultaneously develop the internal staff.

Figure 5 diagrams the process, which can be seen in the following example: A newly appointed secretary of aging immediately went on the road to speak at each of the county organizations for the aged. At each of these town meetings, he struck his strategic themes, always getting loud applause when he called for "more advocacy and less bureaucracy." As he came into contact with the

Figure 5. Potential Consequences of Overly Attending to External Constituencies Before Developing Inside Staff.

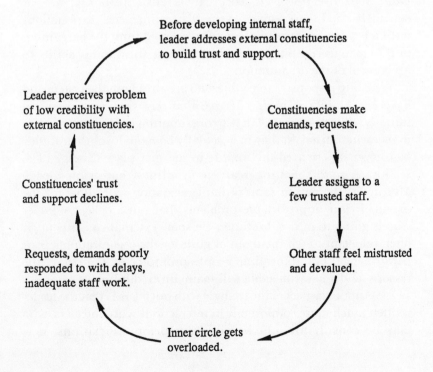

Before developing internal staff, leader addresses external constituencies to build trust and support.

Leader perceives problem of low credibility with external constituencies.

Constituencies make demands, requests.

Constituencies' trust and support declines.

Leader assigns to a few trusted staff.

Requests, demands poorly responded to with delays, inadequate staff work.

Other staff feel mistrusted and devalued.

Inner circle gets overloaded.

clients, he inevitably picked up tasks, questions to follow through on, ideas that he wanted to pursue. Yet he had not yet built his home organization to support him. The people who were needed to deliver on the promise of more advocacy were the very bureaucrats whom he had been attacking. The existing staff felt mistrusted and devalued and became even less available for work. The inner circle became more overloaded. As requests and demands were poorly followed through on, the responsiveness of the organization fell and the constituents' trust and support decreased.

In rebuilding external working alliances, it is probably more effective to promise little and deliver much. Credibility depends on the relationship between promises (or threats) and future actions. When making a promise, a new leader should consider carefully the time necessary for follow-through; it may take only minutes to promise but months (and several people) to deliver. The leader is often well advised to build the capacity and infrastructure that are necessary to be responsive before making new claims. When David Gunn took over the New York City Transit Authority, he was extremely careful to temper external constituencies' expectations until a key level of supervisors was transferred from the bargaining unit to managerial lines, a step he felt was critical to his ability to get control of the organization.

Being responsive to people who are already in the system and have complaints is more effective than creating more demand initially. When people feel that an organization has been responsive to its earlier mistakes, they may actually be more loyal than if they had never experienced the trouble in the first place (Zweig, 1986, section 2, p. 29). Setting realistic deadlines that acknowledge Murphy as the patron saint of implementation will allow for the inevitable but unpredictable problems that cause delay. A leader who is going to miss a deadline with some external constituents is often reluctant to tell them out of guilt for the organization's poor performance, but informing people promptly of the delay, the reasons, and a new timetable will maintain credibility.

Another aspect of the triangle with outsiders is that the leader is often much more comfortable in interactions with outsiders, who may be consultants, old friends from prior associations, new advisers, or in the public sector members of the chief executive's staff or fellow cabinet officers. Or they may be major clients or consumers of the organization's services, who sometimes seem to understand the change agendas quickly and support them (because the changes threaten them less).

One leader commented, "They [outsiders] understand you better than your staff does, and you get misled into thinking that you are understood because you are explaining yourself so well—but maybe not to the right people." Another leader, who had been brought in as a change agent to a children services division, rapidly found critical support externally in the head of a citizen advisory board, a city council member, a private attorney, and a few representatives of private agency service providers. With them, he developed his strategy for changing an ossified civil service bureaucracy—leaving the existing staff feeling abandoned. They felt that the new leader had jumped into an alliance with outside interest groups, who were getting the best part of him—the humor, aliveness, unguardedness, creativity, playfulness. In turn, the new leader felt that the insiders' lack of receptivity was driving him to create his support group externally. The critical developmental challenge that he worked through was to begin to build an internal team.

3. Patterns of Consultation and Resistance to Change. It is very common for the new leader to focus on the change agendas, diagnosing what is currently wrong and can be improved, while the existing staff are more concerned about unintended consequences, things that are going well at present and may be negatively affected by shifts in resources or changes in policy (Gilmore and McCann, 1983). The result is often distortion, in which the new leader hears any discussion of potential negative consequences as "resistance" rather than help, ignoring or rejecting possible constraints. As subordinates sense the new leader not taking into account these realities, they often become more vocal about these issues.

Within this climate, the pattern diagrammed in Figure 6 unfolds. The new leader puts out an initiative and asks for feedback. Existing staff members, sometimes because they care about the idea, give what they believe is constructive input about potential

**Figure 6. Potential Cycle of Misunderstanding Between
New Leader and Staff.**

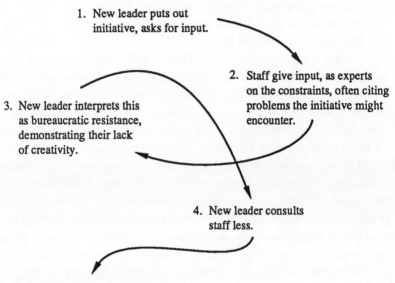

1. New leader puts out
   initiative, asks for input.

2. Staff give input, as experts
   on the constraints, often citing
   problems the initiative might
   encounter.

3. New leader interprets this
   as bureaucratic resistance,
   demonstrating their lack
   of creativity.

4. New leader consults
   staff less.

5. They identify less with initiatives,
   become bystanders, waiting for
   the system to give feedback
   via the failure of the initiative.

problems in implementation. The new leader, filled with hope and having unconsciously delegated to (or projected into) existing staff the work of worry about constraints, interprets their comments as bureaucratic resistance and blames them for not being risk-taking enough, not being creative enough, not being committed enough. The new leader finds consulting the existing staff disappointing and therefore stops listening to them and asks them less. As the existing staff become less involved, they identify less with the initiatives and begin to see the new leader as naive, out of touch with realities. They become bystanders and begin to hope the system will teach the leader a lesson through the failure of the initiative. The leader thinks his initial fears that they are resistant to change have been confirmed and becomes less and less likely to give them new opportunities to change that perception.

This dynamic repeats the pattern of inadvertently creating an outcome that neither party wants yet both cooperate to produce. To understand how such splits can easily develop and become misunderstood, imagine a leader and a key staff member who interact frequently on issues that raise questions about balancing change and the status quo. At the outset, the presumption is that the new leader will introduce new ideas and that the role of the staff member is to flag the potential difficulties. As a particular instance gets discussed, it is likely that after a certain amount of time the staffer will become anxious that the tradeoffs will not be adequately considered and will bring up the costs of change. Over many discussions on many issues, they will experience that the new leader is always pushing the change agendas and the staffer is always raising the costs of change. They might wrongly infer from this pattern that they are far apart on some imaginary continuum of conservation to change. Yet it is possible that they have only slightly different thresholds for raising the costs of change.

If the current staffer rates, say, a 6 on an imaginary conservation-change scale and the new leader a 7 (1 being conservation-oriented and 10 change-oriented), they will repeatedly experience that the current staff member always raises the risks of change, because his threshold is reached first. The way to break the cycle is for the current staffer to hold back and let the issue get talked about long enough to trigger the new leader's threshold of concern for the costs of change. Many bosses and subordinates distort their assessments of each other's concerns because they get caught in repetitive patterns that do not allow them to see just how close their views may be. Like a husband and a wife, they have unconsciously agreed to carry some issue on behalf of the other.

Breaking Out of Traps

When these patterns develop and misunderstandings arise, the working relationships are rarely healthy enough for people to get above the pattern and discuss how things are going. People fail to see the difference between transacting the work and reflecting on the patterns of transacting the work. But just as a plant needs to be shut down periodically for maintenance, so too one needs to find time to reflect on working alliances.

The patterns are like traps in that the more energy people put into them, the more stuck they get. Unless one can get a fresh perspective on the pattern or try a radically different strategy, more effort often simply increases the stuckness. There are, however, some generally useful strategies to avoid or escape from traps.

1. *Explicitly examine whether seemingly attractive goals or positive actions can contain unforeseen problems.* For example, the new leader's positive behavior in responding to a subordinate who comes with a problem, regardless of whether he or she should be spending time on this problem, sows the seeds for the pattern of overload.

2. *Be open to changing one's mind.* Once a person is labeled as resistant to change, it becomes difficult to shed the label. If a leader imagines that a subordinate loyal to a prior leader cannot be trusted and therefore gives that person no meaningful assignments, the subordinate cannot reverse the initial hunch. If the leader takes a risk in trusting the subordinate and the subordinate is *untrustworthy*, then at least he or she was given a chance.

3. *Examine counterintuitive possibilities.* In many traps, more of the same behavior only increases the stuckness, as a fish does struggling on a hook. In many of the patterns that arise, counterintuitive behavior can unlock the trap. For example, if one is nervous about the level of delegation, one can respond by restressing the authorization of the delegation. When one thinks existing staff may be resisting, one can encourage them to think about all the ways that one's favorite new idea will fail. To serve the outside constituencies better, pay attention to the internal staff.

4. *Use networking to get fresh perspectives.* A new leader and existing staff often get into intense relationships that cut them off from the rest of the organization and from outside contact as they work together during the early months. Getting the different parties to talk to outsiders and to bring those new perspectives back to the stalemated situation can be effective. For example, prior to retreats, I have often had people interview outsiders for their views on how the new team is developing and on the critical issues. This information can help the group break out of dysfunctional patterns.

5. *Invest in theorizing.* Too often American pragmatism makes theory building a subversive activity. However, when one understands the dynamics of a situation, it is often relatively easy to escape the situation. Several strategies can be used to help build theories:

- Put the episode in a larger context, looking at more actors. Are people acting as surrogates for one another? Are existing staff carrying the leader's unacknowledged conservatism and vice versa? The concept of triangles discussed in Chapter Eight and the patterns described in this chapter are examples of theories that can help people find ways to break out of the dynamic.
- Look at the historical sequences going back before the obvious beginning and look into the future, beyond the obvious end points.
- Examine carefully who is benefiting from the status quo.
- Try simply commenting on the dilemma; it can unlock new forms of collaboration. For example, acknowledging that one feels burdened by always being the change advocate and letting staff take the conservative role may start a useful dialogue.

Behind many of the failed relationships between talented people in a transition is some misunderstanding like those described. The conclusion is usually the resignation or firing of the subordinate or, more rarely, the departure of the new leader. In either case, valuable human capital is lost.

The next chapter takes up assembling the new team. Clearly the processes of appraising current staff and recruiting new staff begin from the moment of being appointed, but discussion of these issues was delayed because the dynamics explored in Chapter Eight and Nine may be helpful in understanding some of the difficulties of assembling one's own team.

_Chapter 10

Building the New
Management Team

A central challenge of an entering executive is to assemble the right talent in the right positions to lead the organization. Some members of the team will come from within the organization; others will be brought in from the outside. There is pressure to make early decisions; in reflecting on his personnel decisions as he assumed the presidency, John F. Kennedy commented, "I must make the appointments now. A year hence I will know who I really want to appoint" (Brauer, 1986, p. 263).

Important as the other team members are, effective team building begins with the self. The newly appointed leader should start by conducting a ruthless self-appraisal, measuring personal strengths against the challenges of the assignment. Whatever the particular strengths for which he or she was chosen, inevitably there will be aspects of the overall challenge for which the leader is not perfectly suited. A rigorous comparison of actual strengths with the strategic challenges of the position will identify those areas that are critical to success but that the leader, whether because of skill, time, politics, or some other reason, will not be able to handle personally.

Taking an honest look at oneself is a difficult task, and often a new executive needs help from an outsider. An executive recruiter who has been involved in the selection can be a source of useful feedback, as will candid discussions with the appointing authority on the tasks that will require the involvement of others. Past colleagues or knowledgeable external friends can also serve as a sounding board; people outside the organization can be more

146

candid about a new leader's weaknesses than existing staff. Califano got advice from two old friends on the characteristics needed to complement him. "Toughness, you need someone as tough as you are in pressure situations. Otherwise, you'll run over him even when he's right and you're wrong. You can be awfully difficult and demanding to work for. You need someone who knows when to ignore an order you issue out of anger or frustration, someone who is secure enough to tell you to go to hell when he has to" (1981, p. 27).

Without an accurate self-appraisal, a leader can fail. A talented former secretary of a large health and welfare agency was recruited to become the CEO of a major teaching hospital. One of the strengths that he brought was a working knowledge of the external environment and the shifts in the financing patterns of health care. There was a collateral challenge, however: to get control over the internal operations of the hospital, especially the complexities between the academic and business aspects. He did not have the time or detailed knowledge to take the lead on this agenda and therefore should have flagged these as strategic tasks for someone else. His failure to get control over the internal organization resulted in his departure after only two years, a major cost for his career and an even greater trauma for the organization.

Assessing the Roles

Once the new leader has a sense of the critical challenges that will fall on other roles, the next task is to look at how those challenges fit into the existing organizational structure. What other roles will be most critical to success in meeting the strategic challenges? Needed here is a preliminary appraisal of the current organizational structure and how the strategic agenda fits into the existing roles. For example, the new head of a banking consumer group might see the major challenge as rebuilding relationships with the customers. This task might fall into two existing roles— a vice-president for branch banking and a director of training to develop new training strategies. Sometimes the most important strategic challenges will not fit neatly into existing roles and will require some restructuring. In these instances, the new leader must decide either to create a new role or to organize a temporary task group to explore the issue. Ultimately the task group may recommend that a new role be created or that the structure be reorganized to match the strategy.

At this stage, the leader needs to focus on a select few critical roles. A triage process can be useful here, dividing the roles into three categories: (1) downside risks, roles that if mismanaged can lead to substantial harm to the organization; (2) upside gains, roles that offer a favorable ratio of effort to payoff, either because they have great potential for real progress (they add to working capital) or because they are clearly linked to the realization of the overall strategy; and (3) the middle, roles (perhaps relatively self-managing units) that are operating smoothly and relatively stable.

Note that the initial priorities are set in terms of the roles (linked to strategic tasks), not in terms of the current occupants. The leader's limited time for appraising current employees is therefore focused on the jobs that are most critical. For example, when Mayor Green took over the city of Philadelphia, the major issue facing him was a fiscal crisis. He rapidly assembled his fiscal team and a few other key roles, leaving the heads of the major city departments in a holdover status. The department heads were thus in a caretaking rather than an innovating posture while Green focused on the fiscal reforms. As that crisis passed, he began to deal with the department heads, keeping some, changing others, and making decisions that now were based on more direct experience with them and their departments.

Isaacson (1986, p. 14) advises new governors that they need not have a complete cabinet by the time of the inaugural: "No business CEO, not even Lee Iacocca, would fire every corporate, group, and divisional vice president and recruit a completely new team of dozens of executives for every product line, profitable or not, from outside of the company 50 days before he even had the job." He counsels a similar process of identifying the key jobs that will make a major difference, leaving until later situations that are stable and seem likely to remain so.

Once the roles are ranked in priority order, the leader checks the fit of the current staff's skills with both the strategic and the operational aspects of high-priority roles. In a sense, this process combines the assessment work done at the beginning of an executive search and the later matching of finalists against the job's demands. Many of the techniques discussed in Chapters Three, Four, and Six can be useful. These are difficult judgments to make when the leader is new to an organization and still learning it. Paradoxically, one of the teachers is often the executive that the new leader is attempting to appraise. One should not rely on just one person's view of the job but interview key others who relate to the role—outside customers, subordinates, peers—to gain a richer sense of the tasks and challenges. Assessing the demands in roles that do not currently exist can be even more complex.

An added difficulty is distinguishing style differences from more meaningful differences in the conception of the work or the skills necessary to do it. Given the uncertainties that abound during the initial months, new leaders are often drawn to people with similar backgrounds, who allow them to feel comfortable while focusing on the work issues. For example, in an organization with a headquarters/field split, the new leader may find the people in headquarters more congenial and begin to spend more time with them. However, the early emergence of such homogeneous teams can be a major loss for the organization. During the early uncertain months, the organization most needs a variety of different perspectives so that the options are thoroughly considered and the team does not wind up in a cul de sac.

Although the initial focus should be on the high upside and downside roles, the middle category cannot be ignored. Often the best approach here is to speak candidly with the current occupants, explaining that the immediate priorities are elsewhere, that you will get to their situations in the future, and that until that time you would greatly appreciate their remaining in the organization, letting you know if any personal issues should come up requiring them to make decisions about staying or leaving, so that you can give them the best information on which to base a decision. This approach addresses the demoralizing effects of being kept in the dark yet does not fall into the trap of the ritual commitment to everyone, which is rarely believed. Many good people leave because they wrongly interpret hearing nothing from the new leader as criticism. The same strategy of asking executives to stay for a

limited period may also work in both the opportunity and downside
risk roles, if the initial appraisal of their skills suggests they are
adequate.

The process of working through dependence and building
confidence in the capabilities of existing staff is complicated,
fraught with risks both to the new leader and to existing staff. Many
hardworking, loyal staff become casualties during a transition,
often through no fault of their own. Many leaders tell stories about
how close they came to firing some member of holdover staff who
later became an integral part of the team, commenting on what a
major mistake it would have been. There is an asymmetry in
learning to make judgments about who to keep and who to let go.
If you remove someone you should not have, you may never learn
of the contributions that the person might have made. If on the
other hand you make the mistake of keeping someone you should
not have, you learn directly by the person's failure. Because of this
asymmetry, advice will be biased in favor of bringing in a new team,
because the errors of removing someone when you should not have
do not often lead to memorable stories.

Learning the Strengths and Weaknesses of Existing Staff

A new leader has many sources of information about existing
staff: resumes; personnel files, including appraisals, special
commendations, and disciplinary actions, as well as the quality and
thoughtfulness of their appraisals and supervision of their
subordinates; the grapevine from former superiors, colleagues
outside the system, peers, subordinates, and clients; direct experience of people in meetings and one-on-one work sessions, both in
their role and on temporary assignments; assessment interviews;
and present and past staff work. One new executive who was riding
out to the field with his division director as a way of getting to know
him learned much not only from the conversation but also from the
director's difficulty in finding two facilities for which he had been
responsible for four years.

A basic problem in assessing staff is that they will read the
tea leaves to learn the new leader's preferences and styles. They will
wish to appear as loyal as possible, so their current behavior may

not be a valid indicator of their long-term competence in the organization. Information will spread quickly about how the new leader is handling initial transition meetings, what questions are asked, and what signals the leader is sending, and people will shape their presentations of themselves to conform.

Paradoxically, the more the new leader is clear about the information wanted at initial briefings, the less the sessions reveal about the real characteristics of the staff. One newly appointed secretary of a major state agency deliberately did not format the information he wished to cover during his transition briefings. Rather, he told the division heads that he would give each one an hour and a half and that they should structure the time to serve best the interests of their divisions. Some came in with comprehensive books, filled with information, others with a brief list of critical issues, upcoming decisions, and the necessary background for the secretary to make an informed choice about how to get involved. He felt that he learned more about his staff from seeing the variety of ways that they managed the uncertainty of the request than he would have by giving them specifications for the briefing. However, a leader must consider that such actions send messages. Not setting a format may have been considered as evading his responsibilities, or even seen by some subordinates as sadism.

Assessments in Context. Fair assessments of competence must be made in the context of a role and structure. Some roles unconsciously authorize people to be denying, withholding, naysaying; budget and personnel offices often play these roles. A person in one of these roles may be quite different in a different role. If there are problems, they may result from factors and relationships that will inevitably change. At the extreme case, in which a new leader wants to create a different culture, people who have traditionally done poorly on prior appraisals may be promoted. Gabriel and Savage (1978, pp. 177-178) suggest that if one were serious about reforming the military, one would deliberately have to look for people with blemished records, because those who had been promoted under the current policies would not likely be serious about reforms.

Cases of poor performers becoming stars in the new administration are extremely rare; good people are hurt far more often than people with poor reputations are rehabilitated. But in one organization, the new leader sensed real talent in a professional within the organization who was angry about the way he had been treated and had filed suit alleging discrimination in salary. His anger intrigued the new leader, because it represented potential energy in a context of considerable apathy. The new leader initially made a midyear adjustment in his salary and looked for a project to give him. He went to the man's office and asked him to undertake a revision of a field manual. He agreed—if the new leader would collaborate with him on it. Not only did the new leader reclaim the talents of this person for the organization, but the effects on others were great because of the man's role as a symbol of dissatisfaction. Here the leader was intrigued by the challenge. Far too often, leaders would write off someone like this, with consequences for the person and messages for the rest of the staff as well.

In these early assessments, a new leader is trying to judge both a person's capacity to do the work that the role requires and the chemistry of the person's fit with the emerging executive team. One central mark of ability is the person's grasp of the complexity and time horizon of the job. Some people are able to think over the requisite time span for an executive role, others are less able. The new leader also considers whether the person appears to be on top of the job, knowledgeable about the key stakeholders, and able to think about the future consequences of current decisions. These are clues to cognitive capacity (Jaques, 1985). Equally critical is the executive's understanding of the link of the role to the overall strategy.

Assessment Errors. During leadership transitions, the assessments that both leaders and followers make of each other are often distorted by the psychological process called *fundamental attribution error.* In fundamental attribution error, actors attribute their own ineffective behavior to situational factors while observers attribute the same behavior to personality (Jones and Nisbett, 1971 and 1972, p. 80). A new leader will attribute negative outcomes of his or her actions to situational influences, while subordinates will explain them as resulting from the leader's personality. Conversely, subordinates will attribute their negative results to situational constraints, while the new leader explains them in terms of the subordinates' personalities.

Fundamental attribution error also occurs in ongoing organizations, of course. Whenever we appraise someone with whom we are in a work relationship, the relationship is inevitably implicated. For example, if I delegate a task to someone who fails to perform it effectively, I might focus on his or her skills and competencies, but the subordinate might see part of the problem in the clarity of my original delegation. At a broader level, the performance standards for a division are likely to be in question as part of the overall transition, so that the criteria for appraisal are as much an issue in transitions as the behavior of the executive in question, and both have histories that precede the arrival of the new leader.

It feels fundamentally unfair to blame a subordinate for the failings of the prior leader to set the right tasks. Clearly a fair appraisal should begin with some joint planning that sets goals and translates those into performance measures. But, despite the sense of unfairness, few new leaders come to situations in which they can set new standards and then wait before having to make important personnel decisions.

At an even deeper level, sometimes there are unconscious distortions in appraisals. One new leader appointed from within found himself reacting very negatively to a staff member who he felt spent excessive time reading the newspaper each day (arguably justified because of their community-oriented work). He addressed this issue with the subordinate in ways that hurt their ability to work together effectively. Later he came to realize that he was reacting to the behavior because the former leader of the organization, with whom he had had a difficult relationship, had spent inordinate amounts of time reading the newspaper. Because he had never been able to be effectively angry at his predecessor, he now reacted unconsciously to the same behavior in a staff member (whom he perhaps feared was more loyal to his predecessor).

Like so many of the other processes involved in transitions, staff assessments can be self-fulfilling prophecies. The following cycle is common. A staff member is too closely identified with the predecessor for the new leader to trust her initially. She is therefore given fewer important assignments and less access to the intelligence necessary to perform competently. She comes to compare poorly with others and is used even less, and so on, until she is no longer a valuable asset. The difficulty is that the leader labels her lack of value as residing in her—she was unable to cope with the uncertainty of the transition—while the staff member blames the new leader for not giving her a chance.

Retreats as Vehicles of Staff Assessment

Learning the strengths and weaknesses of staff can be dramatically accelerated by the use of retreats in which the new leader spends several days with them, focusing on strategic and team-building issues. If the retreat is facilitated by an outsider, it can afford the leader the opportunity to observe people in action without the inevitable distortions that arise in early direct communications between the leader and staff. Furthermore, retreats often create an informal setting and atmosphere in which people's interactions are less driven by formal roles and relationships. Small group assignments rearrange the people and the issues so that staff get a chance to comment on issues beyond their own roles. I recall one leader being surprised at a fiscal staff member's interest in and knowledge of the substantive work of the agency. In their past transactions, the fiscal issues had always dominated, so that this aspect of the subordinate had never been evident.

Some of the original work in appraisal of leadership potential was undertaken by the British during World War II. Groups of potential officers were assembled and observed as they coped with the ambiguities of the group situation. As Bion wrote about this process: "[The] selecting officers . . . could observe a man's capacity for maintaining personal relationships in a situation of strain that tempted him to disregard the interest of his fellows for his own, . . . the real life situation. . . . [In combat] that is the way in which a man's capacity for personal relationships stands up under the strain of his own and other men's fear of failure and desire for personal success" (Trist, 1985, pp. 8-9).

Similarly, a well-managed retreat places staff in the stressful situation of having to collaborate on tasks linked to the mission of the organization while also competing to stand out in front of the new leader. How each person copes with these challenges is rich data for a new leader in thinking about the human capital available within the organization. If four people are sent off to do a piece of thinking on critical external trends, for example, one not only gets the substantive results but also observes who presents, with what skills, and how others either support or undercut the spokesperson. If well designed and focused on the critical issues facing an organization, retreats can play this double role.

In a retreat that I conducted for a state agency, the new leader participated and was particularly observant of the behavior of the staff members present. In the group were the top twenty-five managers in the system, including about a dozen from field units. In the space of several days and evenings of work, the leader had more time with the people from the field units than he would normally have gotten in six months of routine contact.

We began the retreat by requesting all the participants to line up, from the longest tenure in the agency to the newest arrival (the new leader). People were asked to remember back to their first days in the agency, and describe what the place was like, relating some vivid memories of their arrival. The effect of this exercise was to link the new leader's joining with everyone else's arrival and to allow people to tell their stories. In aggregate it also had the effect of taking the organization's history, as people discussed different critical changes and when they occurred in the organization. Often in this exercise the line of staff members reveals sudden shifts in gender, race, or age that resulted from initiatives of earlier leaders. People tell amusing, poignant stories that give a sense of the person as well as the agency's history.

A second activity during the retreat involved identifying trends and stakeholders. The new leader again had a chance to see the quality of different members' substantive contributions. After critical issues were listed, each participant chose an issue to work on, further signaling interest patterns. The leader circulated to each of the small work groups.

In such small groups, who becomes the leader is revealing, and the group leader's skills in making presentations and responding to questions add to the picture of the person's talents. In one retreat with a newly appointed leader, he and I were making up the groups for a particular activity. He noted that one group seemed to be composed mostly of people who were rumored to be weak. We discussed the pros and cons of redistributing them and ended up leaving them as a group, as an experiment to see what kind of work they would do. It turned out that they did an excellent job, with a skilled presentation of their solid thinking. This experience gave those staff members a fresh start with the new leader and prevented them from being stuck with their rumored image.

At the same retreat, in one of the other groups, a subordinate of one of the division directors did an excellent job on a complicated topic. This person would most likely not have had much direct exposure to the new leader on the job because of the intervening manager. The new leader spotted his potential and gave him a temporary follow-up assignment as a further test of his competence, supervising him directly, and the subordinate performed well on this task. At the same time the new leader had been carefully engineering the removal of a long-tenured executive in another division, the largest and most politically influential in the agency. He was able to transfer the ineffectual division director laterally and move in the person who had just finished the temporary assignment, all with sufficient speed and surprise to prevent potential political resistance.

Informal activities during retreats are also valuable in getting to know people beyond their roles in the organization. Eating, drinking, playing poker, charades, or volleyball—all are occasions for building up richer pictures of staff and for staff to build a more complete image of the leader.

Replacing Key Staff

Firing or removing an executive takes only minutes, but replacing that person thoughtfully can take considerable time and effort, involving all the stages discussed in Chapters Three through Six. Before moving too hastily to move someone out, a leader should think through the following equation:

The difference between the potential new appointment and the old (in competence, loyalty, connec-

tions, symbolism, energy, creativity, and so on) should
be greater than the cost of the search (in terms of your
time and the time of others) plus the inevitable
disruption that results from any transition (lost
momentum, productivity of the staff in the affected
unit).

Unless a replacement has already been identified, this initial
comparison is based on the kind of person that the leader thinks can
be attracted to the organization. It is easy to overestimate the skills
of someone who exists only in the mind and to underestimate the
time a full search will take.

If the decision is to move ahead, three alternatives are
possible:

1. A current job-holder who is a clear liability can be removed
   immediately and someone put in an acting role, pending a
   search, as discussed in Chapter Seven. By taking the role
   oneself, one can immerse oneself in the issues, but at a cost to
   other responsibilities.
2. A current job-holder who is an adequate caretaker can be asked
   to continue to run the division during a search, with a clear
   signal that he or she will not get the job but will be helped
   personally with the transition after the new person is hired.
3. If the current job-holder has some strengths but one thinks that
   a stronger candidate can be found, one can undertake a
   confidential search or announce an open one, with the
   understanding that the individual will be one of the candidates.

The leader should cycle through the stages of an effective
search as discussed in Part Two, thinking carefully about the
strategic challenges in the role and whether it is defined correctly,
translating those insights into desired characteristics for a new
executive, and scanning the potential territories to ascertain
whether or not there are likely to be many good candidates. The
most critical initial problem will be to find someone to take on the
search assignment. In Chapter Five, desired characteristics of an
internal recruiter are listed. In the early stages of new leadership, it

is often difficult to find someone from inside who combines the necessary skills with the trusted personal relationship essential to represent the leader in confidential discussions. Special assistants are the most likely source, but they can easily get caught up in many other assignments. If there are several important roles to be recruited for early on, the new leader is well advised to hire external recruiting help or to dedicate one trusted staff member to the job until it is successfully concluded. Not having key members of the team in place will hold up many other critical activities.

Timing. When a personnel change is necessary, the leader should think carefully about the timing. It may make sense to negotiate with the current occupant for a change in role or even a planned date of termination, but to ask that person to stay through the search process so that the unit has leadership until a replacement is found. One of the advantages of executive search firms is that they can sometimes undertake portions of a search in confidence, so that the unit can continue to operate until the leader is ready with a change in management. A secret search has many drawbacks, however, limiting conversations that are critical to effective recruiting.

Many new leaders, fearing that someone who has been relieved will "act out," want the person to leave as soon as possible. Executives who have been asked to leave, however, have often said they would have preferred a more thoughtful transition that acknowledged their past value to the organization, gave them time to tie up loose ends, and allowed a careful handoff to the incoming person. I suspect that leaders are often uncomfortable with the aggression that terminating employees involves. They displace some of their aggression into the person being fired, who they imagine will inevitably become hostile to the leader and the organization. To be sure, this sometimes happens, but executives who have been fired usually understand the right of a new leader to select his or her own team. Most often, they object to the way it was done rather than to the action itself.

The Wrong Way. To avoid working with the pain of directly terminating employees, two strategies are often used. Either leaders fire people quickly and impersonally or leave them with make-work assignments, hoping that the employees leave because they find the situation increasingly intolerable. In both cases, the leader avoids the harm one must do to others in the service of a mission.

One subordinate had been driven out of an organization to which she was deeply loyal, by a year-long process of signaling from the new leader. She wrote me her advice on how a new leader should handle staff replacements: "If you as the leader plan to bring in your own management team, be honest about it and assist existing staff in working out termination/severance packages. . . . Never confuse your political strategy with the person's competence. Permit the staff to leave in a gracious manner which preserves their self-respect (a quality urgently needed as they face the job market) and recognizes their past accomplishments."

The Right Way. Few actions of a new leader are more powerful than making the "right" choices about whom to keep and whom to let go. When a leader is able to differentiate solid performers from weaker staff, the organization feels the process is fair, that the cuts have been made "with a knowledge of the anatomy," as one key informant put it after a significant change in both leadership and ownership of a company. The cuts had "face validity."

A newspaper account of the turnaround in a corrupt and troubled parking violation bureau illustrates this point: "Mr. Bruno brought an ability to combine hands-on management with the wisdom to leave untouched the people and programs that worked. 'It would have been very easy,' said a bureau official who worked for the bureau's previous administration, 'for him to come in and assume that everybody in the place in any position of responsibility was either corrupt or incompetent and engage in wholesale terminations. He didn't do that. He didn't take the easy way out.' In a recent interview in his office, Mr. Bruno said, 'As soon as they felt, "he's not going to fire or indict us all," then we started building'" (Boorstin, 1987, p. B1).

The manner in which people are let go is also significant. Despite the appearance of winners and losers, those who stay often identify with those who leave. The sense that staff who were let go were handled with respect and dignity has a calming effect on an organization in transition, because remaining staff members realize that if they too end up as casualties, they will be handled fairly. It is shocking how frequently new leaders or their aides handle these matters sadistically, with little attention to the thoughts and feelings of others. People get the first news of their firing from the newspapers or from gossip. They are given little time to wrap up their affairs. Authorities do not admit the responsibility for the decision, leaving it ambiguous whether the firing was called for by the new leader, by someone higher up, by the former leader, or by a key person outside of the organization. People are often not given appropriate transition assistance, although the growing outplacement industry is helping to manage these difficult transitions when organizations use them appropriately.

People leaving an organization may have a considerable amount of important knowledge that can easily become lost to the organization in their exit. In the aftermath of the *Challenger* shuttle disaster, the Rogers Commission uncovered a critical loss of follow-through because of the poorly managed turnover of two executives. Nearly two years before the disaster, two of the highest officials at NASA ordered a full review of trouble with safety seals on the space shuttle's solid-fuel rocket boosters, but they left the agency before following up on the problem. They had scheduled a meeting for a high-level review, but one of them left before the date of the meeting and the other was in the process of transition. As an observer put it, "In the last months at the agency, he insulated himself from most agency affairs and concentrated on the new job he would be taking in Texas" (Sanger, 1986, p. 1).

A leader can sometimes facilitate a structured transition from one role to another. The military has developed such a process for changes in command. The unit works with the former commander in the morning, listing critical pending issues and dealing with the ongoing agenda, and in the afternoon, they go through a structured mutual introduction of people and issues with the new commanding officer (Smith, n.d.).

Few processes are more critical to a successful transition than assembling and building the team. Not only are the choices that the leader makes critical in the competencies that are available to the organization, but they also send signals about how closely the leader is in touch with what is really happening in the organization. Personnel is an elastic resource. A motivated person in the right role and an unmotivated person in the wrong role are several orders of magnitude apart in terms of the value that they can add to an organization. Careful handling of the anxieties surrounding a transition can retain an executive who would otherwise have left and who represents an irreplaceable wealth of history and contacts to the top team. Thoughtful outplacing of an executive who will be disruptive to the team not only is valued by the person leaving but adds to the commitment of those remaining.

If these processes are well handled, a new executive will find himself or herself with a team that is made up of both old and new staff and is well connected to the major units in the organization. Such a team has the capacity to innovate and to translate those innovations into the ongoing changes in policy and operations necessary to realize the dreams, a process we will examine in Part Four.

What New Leaders Must Do to Succeed over Time

If the right leader has been selected and matched to the challenges the organization faces, and if the leader has successfully connected with the existing organization, then follow the ongoing tasks of leading: setting a direction, building the direction into the structure and the people, regulating conflicts, and managing the changes necessary to implement the new direction. Each of these processes has a significantly different character when undertaken by a newly arrived leader. Because leadership changes are opportunities, there will always be an excess of ideas beyond the capacities of the organization to execute. Different people will propose alternative strategies and structures, each offering thoughtful arguments as to their efficacy. Leaders will face making choices often before they feel fully knowledgeable about the business and its people and culture.

Even as leaders commit to directions, structures, and people, they must prepare their organizations for further changes in order to learn from experience and adapt accordingly. One of the changes the leader must prepare the organization for is the next leadership transition. A leader both inherits an office from a predecessor and leaves it for a successor. Only as we more thoughtfully acknowledge both continuity and change will we be able to use leadership transitions as major opportunities for organizational development.

~ Chapter 11

Incorporating a New Vision into the Organization

No matter how thoroughly the appointing authority has thought through the organization's strategic challenges and how wholeheartedly the new leader has agreed to them, the leader always has considerable latitude in deciding what substantive initiatives to raise first and how to do so. Moreover, the new leader often has *not* been perfectly matched to the strategic situation. The appointing authorities may have been too busy with issues at their level to know in detail the substantive issues facing the organization. The appointed leader in turn may have the relevant experience, degrees, and personal characteristics for the job, but may not have examined closely how his or her strengths match the challenges the organization faces (Gerstein and Reisman, 1983).

Even when the appointment affirms the recent directions that an organization has taken, the arrival of the newly appointed leader is almost inevitably an opportunity for rethinking mission and agenda. Long-dormant ideas and coalitions are stirred up, and people who had not been listened to by the prior leader suddenly hope for a new hearing. The question of who will be in the dominant coalition is reopened. Add to this the fact that a new leader brings ideas and values beyond those that the appointing authority affirmed in making the selection. How a particular person, at a specific moment in the history of the organization, will use the authority offered by the role is never fully predictable.

165

Reaching a Shared Vision Through Guiding Themes

New leaders beginning to set new directions must steer between being co-opted by the existing internal interests and being so uncoupled from them that their vision cannot be realized by the organization. Many leaders tend to choose initiatives that are new or on the margins of the organization's mission, sensing that these issues are more manageable and not likely to be challenged by existing groups inside the organization. The result can be a distinctly nonstrategic focus. Lynn and Seidel, discussing the web of influences on top public-sector executives and their complex interactions with career employees, argue that the constraints drive "many—perhaps most—public executives . . . to seek paths of least resistance. . . . They devote their energies to hobbies such as new initiatives and favorite programs, to traveling and speech making, to political gamesmanship, and to passive reliance on advice that comes their way from sources they trust or fear" (1977, pp. 147-148).

A leader in these settings needs to find a way to connect with the core staff of the organization and at the same time to articulate the vision that motivated him or her to take the job in the first place. This tension can be bridged if the leader is able to formulate a vision that (1) positively connotes some aspect of current operations, so that existing staff feel included and realize that the new leader is acknowledging the positive work they have done; (2) touches the core of the agency, not just a peripheral, fashionable issue; and (3) links managerial issues with substantive concerns.

Planning in an Uncertain Climate

Part of the power of a mobilizing vision is its ability to offer guidance, even in the face of considerable uncertainty. Most organizations today must function in ever more complex and rapidly changing settings. The evolution of modifying words with "planning"—from "master" and "comprehensive" to "strategic," "contingency," and "crisis"—shows a clear progression from a world view of certainty and control to a condition of ambiguity and contingency. Most organizations face uncertainty as a result of current business conditions; airlines, for example, must deal with deregulation, and hospitals must cope with shifts in the mode of reimbursement. If the organization is also dealing with the arrival of a new leader, overall uncertainty is dramatically increased.

Leaders therefore need modes of planning that acknowledge ambiguity and uncertainty yet do not try to reduce it prematurely through fiats that may be unresponsive to the culture of the organization. Unless an organization is in a complete state of crisis, the primary task of the new leader with respect to the substantive initiatives is to listen and learn. The more the leader can work in harness with others in the group, the more effective the new leader's interventions will be. Similarly, the new leader must learn how to frame his or her personal agendas in ways that can join with existing staff initiatives or, if this is not possible, to anticipate the consequences of advancing ideas with weak support from others.

One effective strategy is to set broad directions by articulating guiding themes, at the same time allowing for elaboration and participation by others. This type of planning may resemble sailing; one has a clear sense of direction, but currents and prevailing winds make it impossible to predict an unchanging course to the desired destination. One new leader set as a long-term goal the creation of consistent policy across all the institutions in a statewide system, but he could not attack that goal directly because of considerable tension in headquarters-field relationships left over from earlier attempts at centralization. He first needed to introduce some smaller initiatives to create the conditions within which a fresh discussion of policy consistency could take place.

As uncertainty grows, one's ultimate destination may not even be clear. Then the new leader may need to think of several intermediate destinations, perhaps all linked to some overarching direction or set of values, or all characterized by stylistic concerns. For example, a research group in a highly uncertain setting might keep itself open to many different substantive areas with a superordinate goal of keeping together a team whose members enjoy working with one another. Chapter Seven outlined a process for discovering robust issues that will be viable under several different possible futures. Katsenelinboigen (1984) has elaborated on the strategy of investing in the organization's potential while keeping open options. Corporations that husband cash during

turbulent times awaiting a change in business conditions practice
such a strategy. Groups that develop their computer skills increase
their potential without necessarily committing to a single line of
development.

Issues and Themes

Etzioni differentiates between issues and themes: "Issues
concern specific policy differences. . . . Themes are embracing
perspectives: they help people articulate their feelings and think
about such matters as the future. . . . Issues interest mainly that
segment of the public that follows public affairs closely. . . . The
right themes mobilize . . . [broader coalitions]" (1984, p. A31).

The role of guiding themes is receiving increased attention
from theorists. Leaders, it is said, articulate the guiding vision
(Burns, 1978; Bennis and Nanus, 1985); or, in Schon's terms (1971),
leaders create "ideas in good currency"—ideas that are powerful for
action. Peters (1978) discusses the emergence, dominance, and
waning of what he terms "dominating values." These theorists
agree that guiding themes have an affective as well as an intellectual
component, mobilizing commitment (Delucca, 1984). They are not
imposed by or the sole property of the leader but emerge in actions
that relate to genuine concerns of the organization and therefore can
be changed only through interaction with the group that has
embraced them. Themes give direction but also allow experimentation. They permit local creativity and adaptation without the
overcontrol that often results from blueprint methods of project
management. They often address the critical relationship of the
customer or client and the organization, and they offer guidance for
real dilemmas experienced in everyday operations (Delucca, 1984).

A theme has a life cycle that begins with a permissive period
in which it can mean different things to different people; it grows
in strength and focus, reaching a dominant stage during which it
guides hard choices; and finally it loses its dominance during a
declining or institutionalizing period. This cycle can be seen in the
following case study, the revitalization of the juvenile justice agency
whose new leader had actively recruited the head of detention who
we met in Chapter Nine, inspiring her staff with the idea that they

would "fly so high no rat will be able to survive" (Gilmore and Schall, 1986).

Case Study

The dispirited public bureaucracy to which she had been appointed had been attacked in the press for the terrible conditions at its major detention facility, for poor security, and for not doing anything constructive for children. The high-turnover, short-term setting had led to the dominance of an implicit mission of "three hots and a cot," with nothing more. Staff members, originally attracted by the hope of helping children, had become resigned to the dominance of custody over care.

Early in her tenure, the new commissioner began working with the staff to integrate the care and custody missions and to articulate a positive view of detention as an opportunity to detect children with major problems and reconnect them with socializing agents. The idea of "detention as an opportunity to make contact with these children" began to allow staff to think of what those opportunities might be. Case management became the major programmatic vehicle for realizing this vision linking control and service. But in the early months, case management was left quite unspecified as staff groups from the three major divisions began to wrestle with what it would mean for each of them and in what ways they were already using some form of case management. Knowing that resistance would be likely if a case management blueprint were developed in isolation and that producing such a plan would mean a delay, the commissioner sanctioned each of the units to proceed with its own version of case management. At the same time, each unit would be loosely coordinated with the others through a newly created "strategy group," which met monthly to look at the major initiatives. During this phase the theme was honed by the concrete actions of the different units.

Note the relationship between the local actions and the theme. The local initiatives contributed to and shaped the theme and were at the same time guided and shaped by it. For example, one unit developed the service plan. Another concentrated on working out the organizational relationships among multiple functions in a case management system. Cross-unit work began as real needs arose, not as a result of abstract planning work. An ad hoc group studied the intake processes a child might go through and discovered that basic factual information such as name and address was requested by fourteen different people, clearly communicating to the child that the agency was uncoordinated.

As the local work forced cross-unit choices, the commissioner developed the overall guidelines further, imposing more constraints, but only after she had gotten the existing staff actively involved in considering what they wanted case management to mean. Now, several years into the commissioner's tenure, all children experience some elements of the case management system—for example, a full health diagnosis—and over one third have a worker assigned to follow through on a carefully developed service plan, both for the time the child is in detention and, through a newly developed unit, after the child leaves.

Guidelines for Success

Some lessons can be drawn from this work with a guiding theme:

1. Encourage Existing Staff to Sign On. Introducing an important change to an organization takes time, especially if the aim is to get the career staff to own the new processes and procedures. The strongest feature of the case management theme was that it built on what many staff had already been doing, extending it further into a system of care. Furthermore, the theme was left open to multiple interpretations, so that many people could identify with it without any win-lose struggle over who had the "true" interpretation of the concept. By letting the divisions proceed with implementation before the central office was capable of effective coordination, the commissioner unleashed considerable energy and creativity. As a result, the field created the demand for more coordination, a reversal of the usual dynamic, in which the center imposes it and the field resists.

2. Match Themes and Forums. Special forums can help introduce a more strategic perspective. In this case, at an initial retreat staff held philosophical discussions and looked at emerging patterns. Several one-day workshops followed up on the ideas from the retreat. Eventually, these "special events" were replaced by monthly strategy group meetings that encouraged sustained attention to the strategic agenda.

3. Link Vision and Reality. The need for a grand vision or a strategic theme must be balanced with a brutally realistic understanding of what is possible within the constraints of the situation. It is easy for a theme to become uncoupled from reality and to serve as an attractive topic for discussion or as an escape from the real work of the agency (Bion, 1961). Part of the power of the case management theme was that it captured both accountability and service.

4. Elaborate and Specify a Theme over Time. Because leaders have much to learn at the beginning of their tenure, the design for a change should be only as specific as it needs to be at each stage of the implementation process (Herbst, 1974). A new leader should make only those decisions needed to move forward, leaving open the rest for a time when the context for those choices becomes clear. This procedure also allows incoming staff to exert influence over the emerging system. In the juvenile justice case, the use of the overall theme as a mechanism of coordination enabled line staff to participate in design teams for particular procedures and thereby both contribute their expertise and develop ownership of the initiative.

Often, a new leader inadvertently overloads an organization with too many new initiatives, policies, or programs. The power of an authentic guiding theme is that it offers staff a way of linking these changes around a single, coherent idea. Getting the theme right is not magic. It depends on the ability of the leader, in conversation with the organization, both to challenge and to listen.

Strategic Planning Processes

Thus far we have looked at the way a new leader can begin to signal a direction. We now turn to structured planning processes that a newly appointed manager can use to establish a substantive agenda.

The timing of planning processes is critical. If they are begun too early, the new team may not yet have been assembled, the strengths and weaknesses of the staff may be undiscovered, and the points of leverage in the organization may not be fully understood. If they are begun too late, the openness from a leadership transition may be lost.

Menu Model. One model of strategic planning that fits well with uncertainty and with the differing perspectives of the new leader and old staff is a menu, or portfolio, model. The term *menu* suggests that the joint task for the new leader and the existing staff is to create a rich enough set of initiatives that people will be comfortable selecting from that set. This process is particularly valuable in letting all the different parties "invent options for mutual gain" (Fisher and Ury, 1981), decreasing polarization and destructive conflict. As part of this process, the group reviews the external environment, to understand better the links between possible shifts in the environment and options that might be responsive to those shifts. This preparation helps the organization to capitalize on events as they unfold.

The menu planning process consists of several steps: (1) defining the mission and stakeholders, (2) scanning the environment, (3) developing a rich set of options, and (4) selecting an initial set for implementation and determining the status of other options.

Planning Retreat. A quick cycle through this process can be most effectively accomplished at a retreat for top staff members. If people have done careful preparation work, a two-day session can give the new leader a real opportunity to set an initial agenda. A side benefit, as we saw in Chapter Ten, is the opportunity for assessing the staff.

Preparation for the retreat can consist of written responses to several questions. Exhibit 1 shows a questionnaire that probes substantive issues and maps the constituencies. The third question in section 1 is particularly powerful in helping to bridge the gap between the new and the old. It positively acknowledges the veterans' perspective, giving staff the sense that their knowledge is valued and that they have been given a proper opportunity to caution the new leader. A comparison of the lists of what people want the new leader to accomplish and what they want the new

Exhibit 1. Sample Questionnaire.

1.0   *Focusing on Key Tasks, Issues, Problems, or Opportunities.*

One of our most pressing problems is identifying and focusing our scarcest resource—time—on the right issues. We can make two types of mistakes: (1) errors of omission—things that should be addressed but are not; and (2) errors of commission—things that perhaps should not be addressed immediately, but are.

Furthermore, I realize you have invested considerable time on many existing issues. These must be weighed against new initiatives that we develop.

The following three questions address these issues. For each, imagine the time horizon to be the next twelve months.

1.1   Reflect on what you think are the major issues (problems, opportunities, tasks) in our organization today. What do you think are the top three to five that should continue to be our central preoccupations?

1.2   Suggest three to five issues that have not previously been top priorities, but should be. (These can be new issues or issues that have been around but not receiving adequate attention.)

1.3   What new initiatives or changes (substantive, organizational, personnel) that I as the new leader might think make sense for the organization would you as an insider advise against, either because they would require too much effort to accomplish or because they might be no-win, quagmire, or land-mine issues?

2.0   *Managing the Multiple Constituencies.*

Many different outside constituencies watch and pressure our organization to act and change in certain ways. Many of these pressures are contradictory, making it difficult to set goals and objectives. The following section of this questionnaire is designed to tap your views on some of the important external groups. Consider their current perceptions of our organization and their view of what our central thrusts ought to be.

2.1   Below please list five to seven constituencies, organized interest groups, or stakeholders who you believe care enough about our actions and policies to follow what we do and to become active (either in support or opposition).

1. _____
2. _____
3. _____
4. _____
5. _____
6. _____
7. _____

Exhibit 1. Sample Questionnaire, Cont'd.

2.2 To the left of the above list, rank the top five (from first to fifth) in terms of how important you think it is for us to manage that relationship in the coming year.

2.3 On the following two pages, enter each stakeholder's name and describe its *current* perception of the organization (using key words) and its view of what the organization's central thrusts *should be.*

---

leader to avoid often brings out contradictory pressures among existing staff, enabling them to see the triangle that they are placing the new leader in by expecting conflicting actions.

Defining the Mission and Mapping the Stakeholders

Setting directions and defining the mission are challenging tasks. Often there is pressure for unrealistic goals and for overly abstract mission statements. The responses to the presession questionnaire enable the discussions to focus on the key others who either give or withhold necessary inputs (money, staff, clients, information, respect, legitimacy, licenses, and so on). Table 7 shows the stakeholder groups surrounding a corporate research group.

This ecological analysis is not to suggest that the organization's mission is simply the vector that results from all the different directions for which others are pushing. Rather, the challenge is to articulate an authentic mission that can win the support of the necessary others. This process places considerable emphasis on exploring the context of the organization before focusing in on a mission definition. Mapping stakeholders allows the group to explore the consequences of alternate missions as well as the consequences of alternative means to achieving a given mission. By engaging the existing staff in discussions on key outside groups, a leader can also uncover useful staff relationships to these groups.

In highly uncertain environments, the nested logic of ends and means should become less dominant. March (March and Olsen, 1976) suggests the importance of play as a way of experimenting with goals. Planning under conditions of high ambiguity may require high tolerance for lateral thinking (de Bono, 1970), humor,

Table 7. Map of Stakeholders.

Group/Stakeholder	How They See You Now	What They Want
Scientists	Volatile, under attack, unstable	Long-term stability for basic research
Technologists in business units	Arrogant, uncooperative, smart	More support for their technical problems
Business units	Ivory tower, march to own drummer	Research linked to tangible business opportunities
Academics	Competent research colleagues	Opportunities for joint work on interesting problems; chance to publish
Corporate	Expensive, arrogant	More breakthroughs that are relevant to line of business

and suspension of the usual rules of the organization. Yet in conditions of uncertainty, organizations often become more rigid, just at the moment when their survival depends on being able to remain loose.

Careful linking of strategic themes, advance preparation, and a retreat can channel uncertainty and anxiety into productive paths. Chapter Nine examined how a new leader of a research group had articulated the theme of partnership with the staff who were paralyzed during a period of cutbacks. The strategic theme of partnership signaled that the line organization needed to be more effectively coupled to end users, yet the full meaning of this new theme was not yet clear. To help them work constructively with their uncertainty, the new leader organized those who were remaining into six teams to study specific past cases of collaboration with the line, some of which had been successful and some of which had not. Rather than specifying for them what "partnership" was to mean, in ways that most likely would be taken as criticism of their past aloofness, he joined with their research culture to have them study partnership. This gave them a constructive task during the rethinking of the substantive research priorities and put them into direct contact with end users in order to collect the data for their study. They experienced partnership even as they studied what makes it work. The results of the study were reported at a retreat called by the new leader. Some of the end users participated in the first day of the three-day session, confirming the importance of the partnership.

The new leader had demonstrated considerable skill at joining with the existing staff. He realized that his real asset was the human capital and that if he could not mobilize that group around a shared vision, he would not be successful. This leader was both aware of and comfortable with his dependency on the existing staff, despite his superior position in the hierarchy. Leaders who are less comfortable with their dependency often take unilateral and aggressive stances in setting new directions. They pay the price during implementation, when the resistance of the staff comes into play.

Scanning the Environment

In putting an outsider into an organization, appointing authorities often hope that the new leader will shake up the existing complacency. To expect the new leader alone to bring in a fresh perspective is, however, unrealistic. In such a situation an effective strategy is to use some type of scanning process to reconnect staff with the wider environment. People can be assigned different stakeholders to interview. For example, a leader who wants to undertake some new initiatives in labor relations might assign someone to do a series of interviews with labor leaders from other settings, to get their views of new trends, new ideas, and critical issues facing the industry. In this way, the staff person gets outside the normal context and sees the issues from an outsider's point of view. Then, at a retreat or staff planning session, this person can represent the new thinking, taking some of the burden from the leader.

Most organizations do not scan broadly enough, and risk becoming cut off from the wider environment. For example, a prison advocacy organization, when scanning initially, looked only at criminal justice trends and saw that most were unfavorable to the aims they espoused. When people began to scan more broadly, however, one thing they saw was that the mayor was pursuing a major literacy effort. One board member developed a credible argument for how the organization might link with this wider initiative.

Environmental scanning should be done in two phases. First the group scans the widest environment. What is happening in the country? The jurisdiction? People can be asked to list trends that they anticipate over the next five years in the society. The group can then examine the list and look for trends that might be linked to their work. In the second stage, the group can develop a list of trends more closely linked to the sector or focus of the organization. Reviewing both lists, people can identify trends that have implications, either positive or negative, for the agency. One organization, after brainstorming the lists of trends, assigned clusters of trends to different members of the committee with a sheet of questions for further analysis: What is our current response to the trend (if any)? What would be a potential response? What are the positive or negative implications? What resources would be needed? What are the next steps? At the next meeting, the group circulated the sheets and moved toward a consensus on which trends were most likely to lead to new initiatives or to support current program activities and which were interesting or provocative but not as immediately relevant. This process used trends as a means of generating new program ideas.

This type of scanning is not an objective, scientific method (as Naisbitt's [1982] content analysis of publications is). Instead it draws on the direct experience of the participants in their work, their outside reading, and other activities. At one meeting of an organization involved in family planning with teenagers, a health care worker was talking about patterns at the organization's clinic. She recalled that patients would often call to cancel an appointment because they were not feeling well. She was puzzled at the seeming incongruity of not seeing the doctor because one is sick. The group wrestled with alternative explanations of this pattern in a rich discussion about how teenage customers split their contraceptive concerns from wider issues of health. One of this agency's strategic themes was the value of linking teenagers to general health services from their initial visit. Therefore, this split was significant, and when the group recognized it, people began thinking of ways to help their clients see the true links between their service and general health care.

Even within trends that at first glance seem antithetical to one's mission, there may be opportunities. The same prison advocacy group mentioned earlier, watching the growth of the trend toward concern for the victims, initially felt that it made their task more difficult, since the inmates they represented were losing support almost in proportion to growth of support for victims. They learned, however, that in one jurisdiction (Oklahoma) this trend has been linked to themes of mediation, restitution, and the acknowledgment of overcrowding, in a program that brings victims and offenders into a conflict-mediation discussion. During this mediation, the parties arrive at a restitution agreement that can result in a request for sentence modification.

Developing the Menu of Options

The options that make up an organization's menu can come from four sources: (1) current activities, (2) new initiatives suggested by wider trends, (3) initiatives that spring from the personal interests and values of key staff, and (4) initiatives of the new leader. One of the major difficulties in planning at the time of a leadership change is that there is little room for innovation. So many things are going on and competing for time that new ideas cannot be adequately staffed. The result is cynicism and feelings of "Here we go again with lots of talk and no follow-through." People often come up with a long list of possible new initiatives, but few suggestions about which of the organization's current activities could be stopped or cut back. Part of the value of the menu model is that it harnesses the staff's personal energy. For new services, individuals or small groups can be assigned the task of working up proposals. An initial proposal might address the following questions: What is the desired outcome of this initiative? Who would be its clients or customers? Who would be the major stakeholders? What current trends are relevant to this initiative? What resources would be needed to carry it out? What are the risks? What are the next steps? Brief answers to such questions can give a concrete sense of what the initiatives might mean to the organization and help the new initiatives seem as real and concrete as the organization's current programs.

Once the organization has a menu of options, members can assess whether it has the richness needed to be responsive to the shifts in the environment that they had discussed in the scanning. They can then begin to sort them out. Some items will become its current action profile; others can be left, awaiting some stimulus from the environment. Still others can lead to low-cost study groups that develop a proposal or network with others to see if they can develop adequate support. Identification of a particular option often will shape the subsequent scanning, for people will inevitably be more attentive to trends that are relevant to alternatives under active consideration.

Note the power of this process to bridge the inevitable tensions between a new leader and existing staff. In effect, the new leader has sanctioned a planning process that asks people to invent options for mutual gain. Rather than struggling over the leader's pet ideas or those of the existing staff, the group creates a set of potential options, and the selection is linked to external circumstances. Allegations of pure favoritism are avoided.

Selecting the Initial Set for Implementation

The most difficult transition in the planning process is moving from a list of alternatives to the set that the leader wishes to implement. Up until now, divergent thinking had been encouraged. Everyone's pet projects are included, even welcomed. When the moment for convergent thinking arrives, hard choices must be made. There are winners and losers. One of the values of the menu model is that some of the potential conflict is mediated by keeping certain ideas on hold. This feature of the model is valuable because of the importance of personal champions for any idea to survive and thrive. If ideas can be found that are valuable for both the individual and the organization, the benefits are significant (Gilmore and Hirschhorn, 1984). In one legal service program, a board shifted

priorities from veterans' issues to housing issues. Yet the staff for
the veterans' issues were two Vietnam veterans who had personal
passion for this area; they were not passive resources that could
simply be transferred to a new area and expected to perform with
the same enthusiasm. I am not suggesting that a strategic plan
should simply confirm staff interests. The plan should result from
a hard examination of the area of both individual and organizational interest.

One of the difficulties in selecting the initial set of actions
is thinking of the options as a total set, not as a list of separate
initiatives. A set can have characteristics that no item has by itself.
Ackoff (1974) has noted that a set of initiatives can be implemented
when no item by itself is implementable. The set can send messages
to different constituencies and as a whole be balanced by combining
high- and low-risk actions.

Idealized Redesign. A powerful process to integrate the many
different options into a coherent strategy and to link them to the
organization and management of the enterprise is Ackoff's idealized
redesign process (1974), in which people are asked to assume a clean
slate and to redesign the organization subject to two constraints: the
design must be technologically feasible, and it must be operation-
ally viable, able to function on a continuous basis, getting the
necessary resources from the wider environment.

Participants are instructed not to be concerned with implementation difficulties, however, because they often interfere with
creativity. The redesigning can be done in groups or in a modified
Delphi mode in which people develop their designs individually
and a staff person integrates them into a single design, noting the
points of convergence and divergence. One advantage of the Ackoff
process is that it increases the creativity of a group by relaxing
constraints. Furthermore, it leads to consensus, because people
often agree over ideals more readily than over means. Once there is
agreement on the idealized design, the group can work backward to
make the modifications necessary for implementation.

Future Scenario. One other technique to help people knit
together a set of initiatives is to ask them to develop a scenario of
the organization for the coming year, perhaps by projecting
themselves to some future date and developing a story, a "history

of the future" (Hirschhorn, 1980; Weick, 1979). For example, they may be asked, "Imagine it's one year from now, and you are talking with a colleague. You are delighted by how the organization has progressed over the past year, beginning with the strategic planning retreat. Imagine what has been accomplished that leads you to feel so positive. Describe the steps and the new initiatives. How were they linked with existing services and operations?"

After people have been given a few moments to think, pairs of participants can role play the conversation in front of the group. Like idealized design, this process helps people to integrate a variety of initiatives so that a list takes on a life, a texture that can in turn generate provocative discussion. This process also has a playful quality that can lead a group into thinking freshly about its mission and programs.

Process Issues

One test of a planning process is its capacity to engage and revitalize the participants. Ackoff (1974) has suggested that effective planning is like a crusade, motivating people to pursue its newly redefined directions. One of the key issues is the overall rhythm of the planning cycle. Often it begins slowly, with meetings on a monthly basis. Figure 7 suggests the critical stages that a group goes through as it struggles with the collective direction. At first, people willingly defer their need for commensurate payoffs, but as they continue to put time into the effort, they feel that they are not getting benefits commensurate with the effort. They begin to pull back, withhold their commitment, and perhaps move into a wait-and-see posture, especially if the new leader is making promises that they have heard before. Attendance at meetings drops, people arrive late, take fewer risks, appear less psychologically committed, perhaps bring other work to meetings. At this juncture the process can take one of two paths. It can fail, in part because of this disinvestment: a self-fulfilling prophecy. Or it can break through, offering payoffs commensurate with the staff's investments. Then it creates the willingness for another push.

Because of this dynamic, it is often advisable to begin a planning process with a retreat or a long initial session, so that

Figure 7. Stages of Group Development.

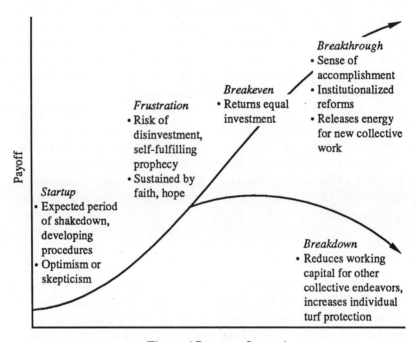

Time and Resources Invested

people build up a head of steam. Once the issues have been structured, an ongoing work group can maintain the momentum. Such initial events should cycle through the entire process, so that all issues are touched on. Effective processes resemble a spiral, getting deeper and more focused with each successive cycle through the process. Early victories, or what Weick (1984) calls "small wins," can be critical in building morale.

    Another effective approach for sustaining momentum is to mix collective and individual assignments. Groups are better than individuals at brainstorming, being creative, and generating rich lists of options. They are less effective at analysis, writing, and doing necessary background work. Too often, strategic planning processes are excessively collective. People begin to feel that they are in a three-legged race—moving in the same direction, perhaps, but always awkwardly. A relay race format may be better, allowing each person to accomplish a segment of the collective work alone and then hand it off to someone else. One person may be assigned a task and a few others designated as resource persons. Individuals are much easier to hold accountable than groups, which, like firing squads, too easily mask who is really responsible for a collective effort.

One new leader used mixed groups at a retreat to do an initial piece of thinking, in each group charging one person with developing notes on the work of the group. The leader met with these spokespersons at a later date—an effective way to link the retreat to the work back home—and reacted to the proposals by making assignments to the person organizationally responsible for the appropriate area. This process nicely mixed individual and group work and allowed fresh thinking to come from outside a particular functional area.

The main benefit of such a planning process lies in the participation rather than the concrete products. If the conversations are stimulating and on the right issues, they begin to shape people's behavior long before any concrete decisions are recorded in a written plan. Furthermore, the various steps offer many opportunities for the leader to reveal his or her thinking and style, so that others can better collaborate with the new leader. Peters (1978) has noted the power of question asking on the part of a new leader in directing staff's attention to the areas and issues of interest. By asking questions, a leader can send clear signals about directions while allowing contributions from others.

One of the major tasks of a leader of a strategic planning process is to keep it from being overly encapsulated in a series of special events. The very mechanisms that are used to buffer the thinking from the press of daily business can become barriers to exporting the ideas and connecting them to the operating realities of the organization. Clear assignments for follow-up and tracking are necessary to ensure completion.

Paradoxically, a good sign of effective strategic planning work can be a somewhat depressive tone, which indicates that group members recognize the difficulties of linking their ideas to a changing reality. By contrast, a manic feeling can suggest that the group has fled from the difficult implementation issues and has remained stuck, playing with ideas but not linking them to existing constraints.

Using strategic themes to give direction and allowing considerable local elaboration and participation, the new leader mobilizes the existing staff, linking their anxieties productively to work. The collaboration of the new leader and existing staff may enhance the organization's overall adaptiveness by enriching the pool of ideas available for action. Inevitably, carrying out these ideas involves new structural patterns within the organization. The next chapter discusses the ways in which a new leader sets these new patterns and assigns people to the new roles the structure offers.

✑ Chapter 12

Handling the Inevitable
Reorganization Effectively

The word *reorganization* is misleading in that it suggests a specific event occurring on a precise date. While such an event may take place in the legal sense, it rarely does in a social and psychological sense. The director of a recently merged organization tells of discovering a retirement party from a division that had not existed for several years since the reorganization. In the hearts and minds of those at the banquet and in the engraving on the gold retirement watch, the division lived on. Boxes and lines can be easily redrawn, but habits, patterns of communication, and informal friendships change more slowly.

Chandler (1962) theorizes that organizations that are structured to fit with the business strategy will outperform those that are not. The new organizational structure is a means to the attainment of a new thrust. Therefore, one would expect reorganizations to take place only in those situations in which a new leader develops a substantially different strategy that calls into question the current structure. Yet many reorganizations seem to flow from a new leader's desire to put his or her stamp on the organization rather than from any clear new goal or strategy. As a result, organizational structures and reporting processes are often closely linked to particular managers and risk being changed or abandoned when a new leader arrives. When Jack Welch took the reins of General Electric, many of the structures and processes that were closely associated with his predecessor, Reginald Jones, were dismantled. As turnover of leaders and the ensuing reorganizing increase (every

185

two to three years for many cabinet officials), staff often adapt by complying only minimally because they do not think the changes will last.

A new leader should proceed cautiously in reorganizing. Lawrence Lynn (1981) has written insightfully on public-sector reorganization and management, drawing on many careful studies as well as on his own experience inside government. He says, "No evidence has yet been produced . . . to suggest that reorganizing government leads to greater competence in the performance of its functions or to specific gains in efficiency or effectiveness. The contrary is probably the case. The instability associated with reorganization efforts often leads to reduced morale and productivity, confusion of assignments, caution in proceeding with important tasks, and defensive behavior in general. Reorganization may aid political executives . . . but it is not a substitute for taking the time to manage" (p. 90). Lynn (1980) notes that reorganization cannot be regarded solely within a technical or managerial frame but must be seen as a fundamentally political act, a reshaping of the coalitions interested in the agency. Reorganizations consume considerable amounts of a leader's scarcest resource—time—yet they often fail because the new roles are not filled with the right people.

Why Reorganize?

A new leader may have one or more reasons to reorganize: to adapt the resources of the organization to a new strategy; to match people and responsibilities, working around an ineffective but protected key employee, for example, or capitalizing on the special competencies of some individual; to symbolize the importance of a new initiative, perhaps by elevating a unit to report directly to the new leader; to get control of an organization, by shortening lines of communications, for example, or altering reporting relationships; to revitalize an organization by shaking people up and giving them new assignments that may remotivate or challenge them; to give groups or divisions more control over the necessary related functions so that they can better control their own work, for example, by decentralizing purchasing; or to integrate and achieve efficiencies by grouping like functions, such as consolidating separate administrative units.

A well-thought-out reorganization must be carefully linked to the specific situation and context. It must take into consideration the organization's recent history, the amount of flexibility the leader has in assigning personnel, the pattern of existing relationships, the leader's style and skills, the constraints in the wider environment—for example, whether approval is necessary and if so whether it is obtainable—and finally the likelihood of finding people to fill the critical roles. Gabarro noted in his study of transition (n.d.) that the most prevalent reason for failed reshapings was "the unavailability of a person or persons needed to fill a key position" (p. 10).

Specific advice on reorganization is therefore impossible to give in the abstract. There are patterns and general considerations, however, that a new leader should take into account. Gabarro (1985) studied in depth four leadership transitions and ten retrospective histories of organizations that had experienced a new leader. He found reorganizations occurring at two distinct time periods: in the first six months, a period that he terms "taking hold," and then, after a period of low reorganizing activity that he labels "immersion," a second wave during what he calls a "reshaping" stage. The first wave of reorganizing is more reactive, fixing immediate problems and assembling a team and working structure good enough to run the organization. The second set of changes appears to be more genuinely strategy driven. Their greater scope and depth are suggested by the increase in the number of associated personnel changes (42 percent of the personnel moves occur during this phase, in contrast to 24 percent in the first six-month phase).

This suggests the potential for using the "taking hold" and "immersion" periods as the time to experiment with different patterns of organizing, mostly via informal processes. Armed with this experience, a new leader is then prepared to make the deeper structural changes during the "reshaping" phase. Table 8 illustrates Gabarro's framework, with the key issues at each stage.

Whether the leader is initially tinkering with the structure or making major changes, the following general points are worth thinking through:

Table 8. Taking Charge: Tasks and Dilemmas.

I	Taking hold: orientation and evaluation, corrective actions	Tasks
		Dilemma
II	Immersion: fine-grained, exploratory learning and managing the business	Tasks

Tasks (I):
- Develop an understanding of the new situation
- Take corrective actions
- Develop initial set of priorities and "map" of the situation
- Develop initial set of expectations with key subordinates
- Establish the basis for effective working relationships

Dilemma:
How quickly to act on apparent problems?

Act too quickly—risks:
- Make a poor decision because of lack of adequate information or knowledge
- Take actions that constrain subsequent decisions that cannot be anticipated yet
- Lose advantages of the "honeymoon" period

Act too slowly—risks:
- Lose credibility because of apparent indecisiveness
- Lose valuable time

Tasks (II):
- Develop a deeper, finer grained understanding of the new situation and the people

			Tasks
			Assess consequences of taking-hold period actions
			Reassess priorities
			Settle questions and problems concerning key personnel
			Reconfigure "map" of the situation; fill out or revise the concept
			Prepare for reshaping actions
III	Reshaping: acting on the revised concept	Tasks	Reconfigure organization based on finer grained understanding
			Deal with underlying causes of residual problems
			Be open to unanticipated problems that emerge as a result of second-wave changes
IV	Consolidation: evaluative learning, follow-through, and corrective action	Tasks	Follow through on reshaping actions
			Deal with unanticipated problems of reshaping stage
			Remain open to new developments
V	Refinement: refining operations, looking for new opportunities		

Source: Garbarro, 1985, p. 121. (Reprinted by permission of *Harvard Business Review*, "When a New Manager Takes Charge" by J. Gabarro, May-June 1985.)

1. *Work to clarify and get agreement on the reasons for the reorganization.* The better they understand the purposes, the easier it is for people to accept a reorganization. Reorganization is often received with initial skepticism, because people have experienced prior changes as more symbolic than real. One should think carefully about the links between the reorganization and the problems that it will supposedly solve. Be prepared for arguments that there are other, less costly ways of resolving those problems— ad hoc task forces, new liaison roles, new promises of cooperation, and so on.

In a major urban probation department, for example, a new leader sponsored a comprehensive reorganization to break down the rigid bureaucratic separations among the different divisions and get more cross-unit cooperation. The reorganization foundered because key division heads were not convinced that such an extensive redesign was necessary. They were able to point to several special cross-division projects that were working well. Here there was agreement over the presenting problem but disagreement over the appropriate response. Rather than simply blaming resistance to change, an effective leader must examine carefully the nature of the resistance and consider what aspects may be adaptive.

2. *Keep a balanced view of the benefits and costs.* In proposing a new structure, a new director often sees only the problems in the present that will be improved under the new design, while existing staff may focus exclusively on what is good about the present and may suffer in the new design. Organizations work only when they appropriately balance change and stability. During the discussion of a reorganization, new leaders should help all parties see all sides. Any organizational structure involves tradeoffs. The biased comparisons of a new organization's strengths with a current structure's weaknesses should be replaced by a careful review of the strengths and weaknesses of both the existing and the proposed alternatives.

3. *Remember that organizations rarely function as they are set forth on paper.* This statement applies to both the current and the proposed structures. A leader should make organizational decisions based on how the organization is actually functioning rather than on paper diagrams and should be sure that the

predictable ways the proposed structure will function will indeed be superior to the current ones. It may be possible to improve the current structure substantially simply by enforcing compliance with its design. For example, in the formal structure of one organization, the president focused predominantly on the external issues and the vice-president integrated the major internal divisions. In practice, the vice-president was frequently bypassed. The organization had the options of changing the person in the role or enforcing the way the structure was supposed to function; substantial improvements would result from either course without reorganizing.

4. *Consider altering aspects of the organizational design other than the structure.* Galbraith (1977) has proposed a model for thinking about organizational design choices that is illustrated in Figure 8. This model is useful in scanning the many options that are open for altering organizational behavior. For example, altering planning processes, such as budget development, by involving different units earlier is a way of increasing their influence without any structural change. Reward systems can be powerful means of creating change without structural alterations by creating incentives for the desired behavior. Replacing or retraining people in existing roles can alter an organization significantly. Galbraith stresses that there is no one best way to organize but that not all ways are equally effective. The key is a design in which the components fit with one another.

Leaders should resist the temptation to undertake a major reorganization early on unless they have a clear sense of the guiding strategy or unless a major crisis demands it. Outsiders in particular should proceed with caution, for the effectiveness of an organization depends on a deep understanding of the strategy, the people, and the existing culture. There are many ways to alter an organization's performance short of redrawing reporting relationships, and they are more easily implemented than a major reorganization. They may offer opportunities to learn about the organization and high-leverage ways to improve it. Successful organization changes often come about after the new behaviors have already become established in ad hoc ways, the formal reorganization simply ratifying changes that are already well under way. Another advantage of waiting is

Figure 8. Organizational Elements.

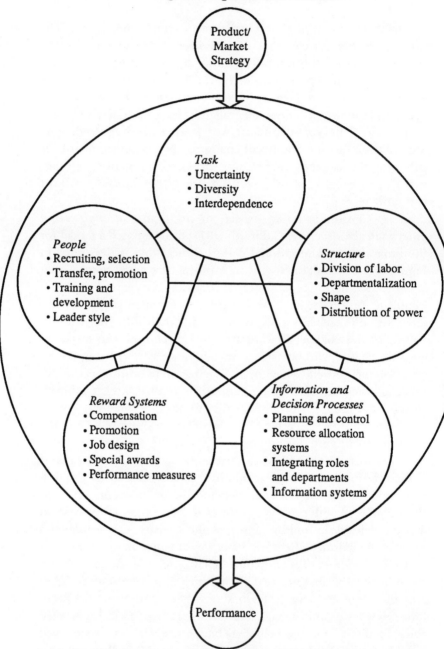

Source: Galbraith, 1977. (© 1977 by Addison Wesley Publishing Co., Inc., Reading, Mass. Reprinted with permission.)

that staff cannot use the confusion of a new structure to excuse unacceptable performance.

Managing the Process of Reorganization

Once a new leader has determined that a reorganization will increase effectiveness, the next task is to implement the new structure. Beckhard and Harris (1977) have called attention to the need to manage carefully the process of transition. They suggest that one needs to think not just of the current and the desired states but also of a transition stage that might even require its own temporary structure, a scaffolding that will provide support until the finished structure can stand on its own. For example, if several new roles will be created, someone might be assigned the responsibility for executive search during the transition phase. Political elections provide for a discrete time between being elected and taking office that often give rise to temporary transition teams, complete with their own organization. Other organizations might learn from the model, perhaps allowing more than the three months elected executives have to bring into being a complicated organizational transformation.

The overall transition might have a project manager and an advisory board made up of representatives of different levels and functions who would both detect and resolve some of the expected misunderstandings or problems in the reorganization. Extensive training may be necessary. For example, if the new structure puts people into dual reporting relationships, people may need to improve their skills in communication, conflict resolving, and negotiating in order to function effectively. These skills do not appear magically on the date of implementation of a new organization but must be systematically developed.

One way of thinking about the process of creating a new organizational structure is to look at the degree of disruption that will be experienced overall and within specific units. Disruption will vary along two dimensions: internal, the change within a given unit, and external, the change in the relationships among units that creates boundary uncertainties. Some units in a reorganization will face high amounts of external change with little internal disruption. For example, a training unit might be shifted intact from the personnel department to a vice-president for human resources. Its members will have to build new working alliances in the new location and alter their relations to the area from which they were shifted, and if the unit's level has been changed as well, there may be shifts in others' perceptions of its influence. Internally, however, there may be little change.

On the other hand, a unit may face little external change but considerable internal reorganization. For example, it may have the same leader and location but a different division of labor among the team. The most trauma is experienced by units that face both high internal and high external change, such as being split apart or merged. Members must cope with reassigning tasks and responsibilities, shifting loyalties, sorting out hierarchical issues, clearly informing outside stakeholders of the new alignments, and so on. Furthermore, they often face these challenges with new unit leadership.

Given the challenges in managing the process of reorganization, new leaders are offered the following advice:

1. *Carefully allocate your time to the units that are most traumatized.* Scanning a proposed reorganization will make clear the units that are most affected and may therefore require the most assistance. Units whose leadership and boundaries remain the same at least have an internal stability that will serve as a base for negotiation of new boundary relationships. Units that face both internal confusion and new boundary relationships are most at risk of becoming dysfunctional. The leader will need to be involved to resolve conflicts in relationships among units. Responsibility charting, which is discussed in the next section of this chapter, can be a powerful way of exploring these issues. If a unit facing considerable internal reorganization also lacks a leader, its ability to become effective in its new role can be damaged.

2. *Coordinate the implementing of new structure with the filling of new positions.* If a reorganization creates new positions, the timing of implementing it is important. In one case, a new secretary created a thoughtful new structure that consolidated administration under a single deputy but did not readily find an acceptable candidate. Without having anyone in that job, he found

himself in a vicious cycle of being too busy to give adequate time to the search for a candidate. The failure to fill a key role in a new structure for a prolonged period of time also leads to distorted patterns of relationships that may impair the effectiveness of the role when it is eventually filled. People become used to talking directly with the leader or working through lateral disagreements without a supervisor. An effective strategy to prevent this from happening is to place a staffer in charge of executive recruiting on an almost full-time basis until the position is filled.

Sometimes structural issues can be held open until a particular role is filled, so that the structure can take into account the specific characteristics and strengths of the person hired. In one organization, the organizational location of the training unit was at issue. The leader did not wait until it was clear who would be in what roles, and an opportunity was lost to put training under a newly hired deputy who would have been able to give it particularly skillful oversight.

3. *Favor "confusion" and "error" over "resistance" and "conspiracy" as theories of why things are not going well.* People do often resist change in subtle, political ways, but experience suggests that these explanations are overused. One can make two kinds of mistakes in this area: treating someone who is really only confused as a resister, and treating someone who is really resisting politically as simply confused. Table 9 examines these two types of errors. This analysis suggests that the easier error to recover from is labeling behavior as confusion. One can easily move from educative to power strategies with the added authority that comes from having given a person the benefit of the doubt, but it is more difficult to switch from power strategies to reeducation, because you have poisoned the relationship that is necessary for reeducative strategies to be effective. Power approaches also run the risk of creating the very opposition that one imagined was there in the first place; people who feel unfairly blamed often respond by going underground with resistance.

4. *Label the various phases and time periods of the overall organization transition.* When change is introduced people may attribute initial problems in the transition to the structure or idea itself. Phrases like "shakedown cruise" and "pilot program" help

Table 9. Consequences of Error.

You Take It As:	Trouble Really Is:	
	Resistance	*Confusion*
Resistance	No error: You correctly use power strategies.	Error: You react with power strategies, and person feels unfairly blamed, still in the dark on what is expected and less likely to ask. Person may go underground and create resistance (self-fulfilling). Hard to switch to educative strategies.
Confusion	Error: You react with education and guidance. Person plays along, thinks you are naive, suspects they're winning. Time is lost, but there are few self-fulfilling dynamics. After you are sure of error, easy to switch to power strategies, given the clear record of resistance.	No error: You correctly use reeducative strategies.

people to see a time-limited period in which errors are expected and are appropriately charged off to the break-in process and not to the idea itself.

5. *Create outlets for assessment and reflection on the transition.* If people know that the leader wants feedback and that special meetings have been scheduled, grievances will be appropriately channeled instead of going underground. The new leader should acknowledge the problems that will be experienced.

A very effective kickoff to a reorganization is to get a knowledgeable group of people together and ask them to respond to the following questions: "Given your experience in past reorganizations, what are three to five predictable ways in which this one might fail? For each way, what are some of the ways we might prevent or respond to these problems as they emerge?" This approach allows people to discharge their cynicism and plan constructively, perhaps setting up a monitoring and problem-solving group that can deal with ongoing problems as they are detected. Tunstall (1985), discussing the lessons learned from managing the breakup of AT&T, noted the critical importance of having a "mechanism for rapid escalation of stalemated issues," which will enable lower-ranking participants—often the first to encounter a novel situation that was not fully anticipated by the planners of the reorganization—to get a hearing quickly so that troubles do not build up.

6. *Prior to initiating any major discussion of reorganizing, check closely into the constraints that might exist.* Subunits sometimes have different standings, one created by an executive order, another with a legislative base. Before getting into a reorganization, know what approvals are required to put a new structure in place. The power of internal groups to resist some changes is often more closely related to their external allies than their internal clout. Even when there are no formal requirements, there may be powerful alliances that are important to know about before undertaking a restructuring. Often knowing the sponsor or reason for an earlier reorganization can be useful.

7. *Balance appropriate direction setting with effective participation.* Often a small group of insiders develops a reorganization proposal and fails to test it against the vast operational knowledge of the career employees. On the other hand, too much consultation can result in a stalemate, with no support for a new structure. An effective compromise is for the leader to work out the major outlines or criteria for a reorganization and then invite widespread participation within some established givens. For example, a utility director created five new major divisions (Ahern, 1983). He invited his senior managers to say which division they wanted to be considered for and to help specify the tasks and responsibilities within each division that would make them function effectively. Through an informal collegial bargaining process, each was able to get one of his or her top two preferences and feel some ownership of the specification of responsibilities. The leader was able to communicate his strategic priorities by resolving conflicts in favor of the more important functions, yet give his managers considerable latitude in structuring their divisions.

In sum, how a leader manages a reorganization has considerable impact on the ultimate effectiveness of the new structure. If the process is well managed, people will actively solve the normal problems that occur, elaborating policies to make the new patterns work and developing the new understandings and behaviors that will make the reorganization operational. If it is poorly managed, the chaos will create low morale and productivity and may cripple the new structure permanently.

Responsibility Charting

Responsibility charting (Gilmore, 1977; McCann and Gilmore, 1983) is a process for analyzing and establishing how multiple actors participate in specific decisions or strategic initiatives. The process has many valuable uses at several different stages of a reorganization process, especially for diagnosing organizational confusion and testing whether reorganization is necessary, as well as for the design, implementation, and debugging of a new organization structure.

The process involves creating a decision matrix, showing actors across the top and decisions or initiatives down the side, and using a code to describe how each actor participates in each decision. The following four modes can be used to describe how different people collaborate on any given decision:

A = Approves, signs off, vetoes. Accountable for the quality of the decision.

R = Responsible. Expected to detect relevant trends in the area of the decision, to shape the definition of the problem, to assemble the necessary analytical information, and to make a recommendation or suggest options. This role is accountable for errors of omission, as well as for the quality of a decision when the approving role accepts the recommendation.

C = Must be consulted. This is not a veto role, nor actively responsible, but it has some information relevant to the decision or a critical role in implementation that makes its input valuable.

I = Must be informed before public announcement of the decision. This role needs to know the results of a decision in order to do its work but does not need to participate in the decision.

Responsibility charting with a group of the top managers early in a leader's transition can be a most efficient way for the leader to learn about the patterns of responsibility, how centralized or decentralized different people see the organization at present. Because one can do it with relatively infrequent decisions or with some annual process such as budget development, it is a way to explore issues long before they come up in actuality, when egos and difficult issues obscure the principles of how the organization is supposed to function.

Developing and Using the Matrix

Responsibility charting consists of the following steps:

1. Creation of a decision matrix (see Figure 9). The decisions that one wishes to examine are identified. These may be a sample of the key decisions in major areas, such as marketing, production, personnel, budget, planning, and so on, or those relevant to a particular organizational option one is examining, such as a new role. The actors relevant to the decisions are also identified.
2. Development of a set of definitions describing types of participation.
3. Individual balloting on the decisions. In the early stages of a leadership transition, individual balloting prevents staff from following the leader's indicated preference. People must work through their own opinions of how the structure would work best and then use the differences that result to challenge each other and learn more about the issues that surround these decisions.
4. Tabulation and analysis. Participants can work through each decision, sharing their perceptions, or a staffer or outside consultant can do the analysis and prepare the data on overheads for a separate discussion and negotiation session. When there are many decisions and many participants, the

Figure 9. Sample Ballot.

Decision	Actors			
	Director	Director Adult Services	Director Juvenile Services	Director Program Planning
1. Develop new programs				
2. Hire staff for a division				
3. Develop unit budget				
4. Respond to news media about a new program in juvenile sentences				

Instructions: For each decision and each role, fill in the letter that best represents your view of the participation of that role in that decision.

A = Approves   C = Consulted

R = Responsible   I = Informed

amount of data can be considerable. It is best to begin with a modest number of decisions (eight to twelve) and as few key actors or roles as possible. Later, finer distinctions such as who within an office actually does the work can be examined as a second stage, once the role of the overall unit is clear.

5. Discussion and negotiation of the new patterns of involvement. This session often takes several hours, especially if there are substantial differences of opinion, either in how the structure is currently working or how it should be working. The first decisions often take considerable time, but as the group moves along it begins to develop precedents that make the later decisions move more rapidly. A useful ground rule is to

separate the discussion from the final decision making. The senior executive takes under advisement the recommended patterns of responsibility and, after studying the outcomes, issues a memorandum that summarizes the major results.

A brief example will illustrate this process. A probation department had recently reorganized by creating a new role, director of program planning, in addition to the existing directors for adult and juvenile services, so that now three executives reported to the director. There had been some confusion about the new role. Using the ballot excerpted in Figure 9, the group charted some decisions and in doing so surfaced a significantly different understanding of the planning role. When the data were tabulated, it was clear that while all four participants saw the leader's role as one of approval (four A's), there was a three-to-one split in their view of the other three roles.

		Actors		
Decision	*Director*	*Adult*	*Juvenile*	*Planner*
Develop new	4 A	3 C	3 C	3 R
programs		1 R	1 R	1 C

The discussion revealed that the director and the heads of the adult and juvenile divisions saw the situation in the same way and that the new program planner had a very different view of the situation; he saw his role as a resource and support to the line divisions when it came to developing new programs. The division directors (and the agency director), on the contrary, expected him to develop new programs and to use the division directors for necessary input. This difference in perception of the role was critical, because the planner would be evaluated on the basis of responsibilities that he was not clear he had been given. When the group members turned to specific examples to support their perceptions, the planner was able to cite instances in which he had clearly been in a consulting capacity. When they then discussed how they wanted things to be, they were unanimous in wanting the planner to take an active, initiating (R) role. Responsibility charting thus enabled the group to correct a basic misunderstanding before it ended in an unfair negative appraisal of the planner.

Ongoing Value

The group process in responsibility charting does not end with the initial chart of decisions but becomes infused in the team's continuing work. As people face new, undiscussed decisions, they relate back to the workshop discussions and think through analogies with issues decided there.

Furthermore, the experience leaves the new top group with a shared language for rapidly communicating how they want to relate to a particular issue. For example, at the end of a meeting, the group can quickly review who will take the lead (R) role, who will be consulted (C), and who approves (A). They will quickly achieve clarity about who is responsible for follow-through because of their common language.

One powerful feature of responsibility charting is that it makes the difficult issues of power and authority discussable in a group. The all-pervasive complaints about poor communication, especially during the early months of a new team, are usually best interpreted as masked complaints about the distribution of influence. Complaining about communication is considered legitimate, but complaining about power is viewed as self-serving. Yet all the literature on job satisfaction (Trist, 1981) suggests that people want to feel some elbow room in their jobs, a well-defined area in which they are responsible and have the requisite authority to meet the challenges of the task. Responsibility charting harnesses the discussions about participation and influence to specific tasks and allows people to evaluate both the benefits and the costs of their involvement, which are summarized in Table 10.

Furthermore, responsibility charting opens up discussions of power and authority because it allows a rich range of potential solutions beyond the win/lose dynamics of discussing boxes and lines of a structure. For example, a role with a stake can be given approval power (A), even though the responsible (R) role is not directly in that chain of command. People's involvement can be

Table 10. Costs and Benefits of Participation in a Decision.

Costs	Benefits
• Information overload.	• New information about the issue.
• Lost time from delivering service or working on more important decisions.	• New perspectives on the issue.
• Interruption and diffusion of focus from other tasks one is working on.	
• Potential cynicism from being consulted but not seeing the impact of one's ideas.	• More ownership of the eventual decision, understanding the reasons behind it, leading to more effective implementation.
• Delay from waiting for different people to get the issue.	
• Diffusion of accountability.	• Accountability, giving those responsible for an area some say in the decisions.

negotiated and changed; someone may be given more influence in some decisions because he or she will have more time as a result of being cut out of some other decisions. Most managers would willingly trade pseudoparticipation in a broad range of decisions for authentic involvement in the few that they regard as essential to their goals. For example, a clear guarantee that one will be promptly informed of a decision enables one to opt out of more active participation, which often may have been the only way to stay abreast of the area.

I should clarify that this process, especially when used early in a new leader's tenure, in no way implies democratic decision making about the allocation of authority. The leader sets the ground rules. Some treat the diagnostic discussions as inputs to their decisions; others establish a preference for consensus, acting as tie breakers when stalemates have been reached. In either case, the patterns of authority are the prerogative of the leader. Sometimes leaders deliberately choose to leave certain decisions vague, with effective results.

Another desirable feature of using this process early is that it is easy to communicate the outcomes of the discussions to those not present. Often in a new administration there are in-groups and out-groups, and key meetings take place before the new team is fully in place. Responsibility charting leaves a clear record of the results that can be rapidly reviewed with subordinates who did not attend the session or with a newly hired executive who joins the team some weeks later. Moreover, the public nature of the discussions can add some pressure for people to live up to agreements. It is much easier for lower-status people to hold higher-status people accountable. Rather than confronting a vague promise to delegate, a subordinate can call a superior on a particular decision for task-related reasons, not interpersonal jockeying for power. The confrontation may lead both sides to learn that the earlier agreement may not be feasible or may not apply in the special circumstances surrounding this issue, but it keeps the dialogue about patterns of participation aboveboard rather than driving it into a subterranean political level where it is harder to harness for work.

Three Phases of Planning

Let us now look at how this process of responsibility charting is used at three different stages of thinking about organizational patterns.

1. *Diagnosis.* Responsibility charting can help a new leader who wishes to tone up an organization and highlight possible misunderstandings that are leading to reduced performance. Using the existing roles and a list of typical decisions, or perhaps a set of strategic initiatives, the leader can ask top staff to ballot on how they see those initiatives being allocated across the existing structure. If there are major confusions or disagreements, the data will reveal them and the leader can then clarify or reallocate assignments.

It is far easier to clarify within an existing structure than to reorganize. If a few new initiatives do not fit comfortably in the existing structure, often an ad hoc solution can be developed.

Perhaps a task group can be given major responsibility, or one role can be given lead responsibility despite the structure. These adjustments can constitute experiments. If they work, then a major reorganization might not be necessary. If they do not, then others may see the need for some restructuring. In either case, the organization is learning about how best to allocate responsibilities.

On the other hand, the analysis may reveal that reorganization is necessary. For example, the charting might suggest that a unit under one side of the organization might be more appropriately placed on the other side. What is powerful about responsibility charting is that it works at the level of specific decisions.

In a workshop for a newly elected governor only two weeks into his administration, the group was focusing on the roles of the different staff members. The governor had three major aides and wanted each to take liaison responsibilities for several cabinet departments. In a few selected areas he had a more junior staff specialist as a substantive expert. As the group worked through some hypothetical decisions in the area of education, it became clear that the governor, the senior aide, and the educational specialist had very different conceptions of how the specialist would function, both upward in relation to the governor's staff and outward with the secretary of education and the educational stakeholders.

Because participants filled out their charts individually, the extreme differences in power among the respondents could not unduly influence the balloting. When the issues were discussed, the governor's support for a more active role for the educational specialist (in many decisions he wanted her to be in an active, initiating role) surfaced, in marked contrast to the senior staff's more limited conception of the role (mostly consultative and informed). After a discussion of several issues that would involve the specialist in major policy issues with significant fiscal impacts, a consensus was reached. The group agreed that the function was to be a noninstitutional voice, with a bigger perspective. The assistant could second guess a secretary, coming up with more options, and could use independent judgment. It was clearly understood that in some situations there would be conflicts between the relevant secretary and the special assistant.

This process enabled the group to work through just how the

role was intended to function, rather than setting up the junior aide in a triangle, with the governor and her immediate boss disagreeing over her role. Imagine how difficult it would have been for the specialist to work this issue out if the confusion had led to performance problems early in the administration. She would have faced the difficult choice of going around her immediate superior to the governor, who also would have been in a difficult bind to address the issue without hurting his relationship with a key adviser. Because all these issues had surfaced around hypothetical issues, during a planning and organizing meeting, before key participants' egos were involved, it was much easier to address.

2. *Developing a New Design.* When careful diagnosis indicates a new organization, responsibility charting can be a powerful aid to design. In this case, the leader does not have the managers ballot but instead examines a selection of major decisions against the proposed new roles. When a new level or division is created, it must draw its clout either down from levels above it or up from levels below. By charting one can easily see what types of issues will be decided in the new role, readjusting them if necessary either to build the role up to be more influential or to keep the role from being overloaded. These modifications are much easier to make in the planning stage than when the reorganization is being implemented. Furthermore, the level of specificity that responsibility charting reveals often helps in recruiting for the job.

A new juvenile commissioner had been through her first year without a deputy for operations and was now meeting with her top staff to consider whether to add such a role. The participants were the commissioner, the deputy for administration, the deputy for planning, and the director of secure detention. They identified twenty-four decisions that would clearly involve a deputy for operations if that role existed, including "responding to the press on a problem in an operational unit," "overall management information system strategy," "program planning within a unit," "union issues," and so on. All four voted on their perceptions of how a deputy director for operations would be involved in each of the twenty-four decisions.

As a consultant to the group, I tabulated the ballots. In addition to showing the patterns of letters for each decision, I created an overall score for each participant's perception of each role's influence by assigning weights to the letters as follows: A (approve) = 4, R (responsible) = 3, C (consulted) = 2. The results are summarized in Table 11.

As is clear from the totals, the amount of influence that each person assigned across all twenty-four decisions was reasonably close (206 to 239). But within various roles, the differences are significant. One person saw the deputy for operations as having an influence score of 85, whereas someone else saw it as having approximately half as much influence, 43. All but one saw this role as the most influential. These overall patterns and the specific responses on each of the twenty-four decisions helped the group work through their different conceptions of what value the deputy role would bring and at what cost to current working relationships.

Table 11. Perception of Influence.

Influence Scores   Approve (A) = 4
Responsible (R) = 3
Consulted (C) = 2

	As Seen by			
Role	Commissioner	Administration Deputy	Planning Deputy	Secure Detention Deputy
Commissioner	22	38	24	48
Operations Deputy	66	56	85	43
Administration Deputy	28	33	27	16
Planning Deputy	12	34	17	23
Secure Detention Deputy	32	31	33	27
Nonsecure Detention	26	16	26	20
Other	25	17	27	29
Total	211	225	239	206

The high influence scores suggested that the role would centralize considerable power. They ended up with a decision *not* to fill the role. Instead they developed alternative mechanisms to ensure the integration across program units that was a critical element in the overall strategy.

The specificity of the process helps people envision the future with the new role included and explore how different people imagine it will alter the way key decisions are reached. It prevents the situation where everyone imagines that the future will bring improvements but each one envisages different (and sometimes incompatible) benefits. It is particularly powerful as a part of the preparation for recruiting for the role, as described in Chapters Three and Four, because the key interrelationships and the patterns of authority are so vividly identified. When the role is filled, the chart can be used as part of the orientation.

3. *Effective Implementation.* As Lynn suggested in the quotation earlier in this chapter, reorganizations are often associated with confusion. Responsibility charting can be used in a number of ways as part of the implementation of a new structure. First, a leader can use decision charts to brief key staff members on how the reorganization is to function. Here, the process of balloting is not used, but only a completed chart, which might have been developed by the reorganization planning committee and approved by the leader. Again, the specificity of a decision chart offers much more guidance than an overall description of the functions of the new divisions. Because responsibility charting, unlike a job description, shows each role's assignments in the context of others, it is like a play book for a football team, showing how the roles interact.

After a reorganization has been in effect for a month or so, a leader can conduct a responsibility-charting process to reveal some of the implementation problems and make necessary adjustments. In this model, participants first develop the chart, perhaps by responding to a questionnaire asking them which decisions they find either confusing or not working effectively. Then the key staff members ballot, using an agreed-upon set of codes. A third-party consultant or staffperson tabulates the data, and the group discusses the patterns at a workshop. This process was used by Richard

Nelson several months after his reorganization of field services in Michigan (Gilmore and Nelson, 1978). A useful ground rule at such sessions is to separate the discussion and the decision making. The group works through all the confusion and lists the pros and cons of alternative adjustments. Then the leader should take a week or so to reflect on the patterns before issuing a memorandum. This use of responsibility charting is particularly valuable in clarifying how people will relate to crucial annual processes such as budget development, planning, and legislative initiatives, areas in which learning on the job is particularly costly.

In sum, responsibility charting can be valuable both before, during, and after a reorganization. Organizations are complex. Just as we are limited in our ability to do complicated mathematical problems in our heads, we can think through only a limited number of organizational changes. Responsibility charting offers a language for handling much greater complexity and can speed up the transition from an old to a new structure.

Reorganizations are complex processes, not one-time events. For their success, they depend not only on an appropriate design but on building good working alliances with the people who will carry them out, a topic to be addressed in the next chapter.

⌐ Chapter 13

Cultivating Productive
Working Alliances

Just as the appointment of a new leader is a strategic act, so too is the leader's development of working alliances. Too often, process and interpersonal issues are split off from strategic and substantive issues. The former are regarded as soft and difficult to measure, the latter as hard, bottom-line business issues. In truth, they are critically intertwined. If the strategic challenge is to get control over a major division, the working relationship downward with the head of that division will be critical. If it is to link a basic science lab with the applied technology groups and the line businesses, those lateral relationships will be critical. If the organization is in disrepute with its parent unit because of poor performance, then the new leader must rebuild the upward relationships. Even if the leader ascended to the role from within, transforming what were peer relationships into hierarchical ones is a substantial challenge.

Gabarro (1985, p. 119) reflects on his study of successful and unsuccessful transitions: "Perhaps the single most salient difference between the successful and the failed transitions was the quality of the new manager's working relationships at the end of his first year. For example, at this point, three of the four managers in the failed successions had poor working relationships with two or more of their key subordinates and with two or more peers, and all had poor working relationships with their superiors. . . . The underlying common problem, however, was the new manager's failure to develop a set of shared expectations with their key subordinates or their bosses."

Working Alliances as Strategic Planning

Strategic issues are often best understood in terms of shifts in critical stakeholders. For example, hospitals during the 1960s and 1970s cultivated their relationships with doctors internally and regulatory bodies externally. The doctor controlled the flow of patients. External bodies set the allowable reimbursement rates. Recently, however, with prospective payment plans, health maintenance organizations, corporate and labor initiatives to control costs, and a consumer revolution, hospitals have had to alter their framework to be successful in an extremely competitive market. Like others in the service sector, they have rushed to embrace the popular texts that preach excellence and a customer orientation (Peters and Austin, 1985; Peters and Waterman, 1982). But a mission statement or an advertising campaign is worthless without the work relationships to implement the strategy. Working relationships are the channel connecting the point where strategic decisions are made with the hundreds of patient transactions. For example, internally, the link with the top nursing executive will be critical as the channel into the largest (almost half of the work force) and most pervasive group in the hospital, the critical link to the customer. Externally, the emergence of managed care makes collaborative relationships with insurers and employers critical.

Nor should these working alliances be regarded solely as means for carrying out a set direction. The quality of thinking and the quality of information on which plans are made are critically linked to interpersonal relationships. The process is circular: who one knows at the moment of one's appointment will determine the information that one has access to, which in turn will shape one's ideas about the critical relationships to focus on. A leader's skill at forming effective interpersonal relationships will be a critical factor in gaining access to the relevant information to lead the organization.

I recall meeting with a newly elected governor on his tenth day in office, as part of helping him clarify working relationships in his administration. He noted that in those ten days, the only people who had come into his office were those he had made an explicit choice to see. As a member of Congress and during his gubernatorial campaign, he had been bombarded by unsolicited encounters and had far less control over the boundary. He was worried about how the new pattern of working relationships might affect his ability to hear bad news quickly, get early intelligence on emergent issues, and take the measure of a wider array of people as potential resources for his goals.

Because of the importance of working relationships to the success of a new leader, this chapter focuses on effective working alliances, including how anxiety can distort interpersonal communications, the difficulty of managing upward, and role negotiation as a way of diagnosing difficulties.

Underlying Anxieties in Working Alliances

Several types of anxiety seem to be particularly salient in hierarchical relationships, especially during the upset of leadership transitions.

Anxieties About Aggression. Leaders often fear being too harsh, too mean, too tough, fantasizing that they might destroy someone or provoke someone to retaliate. Aggression is necessary to work and is particularly required when taking leadership of a large, complex organization. In reality, people do get hurt during transitions; careers are derailed, people are fired, reputations are tarnished, and influence is substantially reduced. Leaders have to attend to the mission of the organization, accepting the inevitability of some casualties. The task is to join with the organization and create the capacity to lead it, not to ensure that no one is hurt.

Aggressive feelings are often rampant in relationships between the new leader and subordinates. The critical task is to keep the aggression from both sides harnessed to work. When leaders lose the link to the task, people experience the aggression punitively, sadistically, as though the leader is "breaking" the organization in order to establish leadership. When followers lose the link of aggression to work, they become passive-aggressive, diverting their energy into resistance and remaining, in Schon's framework (1971), "dynamically conservative." As an outsider moving between a new leader and the key subordinates, I often see both sides feeling attacked.

Jerome Weisner, a board member, distinguished between tough and mean, as he reflected on Jean Riboud, the respected head of Schlumberger. "Tough has a connotation of being mean to me. I don't think that there's a mean side to him. . . . He can separate his human feelings and what he feels is necessary for the company. Any successful chief officer must. The worst failing of any executive is the inability to separate his personal regard for the people from his judgment of what is necessary for the welfare of the company" (Auletta, 1985, p. 62).

Note the similarity to the advice in the popular book on principled negotiation, *Getting to Yes* (Fisher and Ury, 1981): be tough on the issues and soft on the people. Many people link the two, because it is much easier to be tough on someone you have come to see as an enemy. Effective leaders acknowledge the hurt that their actions cause good people yet are still able to do what is required without personally devaluing the other.

Anxieties About Control. These anxieties are also prevalent during a leadership transition. Control issues are a preoccupation on both sides of the relationship between the incoming leader and the existing followers. Gabarro's terms, "taking charge" for the overall process and "taking hold" for the initial phase (1985), both suggest the explicit need to get control over an organization in the early phases. A very common tactic of a new leader from the outside is to remove decision authorizations from subordinates to get control of key decisions involving hiring and committing the organization's resources. One leader who did so cited his desire to establish immediate control and strong personal presence: "It is a means to evaluate staff, learn what's going on, exert control, and establish acceptable performance."

Anxieties about control are particularly salient in lateral or cross-boundary links where the authority relationships are not given but must be negotiated (implicitly or explicitly) as the work gets done. The fear that both the substance and the process of the transaction will be dictated by the other often leads to overstructuring: a tight agenda, or clear procedure, sticking with facts, avoiding spontaneity. The paradox is that the more one controls a situation, the less one learns. One executive of a nonprofit organization boasted that he would never hold a board meeting unless he could write the minutes in advance. Such anxiety over losing control to a board (whose role is to set policy and supervise the leader's work) not only leads to zero learning but in the long run puts the executive at risk from the very people he is so anxious to control.

In developing from one's subordinates a good understanding of the history and information about the prior relationships, the leader also runs the risk of taking in historical affect about the relationships, losing the opportunity for a new beginning. Conversely, as we saw in Chapter Eight, a leader who fears being biased and manipulated by the prior history may remain isolated and aloof, rejecting relevant history and moving to break up established working relationships because of the latent fear of rival power bases. Often those relationships are strategic assets, if they can be influenced. A new secretary of aging rotated all his regional directors, thereby severing all their relationships with local aging groups. His ostensible reason—giving each of them a fresh start— masked his real intent to control them.

Anxieties About Punishment. Anxieties about punishment surround the arrival of the new leader. The most primitive fears about punishment flow from the subordinates, for whom the transition stirs up childlike fears that people above and more powerful will punish them, often with only the vaguest sense of what misdeeds they have done to deserve the punishment. They sometimes use acting-out behavior as an unconscious way of provoking punishment from others because they think they "deserve" it. There may be some residual guilt from the way the prior leader departed. Did some subordinates play an active role in causing the departure? Did they fail to come to the support of the former leader?

The fear of punishment often dominates subordinates' interactions with a new leader. It may lead to ingratiating behavior, seeking out favors. It may also get in the way of giving bad news to a new leader, either facts about the state of current operations, criticism of new ideas, or honest assessments of timetables for change, because of the fear that the messenger will be blamed for the message.

The new leader may also experience anxieties about punishment. Many new leaders in top jobs are for the first time operating without a boss closely overseeing their work. They must make the transition from ongoing supervision to a low-contact, low-feedback situation that stimulates anxieties about performance and fears of being punished by a remote authority figure. Many executives also experience complex feelings about attaining their goals, fearing that their triumph over rivals will lead to punishment, a way of dealing with the guilt that may accompany success. Finally, as a reaction to the aggression involved in taking over an organization and the inevitable harm that a new leader causes some employees, there can often be fears of retaliatory punishment, as if the group will band together and attack the leader. A leader who steps into a difficult situation is prone to see the assault of the task in terms of a personal attack.

One leader who had taken charge of an entrenched and embattled public agency described his early days as follows: "I was in such a godawful state of crisis management that I did not have time for anybody. I did slight them [the existing staff]. For example, I did not have regular sit-down meetings. There was always something disrupting them. I was getting thirty to forty phone calls, hundreds of pieces of mail and memoranda. The whole thing was a joke. It was like the staff had said, 'Here comes the latest deputy commissioner. Let's put him up on the treadmill and then laugh when he falls off, and in the meantime let's take turns spinning the treadmill faster to see how fast this one can run.' " The objectively difficult circumstances of this agency and the leader's own difficulties at building an effective team, given the complexities of an entrenched civil service system, allowed him to view his dilemma as a malevolent personal attack by subordinates.

These are some of the major anxieties that manifest themselves in work systems and are particularly salient during transitions. They play a double role in distorting communications and working relationships. First, they directly alter behavior and communication so that, for example, bad news is not relayed up the chain of command (out of fear of punishment) or an opportunity is not capitalized on (for fear of losing control). At another level, these anxieties also make it unlikely that the parties will ever directly discuss the difficulties in the relationship and correct the misunderstandings. Paradoxically, those with whom one is having the most trouble may be the most powerful sources of information and learning, potentially one's best collaborators. Instead, most people adapt to these anxieties by withdrawing and ultimately exiting from the situation. If the problems are discussed at all, it is most likely to be with some third party, increasing the strength of the emerging dysfunctional coalition.

Managing the Boss

Despite the obvious importance of one's boss, the relationship is often ignored. Drucker (1986, p. 16) notes: "Most managers, including of course most chief executives, have a boss. Few people are as important to the performance and success of a manager as the boss. Yet while management books and courses abound in advice on how to manage subordinates, few if any even mention managing the boss." He suggests that the field has failed to look closely at this relationship because managing is associated with being responsible for the work of subordinates. He offers a better definition of manager as "someone who is responsible for the performance of all the people on whom his own performance depends."

Ignoring the upward relationship during a leadership change is surprisingly common. From the perspective of the appointing executive (or board), relief at finally hiring someone often results in too-rapid disengagement. From the perspective of the newly appointed leader, the enjoyment of attaining powerful leadership positions often leads them to focus downward, on their subordinates, not upward. Reflecting back on the crisis that tore E. F. Hutton apart, Robert Rittereiser noted, "To get this firm back on its feet after I got here [recruited from Merrill Lynch in 1985], I had to work from the bottom up. I didn't think I was going to have to worry about what was happening above me. My assumption was wrong" (Sterngold, 1988, p. 6).

Managing a boss is critically linked to the strategic directing of the organization. In the case of an appointing authority and a new leader, the initial work on the relationship begins before the final appointment is made. One reason why it is so important for the appointing authority to think strategically before undertaking a search and to translate the strategic imperatives into desired characteristics is that the relationship with the new leader can begin with an explicit understanding of the challenges. Recall the example in Chapter Six in which Gregorian rejected a university presidency because he felt that the board did not realistically understand the challenges. Had he accepted that job, his working alliance with that group would have been shaped by their initial differences in perceptions about the critical tasks.

The following suggestions will aid the new leader in establishing and maintaining a good upward relationship.

1. *Negotiate shared expectations of the strategic challenges.* Regardless of how well the issues have been explored during the selection process, the strategic challenges will still need clarification after a new leader arrives. Appointing authorities often avoid setting hard priorities, hoping for a miracle worker who will magically be able to do everything. Once a flesh-and-blood person has arrived, priorities will have to be set for these challenges and other problems that the new leader discovers. This work takes place over the first half year, as the new leader begins to work with the organization and external stakeholders to set directions.

One of the difficulties in these upward discussions can be the struggle over who has the authority to set the directions for the organization. Many executives either present a completed plan for perfunctory approval or merely keep the board or boss informed, fearing active consultation because of the potential for the higher level to become involved inappropriately. When a large social services agency did some responsibility charting, this pattern emerged clearly, with the board getting some "approvals" (A's) and some "informed" (I's) but no "consulted" (C's).

The discussion of this data raised the issue of whether one can consult upward and not take the advice. I think the answer is clearly yes, but it requires careful managing. Like downward consultation, it is very dangerous to do if you have made up your mind and are consulting manipulatively to get a commitment. You need to focus carefully on just what aspect you want the advice about. Often by requesting that the boss consider both sides of an issue (the advantages and disadvantages of a strategy) or by asking for input during the divergent, option-generating phases of strategic planning, you can reduce the chances of getting a single answer that might be difficult to reject.

2. *Think explicitly about the style differences between your old boss and the new one.* It can be helpful simply to list the preferred work style of your boss, looking at dimensions such as formal/informal, listener/reader, thrives on conflict/minimizes conflict, task-focused/people-focused, discursive/focused, high involvement/low involvement, tolerates ambiguity/likes certainty, sets clear expectations/vague about expectations. Style differences can amplify substantive differences, so adapting to the desired style can make it easier to keep the relationship focused on the real substantive issues.

3. *Build up a picture of the boss's world and assess the relative stakes that are located in your area of responsibility.* All leaders, especially in the beginning of their tenure, become immersed in their organizations. At the same time, the boss or board may be disengaging, delighted that the new leader has taken over worrying about this area. A healthy antidote to an excessive preoccupation with your unit is to look at it from the perspective of one level higher. A boss relates differently to a unit that contains the key to a turnaround in profitability than to a division that is less significant. What other issues are on the boss's plate? If you have explored the context of the next level up, you can present your issues with greater sensitivity to the other issues that are competing for attention.

4. *Assess the boss's strengths and weaknesses and how they fit with your own.* Some leaders, because of the anxiety of actually confronting the boss's mix of characteristics, turn the boss into an abstraction resembling the normative image of a good leader in textbooks. A subordinate's task is not to change the leader, but to work with the leader as he or she actually is.

A critical part of your role is to buffer your own work group from those parts of your own superior that you experience as dysfunctional, rather than simply transmitting the difficulties downward. For example, a newly appointed deputy began to see the relationships between how he experienced his boss and how his subordinates might perceive him. He noted, "My boss's unreliability makes me hedge my bets a little, not move as assertively and directly as I really ought to in many situations, and sometimes to dodge issues, too. That is guaranteed to make people under you crazy, because the issue is still there. You are just not dealing with it."

5. *Periodically ask your boss for feedback on how you can better support him or her.* Even though it may be the boss's role to initiate coaching discussions, it often will not happen unless you take the initiative, especially in interactions with boards. A recent publication of the American College of Hospital Administrators states, "The CEO has the primary responsibility to initiate and guide the development of an evaluation system that will enhance the effectiveness of hospital governance and executive management. Finally, the study recommends that the hospital CEOs take the initiative to collaborate with boards in developing formal systems for evaluating executive performance" (Foundation of the American College of Hospital Administrators, 1984, p. 1). Drucker (1986) suggests that leaders periodically ask their bosses, "What do I do to help you or hamper you?" Note that the question asks the boss how the subordinate's performance is linked to the boss's effectiveness, not gratuitous inquiry into how the boss can be more effective in his or her job.

Amazingly, few new leaders have a clear sense of how their bosses (or board members) might appraise them. They usually are very curious, but they have not found the way to initiate the conversation. One leader mentioned that he had kept "bugging" his boss to have such a conversation, but it is very likely that the relationship difficulties he was having were being enacted in the very request to have a meeting to discuss the difficulties. One needs to separate clearly a meeting to discuss the substantive issues from one to examine the patterns of working together. An issue that might be trivial in a conversation about the actual work can be very significant in the context of a discussion of the patterns.

For example, in the work discussed earlier with a governor and his cabinet, many secretaries felt overcontrolled by the budget office, which held up expenditures for items that were already in their budgets. On any one item, the secretaries felt it would be inappropriate to go to the governor, yet in aggregate these episodes were beginning to demotivate them. It was only in the context of a retreat focusing on the working alliances that the issue surfaced and could be effectively addressed.

6. *Work explicitly on followership.* New leaders sometimes tend to overconcentrate on the challenge of leading and underattend to that of following, especially if they have been upwardly oriented, watching their prior bosses to learn how to lead, reading about leadership, and fantasizing about what they would do when they took charge. In that frame of mind, it can be difficult to confront honestly those aspects of one's role in which the challenge is to be a good follower, aspects that may not have been visible in role models. In some work with correctional executives, when we asked top leaders what aspects of their jobs they were the least prepared for, they pointed to the political aspects in which they had to accommodate to the governor and others. It turned out that few of them in turn shared those burdens with their subordinates, thus keeping this issue of followership a secret from aspiring leaders.

Dealing with the "Bad" Boss

A special situation results when the new leader finds himself or herself taking a leadership role under erratic conditions at the next level. The leader may have been blinded by the attractiveness of the leadership role and failed to detect the true character of the appointing executive. Or a new boss may have replaced the appointing executive, requiring the leadership mandate to be renegotiated. Finally, a split board—possibly even anticipated, as we saw in Chapter Two—may be unreliable in its support. In all these situations, the challenge is the same: to take leadership in the context of a difficult boundary above.

All the earlier suggestions come into play, but now under the stress of a difficult and strained relationship. When a new boss has been appointed above, a useful strategy is to find the time and place for the type of conversations that would have occurred in a hiring process so that both parties feel they have recontracted and affirmatively chosen, rather than simply inherited, the working relationship.

The "bad" boss is best regarded as a stereotype; real bosses always have some mix of good and bad characteristics that inevitably depend on one's vantage point. In a study of bosses, one fifth of the bosses who were voted "best" shared qualities with those voted "worst" (Goleman, 1986). The first strategy is to respond to and reinforce the good qualities and be less reactive to the bad. One nursing executive with an intrusive and impulsive boss found that when she controlled her reactiveness, not interrupting what she was doing when it was inappropriate to do so, he became less impulsive in his dealings with her. Yet one has to be alive to unconscious patterns. In this relationship, often the more worried he became, the calmer she would become, which stimulated his worry, and so on. In such a situation, one may have to shift behavior to break out of the cycle.

An important rule to observe is to avoid joining the inevitable gossip and back-channel communication about the difficult boss. One needs someone to vent to, but it should be someone outside the work system. Gossip in the work setting will only reinforce the pathological triangles that are actively maintained by the high volume of communication *about* the difficult person and the low amount of direct communication *with* the difficult person.

Acknowledging honestly one's followership, even in the moment of taking leadership, entails working through the inevitable dependencies on an all too human, fallible boss. This thinking is an invaluable opportunity for the new leader to have a glimpse of how, in turn, his or her subordinates may be viewing their new leader.

Role Negotiation

As the new team takes shape, the leader periodically needs to ensure that all are working well together in support of the purposes of the organization. A structured process known as role negotiation can be used in a variety of ways to keep working alliances in good repair. It is often used as a structured intervention with the assistance of an outside third party, but variants of the process can also be used in a number of ways individually, with one key relationship, or even to work through intergroup or interdivisional problems.

The Process. In role negotiation (Harrison, 1976), interdependent members of a work group exchange messages about critical behaviors that they want from each other in order to be effective in their roles. The steps are:

1. The leader briefly introduces the process and establishes the ground rules. This would most often be at a retreat or at a staff meeting set aside for team development.
2. Each participant makes up a separate sheet of paper for each of the others, listing the behaviors that he or she wants from that person in order to be more effective. The form calls for three categories: (1) behaviors that are helpful and one wants *more of,* (2) behaviors that one wants *less of,* and (3) behaviors that help one be effective and one wants the other to *keep doing.* If the group is large, people can be allowed several days to complete the role-message sheets. Note that each sheet is signed, so people must be willing to be honest about what they want from one another. It is critical to stress that one asks for behaviors that help *oneself,* not the other, to be more effective. This is especially important in sending messages laterally and upward, when the authority of a supervisory relationship is lacking. During this part of the process, people may need some reminding about the requisites for good feedback. The messages should be *hearable:* the other should be able to tolerate being told about the behavior; *testable:* the other should be able to test the meaning of the statement by linking it to observable data (for example, "giving me more lead time" can actually be measured, specific cases can be discussed, and others can offer their perceptions, whereas "trusting me more" cannot be observed objectively); and *actionable:* the other should be able to modify the behavior.
3. The sheets are exchanged so that each person has the messages from all the other participants. This often gives people much more feedback than they have ever had.
4. Each person summarizes the messages and posts those he or she is willing to work on. Note that each participant can screen the messages at this stage. If, for example, one feels that a message is inappropriate or best dealt with privately with the person who sent it, then it need not be posted.
5. Anyone can ask clarifying questions. People can scan the

posted messages. At this stage, the group pauses to make sure that the intent of various messages is clear.

6. In twos or threes, participants begin to negotiate changes in some aspects of their behavior in return for changes on the part of the other. Experience suggests that the most viable agreements are ones in which each party gets something rather than those in which one person graciously offers to change with nothing in return. Despite the good intentions, the latter are often not carried out, in part because team behaviors are interlocked in ways that are difficult to change without movement on both sides of a relationship. For example, if one person wants more time from someone else, that person may need to have someone else take over some responsibilities in order to gain the time to give. Sometimes the agreements can involve three or four people recontracting their responsibilities.

7. Once mutually acceptable agreements have been reached, they are written down so that all parties can monitor them over the coming weeks and can evaluate the success of the discussions at a review session several months later.

Multiple Uses. This process of role negotiation is used in structured team-building situations. It can also be adapted to other uses. In one variation, it is used anonymously in preparation for a retreat that is to focus on one or two roles critical to the team. The consultant tabulates the messages (either oral or written) and at the retreat the group discusses them with the key roles that are being focused on. For example, in work with a governor and his cabinet after the first year, each respondent (staff, cabinet, and the governor) was asked to name the five people with whom he or she was most interdependent and then to give role messages to each. Observing who was most frequently sent messages provided useful information. As would be expected, the patterns showed the asymmetry of many of the relationships: operating secretaries were highly dependent on support or control secretaries (budget, general services, personnel) but not vice versa. In this instance, the patterns from the operating secretaries helped the group reach some useful understandings about the ways they interacted with the budget office. Furthermore, the session sent the governor the message that his cabinet wanted him to spend more time out in the field with them rather than in the state capitol in bureaucratic meetings. It would have been harder for any single secretary to make the point as convincingly, given the asymmetry of power with the governor.

One can also use role negotiation individually to think concretely about a variety of stakeholders, replacing vague feelings of dissatisfaction with a focus on exactly what one wants from them. The specificity often helps one find openings in the normal course of work for bringing up the issue and dealing constructively with it. For example, a director of nursing who was experiencing difficulty with her CEO privately wrote down role messages to him as a way of specifying what she valued and what she wanted changed. One of the behaviors that she wanted was greater clarity about which issues he wanted to be involved in and which he wanted others to take the lead on. She then looked for opportunities to present this request in a hearable way. A new chief operating officer was being recruited, and she developed a plan to use his arrival as a natural entry point into the discussion with the CEO about his patterns of involvement.

A powerful addition to this use of role negotiation is to reverse it, imagining that each of the other stakeholders is giving one feedback about what they want to be more effective in their roles. Often one discovers a woeful ignorance of what the other wants. A new leader, asked what role messages he thought his boss would send to him, replied, "That's a wonderful question. I am not sure." He then began to piece together the fragmentary evidence, but more important he began to strategize how to have a conversation with her about what she wanted from him.

Another variant of the role-negotiation process can be used to explore intergroup issues, such as issues between headquarters and field or the working relationships between engineers and scientists. In this version, it can be incorporated into a questionnaire or an interview schedule. It has been used very successfully in getting staff and line departments to bring out difficulties in their collaboration.

Figure 10 shows the role messages that the staff of a new city manager sent to him and his deputy as part of a retreat to assess the working relationships after the first year. These illustrate the kind of upward feedback that can safely be given to a leader through the anonymous questionnaire method. It is extremely rare that someone uses the process inappropriately to send an attacking, unconstructive comment. It is particularly useful for leaders to get this pattern of feedback from below, to consider what aspects of subordinates' performance may be linked to their own behavior or at least partially explained by some difficulty in the relationship.

The fact that this process communicates what people would like in a relationship does not mean that it is necessarily appropriate or realistic for the leader to make the changes requested. It may simply lead to clarification of the constraints or the reasons behind a particular behavior. Even then such discussions can create a climate where problems are more discussable.

Role negotiation sometimes uncovers vicious circles that have not been visible to all the parties. For example, during an exchange among a top corrections team, it turned out that the deputy wanted to be more involved with prison industries and the secretary wanted him to be more involved, but they had both misunderstood the other's intentions.

A final use of this process is in mediating relationships among subordinates. When two people are experiencing difficulty with each other, the leader can ask both to think about what they want from the other, using the categories from the role-negotiation process (more of, less of, the same). Then asking each to think what the *other* might want may trigger some insights into the failing relationship. In my own work as a third party in many of these triangles, I have found that once people have practiced saying what is on their mind with me and discovered that it is not as devastating as they imagined it to be, they often find ways to communicate it directly to the other person. In the process of giving voice to one's thoughts, they become less frightening. The primitive anxieties over punishments and aggression are lowered as people sort out the thoughts they feel comfortable communicating from those that are too deep to address constructively. Rehearsing the messages ensures that the phrasing will be least likely to contribute to the misunderstandings.

The parties at the top of complex, fast-changing organizations need to find the time to reflect on roles and relationships and how new strategic challenges are reshaping them. Many people who work together every day have never had a reflective conversation on their patterns of interaction directly with each other, although they may have complained frequently to a spouse or colleague. People need to take greater risks in raising these issues because the stakes are high. New leaders need to think more about the distortions they

Figure 10. Role Messages.

To: Director

From: Staff

More:

- Specific assignments, good background and context, what he wants.
- Feedback on work, why he likes some projects, not others.
- Policy clarity, long-term priorities, big picture.
- Overall framework, city's problems.
- Staff involvement in decision making, delegation.
- Accessibility for ad hoc consultation, dialogue.

Less:

- Not clarifying priority rankings, not understanding priority conflicts and complexity of projects, expecting us to jump when requested.
- Cold atmosphere, control, insensitivity to human dimensions, tenseness.
- Withholding information, informing team after the fact.
- Mixed messages; e.g., followup on X requires direct contact but standing policy says no; says work with committee, later thinks he said abolish it.
- Appearance of predisposition, jumping to conclusions.
- Meeting with commissioners and deciding without staff awareness.
- Formality with staff.
- Staff meetings.

The Same:

- Staff contact, availability.
- Open to feedback, involving staff.
- Praise.
- Can-do climate, big picture.
- Moral leadership, activism.
- Meetings.

Figure 10. Role Messages, Cont'd.

To: Deputy Director

From: Staff

More:

- Framework, context, brokering between the director and teams.
  - Brainstorming.
  - Openness and flexibility.
  - Feedback, sharing insights.
  - Individual communication and feedback.
  - Delegation of responsibility.
  - Understanding civil service system.

Less:

- Unclear assignments, withholding information.
- Overattention to detail in writing style of our written work.
- Inability to make decisions.
- Cursory contact.
- Arbitrary deadline setting.

The Same:

- Coordination.
- Accessibility, willingness to listen.
- Confronting issues, focusing, planting seeds for a project.
- Not afraid to look stupid and ask for clarification of an apparently simple matter.
- Mentoring.

---

feel in having these conversations upward and find more effective ways to help their subordinates give them feedback. We too often begin with what we want to tell someone else, instead of working on our inquiry skills to import new perspectives that might have implications for our behavior.

Retreats can be powerful vehicles for reflection on working relationships as well as long-range substantive issues. Particularly when the retreats break the normal daily routines by running into the evening or creating chances to socialize informally, new understandings can result. Third-party facilitation can sometimes be useful in helping a group get perspective on itself or see aspects of its group process that are beneath awareness (Schein, 1969).

The rapid rate of change increases both the difficulties of collaborating and the imperatives of doing so. The top group's investment in critical working alliances can greatly enhance the organization's capacity to implement change effectively, which is discussed in the next chapter.

⌒ Chapter 14

Managing the Pace of Organizational Change

Managing organizational change is a psychological as well as a technical process. The timing of each change and the way it is introduced are as critical to its acceptance by staff and its ultimate success as the substance of the change itself.

Timing Change

In both the public and private sectors, leadership transitions are marked by a honeymoon period. The interest groups that surround the organization grant the new leader an opportunity to resolve major issues. People give the leader the benefit of the doubt and look for positive and hopeful aspects. But a leader is new for only so long. Each decision made will meet with disfavor from one or another constituency. Over time these dissatisfied segments grow and may form blocking coalitions, united in their opposition to the new leader.

Friedman and Friedman (1984, p. 3) have written of new presidential administrations: "A new administration has some six to nine months in which to achieve major changes; if it does not seize the opportunity to act decisively during that period, it will not have another such opportunity. Further changes come slowly or not at all, and counterattacks develop against the initial changes. The temporarily routed political forces regroup, and they tend to mobilize everyone who was adversely affected by the changes, while the proponents of the changes tend to relax after their initial victories."

The honeymoon must be taken as a time to learn about substantive issues, the links to the interest groups both inside and outside the organization, the available levers for the change, and the working alliances needed to run a complex organization. Empirically, Kelly's survey of one hundred new CEOs in 1979 found just such a period of cautious study, suggesting that "new CEOs move slowly in asserting their authority and establishing their imprint on an organization" (1980, p. 37). On the other hand, there are often excellent arguments for moving quickly. We often best understand our goals through concrete trials and reflection on what we have achieved and learned from trying. There is a tradeoff, then, between taking the time to learn what needs to be done and losing the opportunity to do it before the honeymoon is over. The trick for the new leader is to link the growth of the learning curve with the decay of the honeymoon, avoiding the twin errors of moving too quickly and moving slowly. The consequences of making changes too soon are:

- You do not yet fully understand the ramifications of a substantive issue, and therefore miss opportunities to do it right in one step without having to keep tinkering with it.
- You miss political understandings.
- You begin to muddy waters, so you cannot differentiate between what is really going on and reactions to your initial moves.
- You become isolated and encapsulated, losing allies that could have been developed with more time and attention.
- You get out in front of infrastructure, unable to sustain the change.

On the other hand, moving too slowly can mean that:

- You miss a window of opportunity when people are looking to you for new directions, and therefore lose their support.
- You build higher expectations that changes will be fully thought through, and are given less tolerance for mistakes.
- You become socialized to the existing culture, no longer capable of being shocked by its practices or naive about potentially self-imposed limits.

- You begin to own the status quo instead of being able to hold your predecessor responsible for it.

In pacing the change efforts, it is well to recognize the different emotional climates of the succeeding periods of a new administration. The first few months are flush with optimism, hope, and excitement. This period, as we have seen, is particularly useful for learning the issues, building relationships, and beginning the creative development of options. On the downside, the hopefulness that surrounds any new leader can lead to grandiosity, in which both the leader and the followers lose touch with intractable reality and the difficulty of changing even a few aspects of the system, let alone many at once. Working with a governor, his staff, and his cabinet one year into his first term, my colleagues and I saw three shifts: (1) from dreams of what they could do once in power, to a focus on a few issues and an awareness of constraints; (2) from a sense of basic good will and belief in an invisible organization, in which all would carry out their assignments without any oversight or management, to the development of rules, procedures, discipline, and hierarchy; and (3) from a sense of the administration as one big happy family, taking on the world, to a discovery of differences, even opposing points of view, and frustrations with shared issues. The confluence of these three shifts was a turning point in the administration.

This pattern is more pronounced in political administrations or in situations in which a whole new group comes to power at the same time, but all new leaders and their teams come face to face with realities. Sarason (1972) writes that the fantasy of a clean slate gradually erodes as the new team learns that prior events constrain what is currently possible.

Often the very forums that are used to strategize and discuss mission and directions can accentuate the tendency to dream beyond one's capacities. I was working with the leadership of a corporate research laboratory, mentioned in Chapters Nine and Eleven, to revitalize the group after a dramatic cutback in personnel. As the group began to prepare for a three-day, off-site retreat, the list of goals grew longer and more comprehensive until one person commented, "After we finish up these items, we might want to stay an extra day and cure cancer." That joke brought the group back to a more sober sense of the possible.

Not only is there a risk of a surfeit of good ideas, but even those selected for follow-through may overload the change capabilities of the system. New leaders can initiate change with a relatively low investment of their time. It takes only a few hours for a chief executive to think through and decide among several well-staffed options for a problem, but it may require years of effort for others in the organization to implement a solution.

A new superintendent took over a school system with over two hundred schools and an entrenched central bureaucracy that many felt had become uncoupled from the individual schools, each of which had gone its own way on curricular matters and internal policies. The superintendent saw her initial task as rebuilding working relationships among all the elements of the school system and reestablishing some accountability for performance. She launched four major initiatives: (1) a cornerstone initiative of instructional improvement with a standardized curriculum and new testing program that assessed progress with curriculum-referenced tests rather than with achievement tests in only math and English; (2) a strategy for dealing with desegregation that combined limited voluntary busing with focused efforts on improving schools in racially isolated areas of the city; (3) a reorganization of special education to get control of rapidly escalating costs and numbers of students labeled mildly retarded or learning disabled; and (4) accountability through evaluations within the line organization, beginning with a requirement for all principals to observe teachers twice a year and the district superintendent to visit schools and evaluate the principals.

Because she had been an insider, she was able to move quickly to put her team in place, drawing talent from several levels down in the organization and launching the initiatives early in her first year. The planning and development of the initiatives consumed much of that year, and concrete programs and changes moved toward implementation at the beginning of her second year. However, the number and complexity of the initiatives caused a significant bottleneck—they all reached the implementation stage at the same time. Some twenty central divisions such as math curricular specialists, management information systems, and special education needed access to the line side—district superintendents, the principals, and the teachers—for orientation and training. The demand for their time exceeded its availability by several orders of magnitude.

Training time for teachers was in short supply and difficult to create. The union contract limited the uses to which allocated class-preparation hours could be put: shutting down school for training days would provoke outcries from the parents (as the latent custodial function of schools came to the surface) and overtime pay for 11,000 teachers was an impossibility. Even if the time could have been found, some schools were ill equipped to provide the training. Many principals who are excellent administrators do not have the skills to facilitate a curricular planning session on elementary science. Finally, people needed time to digest and assimilate the new initiatives. It is easy to comprehend intellectually that one will be teaching fifth-grade science (perhaps for the first time in ten years) and the rationale behind it. But to actually do it, one needs time to talk it through with colleagues, to get ready to implement.

Identifying and Reallocating Overload

New leaders are often enveloped by a groupthink (Janis, 1982) that makes it difficult for people to question the scope of an agenda. Anyone who suggests that the task is too great or time too short risks being thought disloyal. Quips such as "when the going gets tough, the tough get going" or "the merely difficult we can do today, the impossible tomorrow" suggest this dynamic. The psychological climate is often a heroic culture in which all is regarded as possible. In such a climate, what Schon (1983) calls "undetectable error" may occur. Systems actively work to keep information so diffuse that people can avoid coming to terms with the threat it might contain. The leader keeps the information distributed by discussing different initiatives with different people. Those who set the agenda (the doers) may be unaware of the overload that is created in the followers (the done-bys).

In the work with the school system, we used a structured process that assisted the new leaders and their staffs in making sense of the load that resulted from the new initiatives. The strength of a

structured process is that it formats the information in such a way
that the group is forced to deal with clearly evident patterns. The
process is similar to responsibility charting. A group of managers lists
the major initiatives down the left side of a flip chart and arrays the
major roles and levels across the top. The task then is to fill in the
matrix showing how each role and level will relate to each initiative.
For example, some roles are involved only in the initial policy
discussions, others in designing the system strategies, some in
monitoring for compliance, others in implementing the new
behaviors and systems, and so on. The discussion itself is valuable for
it makes the group look systematically at all the different stakeholders
in a change and assess how they will be affected, not by a single item
but by the set.

   Once the table is filled out, the group looks down each of the
columns to review the impact of the changes on each level and assess
the capacity of that level against the total load that falls on that
group. For example, in the urban school case (see Table 12), two roles
showed up as overloaded, the principals and the teachers. Many of the
initiatives that had different champions at headquarters (recall there
were twenty central staff units) funneled into the school through eight
deputy superintendents to the principals. Each of the initiatives taken
by itself made sense and appropriately had significant responsibilities
for the principals. When taken together, however, they were not
thoughtfully related, and no guidance was given the principals about
their priorities. In the area of planning alone, this process uncovered
five initiatives for which the principal was supposed to submit a
separate plan (school security, truancy, relationships with local
business, special education, and curriculum).

   Eventually, it was decided to combine the different plans in a
single document that made it much easier for the principals to
develop an integrated school plan. The local authorities, rather than
feeling pulled apart by the different staff interests that surrounded the
superintendent, began to feel supported in the difficult work of
integrating all the different initiatives in a single school. At the same
time, the central planning staff began to develop consultation skills
so that, as the new planning requirements created new demands from
the field, they would be able to play supporting roles.

Table 12. Example of Change Load Matrix for an Urban School System.

Initiatives	Superintendent	Central	District	Principals	Teachers
			Roles		
1. Standardize curriculum	Initiate	Design and develop, do training	Monitor	Participate in planning, do training, oversee implementation	Learn new materials, implement a major new curriculum
2. Testing program	Initiate	Monitor contract with external		Administer	Prepare students; administer
3. Desegregation	Negotiate with courts, take lead	Develop school improvement strategy		Implement complex site improvement plan	Implement
4. Special education		Develop policy		Oversee referral process, develop a plan	Learn and use new procedures for referring students
5. Evaluations of teachers, principals	Set the policy	Develop system	Implement the evaluation of principals	Implement the evaluation of teachers	
6. Truancy initiative				Develop the strategy, submit plan	New reporting requirements
7. Link with businesses	Set the policy			Implement the business-school link, develop a plan	
8. Planning		Develop format, process	Review	Develop plans	Participate in plan development
9. School security		Oversight		Develop and implement plan	

This analysis of the load distribution in the school case suggests several possible responses:

1. Integrate initiatives. Some initiatives may lend themselves to be linked in ways that will make them not only easier to implement but more meaningful as well.
2. Shift responsibilities. A closer inspection may make clear that entire initiatives would be better handled at a different level, one that has more resources available.
3. Beef up underloaded roles. Often people who are underused want to have more involvement in the change agendas.
4. Balance initiatives over time by deferring some and phasing others.
5. Support overloaded roles. For example, central staff can be assigned as consultants; peer groups can be developed or resources can be shared in some unique way.

Leverage and Natural Entry Points

Overload can cause erosion of the limited leverage for change at the top. People experience the inability of people at the top to follow through, and they begin to take the initiatives less seriously. One senior manager in the Califano administration at HEW was tired of working on various initiatives, often at the last minute and under unrealistic deadlines, only to see them go nowhere after an initial burst of enthusiasm. He developed a strategy for dealing with Califano's hyperactivity in suggesting new initiatives. He would ignore the first memorandum that requested some analysis or actions; a full third were never heard of again. When he received a reminder, he ignored that too, and another one third would disappear. When a third followup came, he would give a plausible excuse that someone else had failed to tell him and would promise to get on it right away, which he did.

This strategy was in no way evidence of resistance to Califano's leadership. It was rather a defense against his own disappointment from getting excited about many of these initiatives, putting work into them, only to see them come to nothing. The strategy had the effect of making the leader put some of his resources (persistent followup) on the table, before the subordinate would make his commitments.

This approach is similar to the poker maxim to play with other people's money, the currency in this instance being time. You start slowly and then as you win some resources, you play for the larger stakes. As a new leader, your challenge is to signal your seriousness at the lowest cost of your own time. Since this game unfolds over time, credibility is a major concern. If your initial initiatives are not followed through, you need to expend more effort on the next iteration to establish that you are serious. On the other hand, if you pick an initial set carefully and follow through ruthlessly, you can risk a larger number of initiatives the next time because your credibility is enhanced and you can now bluff. This suggests a policy of beginning with a manageable initial set of initiatives and being meticulously attentive to follow through.

Peters (1985) tell the story of Mayor Schaefer of Baltimore, who sent a message to the department that removes abandoned cars about a specific car that he wanted removed. When he did not get the prompt attention he expected, he was appropriately angry in a way that made the department realize his seriousness. He later followed up by sending a memorandum that he had seen another abandoned car that required attention but "was not going to tell where it was located." The department located over six hundred cars in their zeal to get the one to which the mayor was referring.

The concept of leverage is relevant here. Grove (1983) argues that managerial leverage is high when: (1) a small amount of your time affects many people's behavior; (2) a small amount of your time affects one person's behavior over a long time period (for instance, using a performance appraisal to get a person on the right track); or (3) a large group is affected by a critical piece of information that you give to them.

The first chapter of this book contains the idea that leadership transitions themselves are "natural entry points" (Yin, 1976) for changes that would be far more difficult to achieve at other times. Natural entry points include ongoing organizational processes, often beneath notice, that may be vehicles for introducing change with relatively little resistance. For example, recall the case discussed earlier of an industrial basic science lab that was trying to forge a better link to the applied technology and business groups, and thus developed a strategic theme of partnership. The lab had been significantly reduced in size through the transfer of a number of scientists to the applied groups. The leaders failed to link the strategic theme to these personnel transfers, however, and in missing this link, they missed a real opportunity to build bridges. A small amount of time invested at the time of the transfer and shortly thereafter would have made the people transferred feel like a part of the new strategy. Without such a framing, many of them felt they had not made the cut and entered the applied labs with hostility rather than as links.

Natural entry points often have to do with the organization's yearly rhythms. In working with a state office of policy and planning, we charted the monthly work pressures and found a near state of gridlock through the major phases of the budget cycle. The best window for introducing new elements and more active thinking was during the one to two months immediately after legislative approval of the budget before the work on the next cycle began. By preparing for that window and focusing change efforts there rather than when everyone was overloaded, the secretary was more effective in bringing about the desired changes.

Clear goals and rewards help to shape local behavior without central control over the means. Many local groups can be working in parallel and taking different approaches that are sensitive to local differences. Plans that require the participation of the doers are more powerful. In public-sector organizations, despite the frequent attacks, there are many decent, capable employees. Working with incentives and involving people, leaders can bring out latent capabilities and increase the overall resources of the organization.

Managing Stakeholders in the Change Process

Change often causes dislocations and pain to the members of an organization. An effective leader is able to sense the balance of gains and losses from a particular proposal and to work the politics accordingly. Quinn (1980), in his empirical analysis of major strategy shifts in companies, described effective executives as carefully balancing the "young turks" and the "old guard," making sure to create forums for members of both groups to work through the need for change and for stability. Far too frequently, those in a senior executive group forget how long it took them to overcome their own denial of some new business situation that required major adaptations. They move ahead with the changes with little sensitivity to the working-through process that may be necessary at other levels of the organization.

Despite the hope for "win-win" approaches, leadership inevitably involves working through losses for both others and the leader. Zaleznik (1967, p. 68) quotes Douglas McGregor, the famous proponent of Theory Y—that people are motivated to do good work and develop—reflecting on his own exercise of leadership as a college president: "I thought I could avoid being a 'boss.' Unconsciously, I suspect, I hoped to duck the unpleasant necessity of making difficult decisions, of taking responsibility for one course of action among many uncertain alternatives, of making mistakes and taking the consequences. I thought that maybe I could operate so that everyone would like me—that 'good human relations' would eliminate all discord and disappointment. I could not have been more wrong."

In any strategic realignment, there are likely to be one or more powerful, conservative stakeholders within the organization, perhaps someone who was interested in the top job. Rarely are the needed changes so clear that a thoughtful leader will be totally unambivalent about the choice of strategy. The costs and benefits of a change are not equally distributed and often fall unevenly on different stakeholders. Two common patterns are noteworthy and often coexist.

One pattern is for the costs to be felt by powerful members who have substantial stakes in the status quo, with the benefits going to people on the margins who will become more influential on the tide of the new agenda. For example, when Jerome Miller took over the department of youth services in Massachusetts, he faced powerful institutional interests who were aligned against his plans to humanize the institutions and shift to a predominantly community-based service system. Miller found himself in an alliance with nonprofit-service providers outside the system, who were just beginning to become involved in the delivery system against the historic core of his own agency.

Another common pattern is for the beneficiaries of a change to be concentrated in the new dominant coalition and the losers to be people outside the inner circle. One of the central challenges of a leader is to create working alliances into groups that are bearing the costs of the change so that he or she is at least aware of their thinking and feeling and does not fall prey to simplistic stereotypes of them as "resistors" or "mossbacks." To do so, leaders must be in contact with the casualties of their change initiatives and responsible for managing the processes of winning and losing. This stance can be painful for the leader personally, but it is necessary for effectively managing the transition. By confronting the fact that there are casualties, the leader can deal with them fairly.

I have discussed the process of stakeholder mapping earlier (in Chapters Three, Four, and Eleven) as a way of understanding strategic challenges and imagining the interpersonal context for a role. Stakeholder mapping can also be useful in mapping change. As before, the process begins with a simple list of all the stakeholders, anyone who is affected by or can affect a key change under review. The next step is to rank each stakeholder on three attributes: (1) attitude toward the change; (2) power to adopt or veto; and (3) power to shape implementation significantly. With this map, the group can examine coalitional dynamics by listing who influences whom in the network. The completed table gives a sense of the political dynamics that surround a particular change.

A useful way of examining the points of intervention is to construct a table of the four different groups that result from combining people at either end of the power continuum and either end of the favor-oppose continuum (Cohen, 1983). Figure 11 illustrates these four categories and the major strategy implications for each.

First, powerful people who favor the idea should be *organized*. For this group the leader's task is to ensure that the support is channeled appropriately. The leader provides an infrastructure, ensuring that people are kept informed of key meetings or events in the implementation process.

Weak people who favor the idea should be *empowered*. Saul Alinsky was the master of this strategy, organizing communities of people without power in ways that made the power structure take notice. The organizing may be directed at the focal issue or at an unrelated issue that can then be traded for concessions. When used

Figure 11. Strategy Implications for Stakeholder Types.

Power		Attitude	
		Favor	Oppose
	Strong	*Organize*	*Reframe*
	Weak	*Empower*	*Co-opt*

by a leader to garner support for a change, this strategy often takes the form of creating an advisory panel and appointing these stakeholders to it.

Weak people who oppose the idea may be *co-opted*. Opponents of a change are given access to power in exchange for modifying their views. Lord Acton is often quoted about the corrupting influence of absolute power, but Adlai Stevenson reminds us that powerlessness also corrupts. People on the outside are less well informed and may have distorted views of those in power, who in turn often misunderstand those out of power. Co-opting opponents requires some time, because once a disenfranchised group has been given access and influence the first exchanges are often hostile. The group is likely to vent its bottled-up anger at the previous policy and at the people who excluded them, ignoring that the new leader is giving them access. Furthermore, their thinking on the issue may be less well developed, because they have not had the benefit of open discussion of their views. They also often test the commitment of the leader to listen by being provocative and seeing if the invitation to participate is serious. Once this transition is weathered, co-opting can be effective.

Powerful people who oppose the idea are the most difficult to deal with effectively. Co-opting often fails dramatically, because the stakeholders have little to gain—they are already powerful. Bringing them into the decision only provides another forum in which to express their opposition. *Reframing* involves redefining the issue so that they see it in a different light. One of the most common ways of reframing is through linkage. Someone opposed to a change may withdraw the opposition on discovering that the change is linked to other things he or she greatly desires. The Commission on Social Security was able to develop a package that all could support, but if it had been taken apart and voted on item by item, most of its components would have failed to win a majority (Neustadt and May, 1986). The Harvard Negotiation Project (Fisher and Ury, 1981) explores reframing via a conceptual distinction between positions and interests. The Egyptians and Israelis were stalemated on their positions regarding the Sinai, Israel insisting that keeping it was essential, Egypt that giving it up was unthinkable. When the issue was reframed in terms of their interests—Israel's in security, Egypt's in the historical integrity of its boundaries—a demilitarized Sinai became feasible.

Obviously, not all stakeholders can be neatly slotted into these four categories. In most significant changes, however, there are more stakeholders both inside and outside the organization than we are able to keep intuitively inside our heads. A new team at a state corrections agency was able to list over forty groups of significant players as they formulated their strategy. They then focused on eight relationships that they believed could be substantially improved with relatively little effort and assigned different individuals to take the lead. The discussion helped give all the members of the top team a richer inner map of the players who should be kept in mind as they worked on particular issues.

With many stakeholders, the major opportunities for shaping their response to an initiative come during the early phases of the discussion, before positions become hardened and people feel angry for being excluded. Arraying and sorting all the stakeholders helps the leader affirmatively choose strategies rather than angering some group simply as a result of oversight.

Small Wins and Large Gains

In the literature on change, there is much debate about the relative advantages of large, significant changes and small incremental moves. The best approach depends on the specific context, with some circumstances favoring large changes, others favoring incremental approaches.

One approach to the debate is to look at the amount of "flak" that may come from various levels of change. Figure 12 illustrates the relationship. Observe that flak does not increase in direct proportion to the amount of change. Small amounts of change can often be introduced virtually unnoticed. This is shown in Zone A, where a relatively large amount of change produces relatively little flak. In Zone B, a threshold is crossed, and the growth in the amount of the outcry is disproportionate to the amount of change. Rather than get caught in this zone, it is often better to go for all the change one wants, Zone C, because the amount of flak may reach a plateau. Zone C suggests an advantage to bundling related changes. In any significant change effort, there will be considerable anxiety and disorientation. For the same amount of flak, one can often get a significantly greater amount of change by linking. For example, reorganizing and changing personnel at the same time can combine two traumas effectively. Physical moves can also provide an excellent opportunity to introduce changes.

Weick (1984) has elaborated the strategy of small wins, especially in the context of large, overwhelming social problems. Small wins are defined as concrete, complete, implemented outcomes of moderate importance, similar to those in Zone A. They can be either important changes in unimportant variables or unimportant changes in important variables. Weick argues that the overwhelming feelings of helplessness, frustration, and anxiety associated with the complexity and interdependence of today's problems have the effect of reducing our creativity. He suggests framing problems in focused ways that make us better able to achieve creative responses. The satisfaction gained from real progress early on, Weick says, can

Figure 12. Flak/Change Ratio.

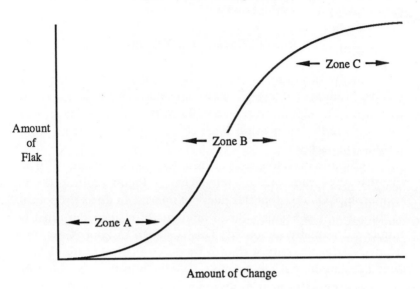

provide the momentum for tackling further problems down the line. Alcoholics Anonymous, for example, emphasizes staying sober "one day at a time." The alcoholic can experience each day as a victory without confronting the overwhelming prospect of staying sober forever. Feminists have focused on convincing prestigious publications to avoid sexism in their style guidelines. At five Du Pont plants, minor technical changes accounted for over two thirds of the cost reductions between 1929 and 1960.

Small wins can significantly alter the stakeholder field around an issue by giving hope to supporters, attracting new allies, lowering resistance to future steps, and changing the frame within which the debate is experienced. They are occasions for learning and adaptation that often test assumed constraints. Because the immediate stakes are low, they do not arouse the anxiety that can lead to rigidity in the introducing of major changes. A sequence of small wins is not easily predictable, because they must be experienced and lived with before the next appropriate step can be determined. They cannot be set out like milestones on a classic project management chart. Yet they are like building blocks, visible accomplishments that cannot be easily taken away, so they help rebuild the organization's sense of its ability to implement.

A small win may in fact be the recognition and celebration of a change that is already occurring but has not been noticed. For example, a magnet high school had fallen on hard times. Its standards had slipped, and its enrollment had declined. A new principal revitalized the school and began to turn the tide, but for some time after the situation improved, the school's reputation lagged. A newspaper article calling attention to the numbers of former private and parochial school students who now attended this high school was a significant small win in the overall strategy of regaining preeminence. Emery (Emery and Trist, 1973) notes that the future is always with us in the present but goes unnoticed because it often is parasitical on some dominant process, drawing resources until it is powerful enough to break out as a trend on its own. The noticing of such a trend can be a significant small win and signal the beginning of a new direction.

Small wins can catch the attention of people who have short time perspectives or who suffer from information overload. They are not so big as to arouse opposition, and they can be subversive. A nice example of a subversive small win is flex time. Initially flex time looks reasonably simple and contained, and it can be implemented reasonably quickly. For many organizations, however, it contains several powerful developmental features. First, it makes supervisors look beyond tardiness as their major way of checking up on employees. Second, if the workers are laterally interdependent, they need to plan more because they cannot take for granted that they will all be available throughout the day. Flex time can make the lateral interdependencies more visible and develop them further. Finally, flex time begins a process of acknowledging differences in people's preferences and motivations that helps everyone capitalize on the different strengths.

A leadership change is itself a window for introducing other changes, yet care must be taken to fully capitalize on the opportunities. The hope that attends a new leader's arrival can be rapidly transformed into despair by errors in timing, initial choices of what to change, and the overall scale and pace of change.

༔ *Chapter 15*

Preparing the Organization for Future Transitions

The organization of this book has imposed a chronological structure on the story of leadership transitions. First, an organization or an individual decides to make a leadership change. Then the appointing authorities think strategically about the organization and the characteristics of the desired leader. An active search is undertaken to find candidates, who are then carefully screened and checked out prior to the final selection. The new leader begins, building the necessary working alliances with existing staff and assembling a team of new and old. The new leadership team sets directions, reorganizes, and manages the change agendas.

Yet in reality these processes are going on simultaneously at various levels in most organizations all the time. At a major teaching hospital, a vice-president for health affairs, who has been in office a year while simultaneously retaining his former role as dean of the medical school, is feeling his way toward the right structure for a new organization of the medical center. After a year, a search begins to fill the dean's role. The hospital has a new CEO after fourteen months of acting leadership, following on a failed new leader from the outside, who served only two years. The director of nursing position has acting leadership while an executive recruiting firm searches for a full-time director. The acting nursing director serves on the search committee for a new chief operating officer; the acting occupant in that role is one of the finalists. A new chief financial officer for the clinical practices, one of the major elements in the medical center, is just starting. At the trustees' level, new leadership of the board subcommittee that oversees the medical center is asking new questions.

It is only from the perspective of one role at one level of an organization that one can hold to a simple story line of a leadership transition. When we turn to the team, we see a pattern of constant change. In any complex organization, little time passes without a change in leader, a change in an important subordinate, a change in an important peer, or a change in a key external relationship. Each of these changes involves not only the dyadic relationship of the new person to others but new triangles and coalitions. We still speak about and collect statistics on the tenure in a role, but increasingly we are beginning to see the importance of thinking about the length of time that key relationships survive. As we saw in Chapter One, almost a third of the key relationships at the top of federal agencies do not survive more than a year (Heclo, 1977). Considering the time it takes to develop the necessary understanding between just two individuals in a complex organization, one is left with a trivially short time for the relationship to deliver value for the organization. The rate of recomposition of key relationships can threaten institutional memory. Organizations may suffer from the kind of problem that John Paul Vann, a retired lieutenant colonel, insightfully diagnosed as critical in Vietnam, that "the United States has not been [there] for ten years, but for one year ten times" (Gabriel and Savage, 1978, p. 87).

We may be approaching the era of what Toffler (1971) calls "adhocracy." Our organizations are no longer the enduring institutions of old but assemblages of parts. The assemblage of a French designer, an American marketing organization, and a Korean manufacturer who join to produce a line of shirts may, within a year, shift some or all of its parts. Like movie producers who assemble and disassemble the elements of a film, leaders and followers have to develop their skills at recruiting, joining, direction setting, organizing, and managing change among short-lived teams of people.

We need to match hopes of finding leaders who can articulate a genuine vision, infuse the organization with a sense of purpose, moderate conflicts, and defend the integrity of the enterprises with the realities of the instabilities of key relationships. We risk replicating in the wider society what Gabriel and Savage (1978) think has happened to the military, with its emphasis on "up and out" and rapid rotation of leaders through units. They cite a study that finds a pattern of the "ambitious, transitory commander— marginally skilled in the complexities of his duties—engulfed in producing transitory results, fearful of personal failure, too busy to talk with or listen to his subordinates, and determined to submit acceptably optimistic reports which reflect faultless completion of a variety of tasks at the expense of the sweat and frustration of his subordinates" (p. 94). The scenario of rapidly rising and rotating leaders, loosely linked to their organizations, is particularly galling to middle managers, who have seen their ranks significantly trimmed and their own rates of advancement slowed considerably.

The argument of this book is that if we wish leaders to deliver on the hopes we project onto them, we need to manage much more intelligently the entire cycle of leadership transitions; for each of the aspects of the transition discussed here, we need to learn more systematically how to improve the handling of that phase. We need to acknowledge that the environment of what Peter Vaill calls "permanent whitewater" requires us to think and act differently in both taking and exercising leadership. If we are to capitalize on leadership transitions as opportunities and prevent the risks they pose, we face new imperatives at many stages in the process.

New Imperatives

1. Leaders must foster a significant increase in the general capacity for "managing change and ambiguity" (McCaskey, 1982) in organizations, reducing the dependency on paternalistic leaders who make unrealistic guarantees of no surprises. In the recent wave of writings about our need for leadership, we see two strains: one nostalgic and regressive that yearns for the "good old days" when people felt protected and cared for by their leaders, the other calling our attention to the need for each of us to shoulder more of the burdens of leadership at all levels of an organization from the shop floor to the board room. John Gardner tells the lovely story of a little girl in kindergarten who tells her teacher she is drawing a picture of God. The teacher replies, "But Mary, no one knows what

God looks like." Little Mary replies confidently, "Well, they will when I get through" (Gardner, 1965). Tunstall (1985) tells of a middle manager who in the early stages of the breakup of AT&T developed a book of planning assumptions that were simply best guesses and ranges of possible outcomes that others could use in beginning to plan on a wide variety of fronts. Leaders from the top must authorize and encourage people at all levels to step forward and absorb relevant uncertainties, thereby creating the necessary conditions for others to take initiative in their areas.

2. Leaders need to stay ruthlessly focused on the mission of the organization and the critical success factors for the organization. As uncertainty increases, the more the leader and others need some guiding north star to orient themselves as the terrain around them seems ever more confusing. When vacancies arise or are created, they can then be examined in relationship to the mission of the organization and used as opportunities to reinforce the desired values and orientation and to import necessary new skills that will add value to the organization's capacity to meet its goals.

3. Leaders need to be more reflective about how committed they are to an organization and when is the right time to let go. If they have had a clear strategic focus, they may have a better sense of when a natural stage of the organization has come to a close. If they experience themselves as not sure about what the next chapter holds for the organization, then it may be time to think about moving on. Boards play a critical role in this process. Few boards take seriously their assessment of the chief executive against the stated mission of the organization. Even more difficult is to think afresh about the mission and end up with a conclusion that the current chief executive is performing adequately against the current plan, but that he or she is poorly equipped to take the organization to the next stage of its development. Yet no one is well served by colluding in sustaining a leader who is not adequate to the task. There has been too little writing or thinking about leaving and letting go. When is the right time? What accomplishments feel stable, and which seem likely to be swept away by a new leader?

Few leaders have people that can help them think about the right time to leave. People inside the organization might misunderstand. Leaders need to find outside confidants with whom they can talk candidly about the right time to leave. Even the microtiming of when to leave within the rhythms of the organization is important to think about. I respect individuals who stay to the end of an outgoing elected leader's term of office. Many jump during the final year, leaving a very difficult situation: the elected leader must make either interim appointments or attempt to attract someone into government for a very short tenure. Part of the reason people leave early is they cannot tolerate the thoughtful working through of the ending of an administration. Because we have too few rituals that surround leavings and endings in organizations, there are many who simply jump ship into the personal excitement of a new situation, leaving others to cope with the important work of a competent, thoughtful transition.

In this world learning to manage these transitions is a core skill for all the stakeholders. One needs to understand what a transition means, not only from one's own perspective but also from the viewpoint of others. Increasingly often, a leader in the midlife of an initiative will face negotiating with a new boss who is flush with the excitement of a beginning. An outgoing leader will need to work with an incoming leader in ways that do not put the organization at risk during the transition, causing critical omissions such as those that led to the *Challenger* tragedy and the Bay of Pigs fiasco.

4. The vitality of boards must be maintained. Boards are particularly vulnerable in light of the increased rate of change. Often a new board member is just becoming comfortable when the leader changes. Alternatively, the slow socialization of new board members may prevent the freshness of their point of view from being brought to bear promptly on the critical issues facing the organization. Here is a particularly important area for inventing processes that speed up the building of the necessary working relationships to get work done.

5. We need to develop the skills of all the parties to a transition to build the necessary working alliances. As Reich (1987) has argued, we need to reconnect leaders and followers and think more about teams than about the individual entrepreneurial hero. Effective teams are resilient. They are capable of absorbing new members, both being revitalized by the new perspectives that

outsiders bring as well as socializing them to the relevant history and norms of the group. Teams are adaptive when the roles are sufficiently flexible that people can cover for the missing skills of a departed member during a transition and can renegotiate tasks and responsibilities to capitalize on the particular competencies of a replacement.

Leaders must get much better at managing departures of key people. They will then be more able to make the personal transition, and remaining team members will feel that if they should end up leaving, they will be handled fairly.

6. Leaders who wish to be effective in managing transitions strategically will need to develop executive recruiting skills. Those who have become skillful at defining the key challenges, translating those into specifications for candidates, searching, screening, and selecting are finding that these skills serve them admirably in their leadership assignments. One executive, who served as an internal recruiter early in his career, keeps a book of names of people who strike him as talented and dips into it whenever he finds himself needing particular competencies. In a sense, leaders must be constantly in the talent-recruiting business, scanning, collecting, and filing away for some unanticipatable occasion when that skill may be needed. Organizations will also have to have more internal people taking executive recruiting roles or working with outside recruiting as a deliberate part of building their future ability to be leaders.

Alternatively, organizations will develop retainer relationships with executive search firms so that they will not lose time in doing a thorough screening of search firms when a vacancy arises. The working alliance between an executive and the recruiter will be in place and a particular search can commence immediately. Organizations will develop standard processes for filling key vacancies that guide who to involve and how, and outline the generic steps. At the close of each recruiting episode, the experience will be systematically reviewed to ensure that the next occasion profits from the lessons.

The choices of which roles a leader focuses on quickly and fills promptly send clear messages about directions. Nothing will undermine an initiative more than a prolonged period of indecision and indirection about how to proceed to fill a key vacancy in that area. An explicit choice not to fill it but to place its functions under another executive, a quick filling of the job with a thoughtfully chosen executive, or a tightly managed executive search each sends a signal that the uncertainties and risks associated with absent leadership are being addressed. People can tolerate ambiguity when they are kept informed about the reasons why decisions cannot yet be reached and when they feel that someone is worrying on their behalf. When they see a vacuum, they rightly become unproductively anxious.

7. Leaders must search actively both within and without. Far too often leaders do not see the broader executive potential of insiders because they have overcategorized an individual in a current assignment. Search processes are an opportunity to see many staff with fresh lenses.

8. All managers will need to work on their joining skills as they take permanent or temporary roles as the head of work groups. Larry Meachum, the former director of corrections in Oklahoma, conducts workshops for subordinates who have recently taken new assignments (Friedman, 1986). He has invented a "learning journey," which each employee takes as part of the transition ritual, building up a picture of the role from outside in by interviewing all the key others who relate to the role and beginning to create the necessary working relationships with them before stepping into the role. Groups of six to eight people who are experiencing transitions at the same time come together to explore common patterns in their experiences. As they reflect on how they and others manage the transitions, they build up their repertoire of skills so that they will be even more effective in subsequent transitions.

9. Leaders must model directness and encourage the relevant parties to talk directly to one another. During leadership transitions, different camps easily emerge: people associated with the old leader, the new dominant coalition, insiders involved in the search process, outsiders not involved, headquarters versus field, and so on. Increased communications within each group and reduced communications among groups both create and sustain these splits in an organization. Leaders must find ways to work against the natural tendencies for people to vent within safe homogeneous groups, and

instead to tap the energy that the talk represents when it can be harnessed constructively to the difficult challenges that the organization faces.

10. Because of the rate of change and the net increase in ambiguity, leaders must redundantly communicate new directions. A new direction is not truly believed until people see the shift embodied in a critical personnel decision—to remove someone or to replace him or her with someone with a significantly different background. Similarly, a reorganization may be viewed as a paper shuffle until followed up with hard decisions about who is included and excluded at executive staff meetings. Physical changes can powerfully underscore new organizational initiatives.

11. Leaders need to acknowledge that one of their central tasks, from the first moment of arrival, is to prepare the organization for future transitions at multiple levels. Leaders are not indispensable and cannot collude with their organizations in making themselves so. From the moment of their arrival, they need to be thinking of their tenure in the context of the organization's history and its future. They need to address the issues of succession, perhaps less by focusing on a particular individual but more by attending to the development of many important team members whose different skills and strengths offer the organization some hedge against future changes that may make one skill more relevant to an emerging future than another.

Leaders must find ways to authorize talented subordinates to represent the organization, thereby getting exposure to critical outside stakeholders as well as having to transcend their particular narrow role and think across the entire organization. Even small occasions can help this process along. Many executives who believe that those under them have been too sheltered from political process will bring along subordinates to critical budget hearings, have them make a presentation to a legislative subcommittee, or have them present departmental legislation relevant to their area so that they get experience in critical forums that are necessary to their development.

12. Leaders need to see themselves as stewards of the role they occupy. They need to think and act on behalf of future occupants, knowing that painful choices they must make, which may result in

personal attacks, may well produce results that some future leader will get credit for. Leaders must be seeking to increase the authority and competence in the organization to match the ambiguities they face. Just as we talk of a weakened or strengthened presidency at the national level, each leader takes a role that has been shaped by predecessors and will be empowered or enfeebled by his or her choices.

The Consequences of Failure

In the end, if our institutions are to survive, there will need to be much more attention to the damage that can result from failed transitions, both to people and to organizations. Martin Davis of Gulf + Western has remarked, "You can't be emotionally bound to any particular asset" (Prokesch, 1987, p. 8). I believe that such an attitude is a maladaptive response to the pain that lies beneath the making and breaking of relationships as one leads any complex organization. Leaders must be attuned to the emotional connections of people to one another and to their work and become more skilled at working through the issues that arise as people come and go.

Just as we have developed a new awareness of the stages of death and dying, just as birth has become more of a process than an event, just as we have developed support groups for helping people cope with difficult personal transitions such as divorce, so too within the organizational world we must invent new ways of helping teams come together and disband that acknowledge the instability of any particular grouping. In well-designed retreats leaders and followers may learn more about one another than they would in months of routine interactions. Third-party assistance can help renegotiate difficult relationships that have been stalemated for years. The rate of change is too great and the costs of not adapting are too high to leave these issues to chance, hoping that time will take care of the difficulties.

We must search for transforming leadership that "ultimately becomes moral in that it raises the level of human conduct and ethical aspiration of both leader and led, and thus it has a transforming effect on both" (Burns, 1978, p. 20). Levinson and Rosenthal (1984, pp. 288–289) write at the end of their study of six major business leaders, "These leaders loved their companies. How else can one understand the narcissistic grandiosity that compelled each to devote his ordinary working life to making his company the best in the world? And, even more significantly, in the service of that grandiosity, when it came time to retire, the ability of each to let go? . . . Only the true leader, like the parent who enables his child to leave home when he grows up, can leave his company in the hands of others, having assured himself that his job is done. Not to let go is to manipulate and exploit in one's own self-interest. To be able to endure the pain of letting go takes deep and abiding affection."

Transitions are critical moments in the lives of organizations and individuals that stir such deep waters that often we can endure them only by failing to confront the opportunities and dangers that they contain.

Appendix: Biographical Interview Sample

by John Isaacson

Generally speaking, managers behave consistently through-out their careers. They repeat many of the same successful and unsuccessful patterns in each succeeding job.

No one comes to management fully equipped to set strategy, to assess risk, to test the real world, to bear pain, to relearn the obvious, to reward loyalty, and to discipline foolishness. Those are learned arts, and they most often include personal learning in which the ardent manager reworks patterns of choice that are deeply rooted in his or her own personality.

Biographical interviews are chronological stories. Candidates generally tell their stories easily and naturally. Candidates with well-formed and stable identities can tell you, in a reflective way, how they have changed with experience. Those are the most attractive candidates.

A biographical interview begins at the beginning, with home, neighborhood, and community. You want to hear some of that story. You are not engaged in psychotherapy and you are not probing deeply into the unconscious mind. You are surveying the landscape, looking for consistent themes. From there, you should take the interview through schools, looking for intellectual development, for the social skills of leadership, and for the signs of independence.

Source: Isaacson, 1983.

"Which town, what kind of community?"

You are looking for a candidate's capacity to describe an environment, particularly one that counts. If you get a brief and meaningless "grew up in the Bronx, it wasn't bad," stop. Ask the person to tell you what it was like. Explain that you have never been there, you would like to understand the setting, or ask if it was different then from now and how it has changed. Push on next to see how the candidate's parents got there.

"Has your family always lived in the Bronx?"
"Did you grow up in a large, extended family?"

The qualities that have to do with the presentation of self are rooted in parents and surrounding family. You probe for them, leading up to them through Dad's career or Mom's career.

As you hear some of Dad's or Mom's character show through, you pop a question:

"Was he or she hard to get along with?"

You will be surprised how often you get the answer,

"Yes," or, "What do you mean?"

Do not leave it there. Follow it:

"Well, was he an easy man? Someone people could talk to easily?"

"Not exactly. Fathers are like that. You only get to know them when you grow up."

You know something. Authority is distant and uninvolved. It does not get in there and grapple with problems. It's the boss. It protects, but does not solve.

You next want to explore the family context. You have two goals: Dad's and Mom's careers and family politics.

"Dad got a job with Acme Bleach. They were located nearby."

"Was it a good job for him?"

"I suppose so."

"What was his career?"

You always want to know the career story of the family, Dad, Mom, grandparents, stepparents, whoever brought this man or woman up. What you want to know about the parents' work is "Did they like their work?" and "What imperative messages did they pass on?"

I remember a brilliant son whose father had had a meteoric career in advertising. At fifty, Dad felt cheated. He did not believe in ads. His work meant nothing to him. He had been loyal for too long, to one company, in one industry. His message to his son was "Do only what you want to do." The son has no institutional loyalties, but has a very deep streak of personal integrity.

Always there are guiding myths. All parents send some fundamental messages about work. Their pathways and successes or failures, the very language that surrounded their careers establish myths. You will find an echo in the son or daughter. Nothing runs deeper. You want to hear and understand the myths. Examine the candidate's awareness of these myths, as well, for the degree to which he or she understands the influence of the parents' stories.

The second set of themes is political. You are probing to find how this candidate views authority. Nothing is more basic to work and nothing is harder. Every twenty-two-year-old launching a career carries a small mountain of unresolved parental conflict. He thinks of fathers as demanding and unresponsive, or weak and uninformed, or informed and unresponsive, or powerful and demanding, or whatever. He thinks of mothers as silent or vocal, as reassuring or frantic, as dependable or as powerful. A large family may have been a tyranny or a fluid and supportive culture for a kid, or both. A young person will automatically, readily, without any conscious thought, project these core assumptions about family politics onto the organization he or she joins. Over time, a person who has the normal capacity to mature will sort out that this boss behaves very differently from Dad and this organization does not look anything like three generations of Italians all living in the Bronx. Alas.

The most important thing to learn about any candidate is how comfortable he or she is with authority. Can she act decisively without demanding personal submission? Can he report decisively, staking out his convictions, without the hint of rebellion? Can she sell in the market without fear of rejection? Can he win and lose, both and readily, and retain composure and friends? Do not let it go:

> "Where are the men in the family reunions?"
>
> "Oh, in the middle. They get feasted. And they lead the singing."

Men are at least ceremonial and engaged. We still do not know who wields discipline (mothers, I guess) and how the world of work connects to the family.

> "Did your mother ever have a career?"
>
> "Now she does. She's got a shop. It does real well. She's made some money, and she really likes it."

We know a bit more. We have confirmed her as an activist and identified a charismatic act.

You cannot push these things too far. Some people just will not talk about their families. Do not press for it. It must be voluntary. Be aware of reticence, though, and in the later discussions of the candidate probe for defensiveness and for anger.

The key themes in college are independence and learning to learn. More precisely, learning to learn technically complex material. Look for some evidence of hard work, of grinding through a topic and mastering it.

The second arena to explore is a social career. People often find a first opportunity for leadership or mastery while in school. It may be in sports, in student politics, or in a job. If a person has any fire, he or she will have done something—and it will have clues for you.

As a career develops and a person acquires depth and the possibilities of command, you want to know to what degree your prospective manager routinely, instinctively, rethinks the obvious. Are the habits of mind necessary to creativity there? Look for involvement in budgets and numbers. Ask how the manager keeps on top of projects or tasks. Ask about personal order—time, files, desk. Early in careers, people do not know how to handle these things. It helps if you can hear some of the struggle of this first managerial role. And it is always reassuring to discover a sense of humor about early failings.

Probe for drive, for the hours, the commitment, the vision, and also for the relationship with the boss.

In mid-career, mature, third, fourth, or subsequent jobs, you want to hear evidence of unusual and penetrating thought, and the capacity to move people, not just subordinates. Mature managers need to wield their authority, to have their presence felt, up, down, and sideways. A manager needs to be a persuasive, balanced, even, harmonious personality, who sells his program—whether political or commercial—in the marketplace, in the front office, and with the staff. At the highest levels of management, getting things done requires the marriage of a flexible, set-breaking mind to a visionary purpose, sufficient to inspire people to do what they would not ordinarily do.

It's an old saying that the world is not run by brilliant people, it is run by sound people. It is surprising how often mediocre intelligences run credible operations for long periods of time. They have learned something basic—that ordinary people, well and responsibly governed, can do great work.

There is one additional quality to probe for. It is more obvious in the public sector than in the private, but it is equally essential in both. A good manager cannot run a first-class institution without profound moral convictions that run deep and true and that the whole organization will recognize and salute. We tend to think of ethics as a private matter, public only for elected officials and cases of theft. It is not so. Moral conviction about the quality of one's work is essential to any decent management.

∽ Bibliography

Ackoff, R. *Redesigning the Future.* New York: Wiley, 1974.

Ahern, W. R. "Reorganizing Without Too Much Pain." *Journal of Policy Analysis and Management,* 1983, *2* (3) (Spring), 462–465.

Alderfer, C. P. "The Invisible Director on Corporate Boards." *Harvard Business Review,* 1986, *64* (6), 38–50.

"Alum Fights in Trenches of State Government." *Wharton News Update,* Dec. 1986, p. 5.

Argyris, C., and Schon, D. *Organizational Learning: A Theory of Action Perspective.* Reading, Mass.: ddison-Wesley, 1978.

Arvey, R. D., and Campion, J. E. "The Employment Interview: A Summary and Review of Recent Research." *Personnel Psychology,* 1982, *35,* 281–322.

Auletta, K. *The Art of Corporate Success.* New York: Penguin Books, 1985.

Beckhard, R., and Harris, R. T. *Organizational Transitions: Managing Complex Change.* Reading, Mass.: Addison-Wesley, 1977.

Behn, R. D. "The Massachusetts Department of Revenue." Unpublished paper, The Governor Center, Institute of Policy Science and Public Affairs, Duke University. Dec. 18, 1985, pp. 1–31.

Bennis, W. *The Unconscious Conspiracy: Why Leaders Can't Lead Associations.* New York: AMACOM, 1976.

Bennis, W., and Nanus, B. *Leaders: The Strategies for Taking Charge.* New York: Harper & Row, 1985.

Bernstein, P. "Going Outside Can Be Dangerous." *Fortune*, 1980, *102* (3), 185.

Bion, W. R. *Experience in Groups and Other Papers*. London: Tavistock Publications, 1961.

Bivens, T. "At the Top the Pink Slip Is Showing." *Philadelphia Inquirer*, May 3, 1987, p. 1.

Boorstin, R. "Parking Bureau: Strides After Turmoil." *New York Times*, Feb. 25, 1987, p. B1.

Bowen, M. "Bowen on Triangles—March 1974 Workshop, Part 1." *The Family*, 1974a, *2* (1) (Fall), 45–48.

Bowen, M. "Bowen on Triangles—March 1974 Workshop, Part 2." *The Family*, 1974b, *2* (1) (Fall), 35–38.

Brauer, C. M. *Presidential Transitions: Eisenhower through Reagan*. New York: Oxford University Press, 1986.

Brettschneider, E. "Remarks." In M. Steeg (ed.), *Strategies for Serving Families with Children in Residential Treatment*. Dobbs Ferry, N.Y.: The Children's Village Symposium, 1985.

Burns, J. M. *Leadership*. New York: Harper & Row, 1978.

Butterfield, F. "Harvard Alters Recruiting of Faculty." *New York Times*, Sept. 2, 1986, p. A14.

Califano, J. A. *Governing America: An Insider's Report from the White House and the Cabinet*. New York: Simon & Schuster, 1981.

Chandler, A. D. *Strategy and Structure*. Cambridge, Mass.: MIT Press, 1962.

Cohen, B. J. "The Planner as Reticulist: Network Interventions in a Human Services Setting." Unpublished doctoral dissertation, Department of Social Systems Science, Wharton School, University of Pennsylvania, 1983.

Cowherd, D. M. "On Executive Succession: A Conversation with Lester B. Korn." *Human Resource Management*, 1986, *25* (2), 335–347.

de Bono, E. *Lateral Thinking*. London: Penguin Books, 1970.

Delucca, J. Presentation at a Wharton School Seminar. Philadelphia, Pennsylvania, 1984.

de Rham, C. Letter to Joseph Featherstone, May 23, 1983.

Drucker, P. F. "How to Manage the Boss." *Wall Street Journal*, Aug. 1, 1986, p. 16.

Emery, F., and Trist, E. L. *Towards a Social Ecology: Contextual Appreciation of the Future in the Present.* New York and London: Plenum, 1973.

Etzioni, A. "The Democrats Need a Unifying Theme." *New York Times,* Oct. 5, 1984, p. A31.

Fancher, C. B. "How Gregorian Lost the Penn Presidency." *The Philadelphia Inquirer,* Oct. 26, 1980, pp. 1b, 4b.

Fisher, R., and Ury, W. *Getting to Yes: Negotiating Agreement Without Giving In.* Boston: Houghton Mifflin, 1981.

Fix, J. L. "Mellon Bank's Course Is Steady: CEO Search Underway." *Philadelphia Inquirer,* May 13, 1987a, p. 7f.

Fix, J. L. "New Mellon Chairman Selects a Finance Chief." *Philadelphia Inquirer,* July 9, 1987b, p. 8b.

"Following the Corporate Legend." *Business Week,* Feb. 11, 1980, pp. 62-67.

Fombrun, C. "Conversation with Reginald H. Jones and Frank Doyle." *Organizational Dynamics,* 1982, *10* (3), 46-63.

Foundation of the American College of Hospital Administrators, Ad Hoc Committee. *Evaluating the Performance of the Hospital Chief Executive Officer.* Chicago, 1984, p. 1.

Fowler, E. M. "Finding Your Way to the Top." *New York Times,* June 13, 1984, p. D19.

Freeman, R. E. *Strategic Management: A Stakeholder Approach.* Boston: Pitman, 1984.

Freund, C. M. "The Tenure of Directors of Nursing." *The Journal of Nursing Administration,* Feb. 1985, pp. 11-15.

Friedman, M., and Friedman, R. *Tyranny of the Status Quo.* New York: Avon Books, 1984.

Friedman, S. D. "Managing Succession Systems." Unpublished working paper, Philadelphia, 1986.

Friedman, S. D., and LeVino, T. P. "Appraisal and Development in the General Electric Company." In C. J. Fombrun, N. M. Tichy, and M. A. Devanna (eds.), *Strategic Human Resource Management.* New York: Wiley, 1984.

Gabarro, J. "Stages in Management Succession: The Process of Taking Charge." Unpublished working paper prepared for Harvard Reunion Weekend Program, n.d.

Gabarro, J. "When a New Manager Takes Charge." *Harvard Business Review*, 1985, *63* (3), 110–123.

Gabriel, R. A., and Savage, P. L. *Crisis in Command: Mismanagement in the Army.* New York: Hill and Wang, 1978.

Galbraith, J. *Designing Complex Organizations.* Reading, Mass.: Addison-Wesley, 1973.

Galbraith, J. *Organizational Design.* Reading, Mass.: Addison-Wesley, 1977.

Gamson, W. A., and Scotch, N. R. "Scapegoating in Baseball." *American Journal of Sociology*, 1964, *70* (1), 69–76.

Gardner, J. W. "Some Maladies of Leadership." *Annual Report.* New York: Carnegie Corporation, 1965.

Gargan, E. A. "The Secret Courting of Robert Kiley." *New York Times*, Oct. 7, 1983, p. 38.

Gaul, G. M., and Bivens, T. "DiBona Says He's Quitting the Chamber." *The Philadelphia Inquirer*, Aug. 8, 1986, p. 8a.

Gerstein, M., and Reisman, H. "Strategic Selection: Matching Executives to Business Conditions." *Sloan Management Review*, 1983, *24* (2) (Winter), 33–49.

Gilbert, M. *Winston Churchill: Finest Hour.* Vol. 6: *1939–1941.* Boston: Houghton Mifflin, 1985.

Gilmore, T. N. "Managing Collaborative Relationships in Complex Organizations." *Administration in Social Work*, 1977, *3* (2) (Summer), 167–180.

Gilmore, T. N., and Brown, R. A. "Effective Leadership Succession as a Critical Event in Social Agencies." *Administration in Social Work*, 1985, *9* (4), 25–35.

Gilmore, T. N., and Hirschhorn, L. "The Downsizing Dilemma: Leadership in the Age of Discontinuity." *The Wharton Annual*, 1984, *8*, 94–104.

Gilmore, T. N., and McCann, J. E., "Designing Effective Leadership Transitions for New Correctional Leaders." In J. W. Doig (ed.), *Criminal Corrections: Ideals and Realities.* Lexington, Mass.: Lexington Books, 1983.

Gilmore, T. N., and Nelson, R. "Responsibility Charting in Corrections." *Federal Probation*, June 1978, pp. 87–94.

Gilmore, T. N., and Schall, E. "The Use of Case Management as a Revitalizing Theme in a Juvenile Justice Agency." *Public Administration Review*, 1986, *46* (3) (May/June), 267-274.

Goldman, A. "Acting Transit Chief." *New York Times*, Aug. 22, 1983, p. B3.

Goleman, D. "When the Boss Is Unbearable." *New York Times*, Dec. 28, 1986, sec. 3, pp. 1, 29.

Grove, A. S. *High Output Management*. New York: Random House, 1983.

Hale, C. D. "Selecting the Right Police Chief: Guidelines for the Municipal Administrator." *Target*, International City Management Association, 1979, *8* (4), 1-2.

Hamburger, P. "Searching for Gregorian I." *New Yorker*, 1986a, *62* (8), 45-61.

Hamburger, P. "Searching for Gregorian II." *New Yorker*, 1986b, *62* (9), 53-68.

Harrison, R. "Role Negotiation: A Tough-Minded Approach to Team Development." In *Social Technology of Organization Development*. La Jolla, Calif.: University Associates, 1976.

Harvey, J. B. "The Abilene Paradox: The Management of Agreement." *Organizational Dynamics*, 1974, *3* (1), 63-80.

Hechinger, F. M. "College Presidencies in State of Decline." *New York Times*, Sept. 18, 1984, sec. C, p. 6.

Hechinger, F. M. "Short Tenures Reflect Troubles of College Chiefs." *New York Times*, Mar. 18, 1986, p. 12.

Heclo, H. *A Government of Strangers: Executive Politics in Washington*. Washington: Brookings Institution, 1977.

Herbst, P. G. *Sociotechnical Design*. London: Tavistock, 1974.

Hirschhorn, L. "Scenario Writing: A Developmental Approach." *APA Journal*, 1980 (Apr.), 172-183.

Hirschman, A. O. *Development Projects Observed*. Washington: Brookings Institution, 1967.

Hirschman, A. O. *Exit, Voice, and Loyalty: Responses to Decline in Firms, Organizations, and States*. Cambridge, Mass.: Harvard University Press, 1970.

Isaacson, J. "Internal Training Materials." Unpublished paper, n.d.

Isaacson, J. "Recruiting Top-Level Appointees." A paper presented at the Conference for Newly Elected Mayors, John F. Kennedy School of Government, Harvard University, Boston, 1977.

Isaacson, J. "Executive Search: A Manual for Commissioner Schall and Her Able and Willing Staff." Unpublished paper, Boston, 1983.

Isaacson, J. "Recruitment of the Governor's Staff and Cabinet." *State Services Management Notes,* Office of State Services, National Governors' Association, Nov. 1986, first draft.

Jaques, E. "Social Systems as a Defense Against Persecutory and Depressive Anxiety." In G. S. Gibbard, J. J. Hartman, and R. D. Mann (eds.), *Analysis of Groups: Contributions to Theory, Research, and Practice.* San Francisco: Jossey-Bass, 1978 (originally published 1955).

Jaques, E. "Too Many Management Levels." *California Management Review,* 1985, *8* (1), 13–20.

Janis, I. L. *Groupthink: Psychological Studies of Policy Decisions and Fiascos.* Boston: Houghton Mifflin, 1982.

Johnson, K. "Why References Aren't." *New York Times,* June 9, 1985, p. 8F.

Jones, E. E., and Nisbett, R. E. "The Actor and the Observer: Divergent Perceptions of the Causes of Behavior." In E. E. Jones and others (eds.), *Attribution: Perceiving the Causes of Behavior.* Morristown, N.J.: General Learning Process, 1971 and 1972.

Kanter, R. M. "Power Failure in Management Circuits." In R. W. Allen and L. W. Porter (eds.), *Organizational Influence Processes.* Glenview, Ill.: Scott, Foresman, 1983.

Katsenelinboigen, A. *Some New Trends in Systems Theory.* The Systems Inquiry Series. Seaside, Calif.: Intersystems Publications, 1984.

Kelly, J. N. "Management Transitions for Newly Appointed CEOs." *Sloan Management Review,* 1980, *22* (1) (Fall), 37–45.

Kleinfield, N. R. "Gentle Persistence Pays Off." *New York Times,* Oct. 30, 1983, p. 6F.

Kotter, J. P. "General Managers Are Not Generalists." *Organizational Dynamics,* 1982, *10* (4), 5–19.

Levinson, H. "Self-Defeat in the Executive Suite." *Addendum,* A Special Feature of *The Levinson Letter,* The Levinson Institute, 1974, pp. 1–6.

Levinson, H., and Rosenthal, S. *CEO: Corporate Leadership in Action*. New York: Basic Books, 1984.

Lewin, K. *Resolving Social Conflicts: Selected Papers on Group Dynamics*. New York: Harper & Row, 1948.

Loving, R. "Bob Six's Long Search for Successor." In R. M. Kanter and B. A. Stein (eds.), *Life in Organizations*. New York: Basic Books, 1979.

Lynn, L. E. *The State and Human Services: Organizational Change in a Political Context*. Cambridge, Mass.: MIT Press, 1980.

Lynn, L. E. *Managing the Public's Business: The Job of the Government Executive*. New York: Basic Books, 1981.

Lynn, L. E., and Seidel, J. W. "Bottomline Management and Public Agencies." *Harvard Business Review*, 1977, *55* (1) (Jan./Feb.), 144-153.

McCann, J. E., and Gilmore, T. N. "Diagnosing Organizational Decision Making Through Responsibility Charting." *Sloan Management Review*, 1983, *24* (2), 3-15.

McCaskey, M. B. *The Executive Challenge: Managing Change and Ambiguity*. Boston: Pitman, 1982.

Maeroff, G. I. "Halverson Named to Act as Head of City Schools." *New York Times*, Jan. 18, 1985, p. B3.

March, J. G., and Olsen, J. *Ambiguity and Choice*. Bergen, Norway: Universitetsforlaget, 1976.

Mechanic, D. "Sources of Power of Lower Participants in Complex Organizations." In H. J. Leavitt and L. R. Pondy (eds.), *Readings in Managerial Psychology*. Chicago: University of Chicago Press, 1964.

Minuchin, S., and Fishman, H. *Family Therapy Techniques*. Cambridge, Mass.: Harvard University Press, 1981.

Morgan, T. "Recent Insights into the Selection Interview." Unpublished paper, n.d.

Naisbitt, J. *Megatrends: Ten New Directions Transforming Our Lives*. New York: Warner Publications, 1982.

National Academy of Public Administration. *Leadership in Jeopardy: The Fraying of the Presidential Appointments System*. Washington: National Academy of Public Administration, Nov. 1985.

Neustadt, R. E., and May, E. R. *Thinking in Time: The Uses of History for Decision Makers.* New York: Free Press, 1986.

Newcomb, T. M. "An Approach to the Study of Communicative Acts." *Psychological Review,* 1953, *60* (6), 393–404.

Onken, W., and Wass, D. L. "Management Time: Who's Got the Money?" *Harvard Business Review,* 1974, *52* (6) (Nov./Dec.), 75–80.

Peters, T. J. "Symbols, Patterns and Settings: An Optimistic Case for Getting Things Done." *Organizational Dynamics,* 1978, *7* (Autumn), 3–23.

Peters, T. J. "Leadership, Sad Facts and Silver Lining." *Harvard Business Review,* 1979, *57* (Nov./Dec.), 164–172.

Peters, T. J. "A Passion for Excellence." (videotape.) Des Plaines, Ill.: Video Publishing House, 1985.

Peters, T. J., and Austin, N. *A Passion for Excellence.* New York: Random House, 1985.

Peters, T. J., and Waterman, R. H. *In Search of Excellence: Lessons from America's Best-Run Companies.* New York: Harper & Row, 1982.

Pollack, A. "BankAmerica's Employees Edgy Over New Chief." *New York Times,* Oct. 12, 1986, p. 36.

Prokesch, S. "America's Imperial Chief Executive." *New York Times,* Oct. 12, 1986, sec. 3, pp. 1, 25.

Prokesch, S. "Remaking the American C.E.O." *New York Times,* Jan. 25, 1987, sec. 3, pp. 1, 8.

Quinn, J. B. *Strategies for Change: Logical Incrementalism.* Homewood, Ill.: Richard D. Irwin, 1980.

Reich, R. B. "Entrepreneurship Reconsidered: The Team as Hero." *Harvard Business Review,* 1987, *65* (3), 77–83.

Sanger, D. E. "Top NASA Aides Knew of Shuttle Flaw in '84." *New York Times,* Dec. 21, 1986, p. 1.

Sarason, S. *The Creation of Settings and the Future Societies.* San Francisco: Jossey-Bass, 1972.

Schein, E. H. *Process Consultation.* Reading, Mass.: Addison-Wesley, 1969.

Schein, E. H. *Organizational Culture and Leadership: A Dynamic View.* San Francisco: Jossey-Bass, 1985.

Schneider, K. "North's Record: A Wide Role in a Host of Sensitive Projects." *New York Times,* Jan. 3, 1987, pp. 1, 4.

Schon, D. A. *Beyond the Stable State.* New York: Random House, 1971.

Schon, D. A. *The Reflective Practitioner: How Professionals Think in Action.* New York: Basic Books, 1983.

Segal, H., and others. *Introduction to the Work of Melanie Klein.* New York: Basic Books, 1974.

Smith, L. J. "Leadership and Management Transition Model: A Different Approach." Organizational Effectiveness Office, U.S. Army, n.d.

Sonnenfeld, J. A. "Heros in Collision: Chief Executive Retirement and the Parade of Future Leaders." *Human Resource Management,* 1986, *25* (2), 305–333.

Span, P. "New Yorker: Transition Plagued by Intransigence." *The Philadelphia Inquirer,* Feb. 11, 1987, p. 8c.

Staw, B., and Ross, J. "Knowing When to Pull the Plug." *Harvard Business Review,* 1987, *65* (2), 68–74.

Sterngold, J. "How They Tore Hutton to Pieces." *New York Times,* Jan. 17, 1988, sec. 3, pp. 1, 6, 7.

"Survey of Business Executives." In *Gallup Poll Report.* Princeton, N.J.: Dow Jones Publications, Oct. 1980.

Tierney, J. "John Isaacson Is Looking for a Few Good Men and Women." *Esquire,* 1985, *106* (12), 356–358.

"Tisch's Regimen Built Trimmer CBS." *New York Times,* Dec. 26, 1986, p. D2.

Toffler, A. *Future Shock.* New York: Bantam Books, 1971.

Townsend, R. *Up the Organization.* Greenwich, Conn.: Fawcett, 1970.

Trist, E. *The Evolution of Socio-technical Systems: A Conceptual Framework and an Action Research Program.* Issues in the Quality of Working Life, A series of occasional papers, No. 2. Ontario Quality of Working Life Center, June 1981.

Trist, E. "Working with Bion in the 1940s: The Group Decade." In M. Pines (ed.), *Bion and Group Psychotherapy.* Boston: Routledge & Kegan Paul, 1985.

Tunstall, W. B. *Disconnecting Parties: Managing the Bell System Break-up: An Inside View.* New York: McGraw-Hill, 1985.

"Turnover at the Top." *Business Week,* Dec. 19, 1983, 104–110.

Vancil, R. F. "A Look at CEO Succession." *Harvard Business Review,* 1987, *65* (2), 107–117.

Waddington, C. H. *Tools for Thought.* New York: Basic Books, 1977.

Webster's New International Dictionary of the English Language. 2nd ed. W. A. Neilson, T. A. Knott, and P. W. Carhart (eds.). Springfield, Mass.: Merriam, 1946.

Weick, K. E. *The Social Psychology of Organizing.* New York: Random House, 1979.

Weick, K. E. "Small Wins: Redesigning the Scale of Social Problems." *American Psychologist,* 1984, *39* (Jan.), 40–49.

Wysocki, B. "The Chief's Personality Can Have a Big Impact for Better or Worse." *Wall Street Journal,* Sept. 11, 1984, p. 1.

Yin, R. K. *R and D Utilization by Local Services: Problems and Proposals for Further Research.* Santa Monica, Calif.: Rand Institute, 1976.

Yu, W. "Firms Tighten Resume Checks of Applicants." *Wall Street Journal,* Aug. 20, 1985, p. 3.

Zald, M. "Who Shall Rule? A Political Analysis of Succession in a Large Welfare Organization." *Pacific Sociological Review,* 1965 (Spring), 52–60.

Zaleznik, A. "Management of Disappointment." *Harvard Business Review,* 1967, *45* (6), 59–70.

Zaleznik, A. "Leaders and Managers: Does It Make a Difference?" *McKinsey Quarterly,* Spring 1978, pp. 2–22.

Zweig, P. L. "Banks Stress Resolving Complaints to Win Small Customer's Favor." *Wall Street Journal,* Dec. 8, 1986, Section 2, p. 29.

ᴄ⌒ Index

273